# Contentious Traditions

# Contentious
## Traditions

### The Debate on *Sati*
### in Colonial India

### Lata Mani

UNIVERSITY OF CALIFORNIA PRESS

*Berkeley / Los Angeles / London*

University of California Press
Berkeley and Los Angeles, California

University of California Press, Ltd.
London, England

Early versions of chapters 1 and 2 were published as Lata Mani, "The Production of
an Official Discourse on *Sati* in Early-Nineteenth-Century Bengal," in *Europe and Its
Others,* ed. F. Barker et al. (Colchester: University of Essex, 1985), vol. 1, 107–127; also
in *Economic and Political Weekly; Review of Women's Studies,* April 26, 1986, 32–40;
"Contentious Traditions: The Debate on *Sati* in Colonial India," *Cultural Critique* 7
(Fall 1987): 119–156; also in *Recasting Women: Essays in Colonial History,* ed. Kumkum
Sangari and Sudesh Vaid (New Delhi: Kali, 1989), 88–126. An early version of chapter 5
was published as Lata Mani, "Cultural Theory, Colonial Texts: Eyewitness Accounts
of Widow Burning," in *Cultural Studies,* ed. Lawrence Grossberg et al. (New York:
Routledge, 1992), 392–405; also as "The Female Subject, the Colonial Gaze: Reading
Eyewitness Accounts of Widow Burning," in *Interrogating Modernity: Culture and
Colonialism in India,* ed. Tejaswini Niranjana et al. (Calcutta: Seagull, 1993), 273–290.

Library of Congress Cataloging-in-Publication Data
Mani, Lata, 1956–
    Contentious traditions : the debate on Sati in colonial India /
Lata Mani.
      p.  cm.
    Includes bibliographic references and index.
    ISBN 0-520-21406-4 (alk. paper). — ISBN 0-520-21407-2 (alk.
paper)
    1. Sati.  I. Title.
GT3370
393'.9—dc21                                                98-21003
                                                  CIP

Printed in the United States of America
9  8  7  6  5  4  3  2  1

*To*
*Devi Amma*
*for awakening my heart*

# Contents

# Illustrations

# Preface

In this preface I would like to briefly explain the special circumstances in which this text was completed. In January 1993, I was within two weeks of sending the manuscript to the publisher. However, plans for finishing it were interrupted when, whilst on my way to work, I was hit by a truck traveling at high speed. As a result of this collision I suffered a serious head injury from which I have even now to recover. The cognitive and visual impairment that was the result of the injury have made reading and writing impossible. Under these circumstances there was of course no question of returning to the book. Recently, however, I was urged and encouraged by my friends Sujata Patel and Avtar Brah to consider publishing the text in its present form, a proposal with which my editor, Naomi Schneider, concurred. I note these circumstances only to explain why work published after January 1993 has not been addressed here. The only exceptions are a few instances in which my familiarity with the unpublished versions of relevant material enabled me to cite their publication without discussion. Completing this work has been a challenging and humbling process, and one which would not have been possible without the tireless assistance of Ruth Frankenberg, who took responsibility for final preparation of the manuscript. I am also grateful to Naomi Schneider for her understanding and enthusiasm.

# Acknowledgments

Numerous people have supported, encouraged, and assisted me during the research and writing of this book. This project was begun as an M.A. thesis in the Comparative World History Program at the University of California, Santa Cruz, and completed as a doctoral dissertation in History of Consciousness, on the same campus. I would like to thank James Clifford, Donna Haraway, and Thomas R. Metcalf, as well as Dilip K. Basu, Terry Burke, Teresa de Lauretis, Susan Mann, and Carolyn Martin Shaw, all of whom served as my advisers at various stages. I would also like to thank all those who were associated with the Group for the Critical Study of Colonial Discourse, which provided an invaluable context for my own work. Thanks are also due to the following people whose presence in my life made graduate school memorable and intellectually invigorating: Lisa Bloom, Satish Deshpande, Vivek Dhareshwar, Inderpal Grewal, Billie Harris, Mary John, Caren Kaplan, Katie King, Tejaswini Niranjana, Chéla Sandoval, the late Rosa Maria Villafañe-Sisolak, and Kamala Visweswaran. I am grateful to the Group for the Critical Study of Colonial Discourse and the Feminist Studies ORA, University of California, Santa Cruz, for research grants, and to the Humanities Division, University of California, Santa Cruz, for a dissertation writing fellowship.

The staff at the following libraries have been enormously helpful: Golden Gate Baptist Seminary, Mill Valley, California; Graduate Theological Union, Berkeley, California; Baptist Missionary Society, London; India Office Library, London; British Museum, London; National

Library, Calcutta; Carey Library, Serampore College, Serampore; and National Archive, New Delhi. I would like to thank Chetan Bhatt, Kum Kum Bhavnani, and Hansa Chudasama for supporting me through two winters of research in England. In Calcutta I received the warmth and welcome of many people, including Jashodara Bagchi, Himani Bannerji, Moinak Biswas, Dipesh Chakrabarty, Partha Chatterjee, Indira Chowdhury, and Alakananda Guha. I would also like to thank Moinak Biswas for assistance in research and translation in Calcutta.

I would like to thank my friends and colleagues in the Women's Studies Program and the Gender and Global Issues Research Group at the University of California, Davis, for intellectual community during my time there. I thank the many people who have been generous enough to share with me over the years their response to my work. Additionally, Avtar Brah, Catherine Hall, Nancy Paxton, Jane Rendall, Kumkum Sangari, Carolyn Steedman, and Sudesh Vaid have read and commented on parts of my written work.

It has been a great pleasure to work with the University of California Press on the publication of this book. Naomi Schneider and Sue Heinemann made the process a very smooth one, and Steve Gilmartin brought grace and thoroughness to copyediting the manuscript. I am honored to be able to use a painting from S. G. Vasudev's *Humanscape* series for the cover of this book.

My parents, N. V. S. and Leela Mani, and my sisters, Meera Mani and Sunita Mani, continually encouraged and supported me through the research and writing process, as did my friends Reyna Cowan, Rosa Linda Fregoso, Ammu Joseph, Vivien Kleiman, Sujata Patel, and Giti Thadani. Last but by no means least, I would like to express my deepest gratitude to my *saheli,* Ruth Frankenberg, with whom I shared this journey of research and discovery, and without whose assistance this book literally could not have been completed.

# Introduction

The prohibition of *sati*—widow burning—in 1829 has been canonized by colonialist and nationalist texts as a founding moment in the history of women's emancipation in modern India. Within the frames of a patriarchal ideology, *sati*, a predominantly upper-caste Hindu practice, is comprehended as the duty of a virtuous wife. By immolating herself, the widow purportedly enables herself as well as her deceased husband to enjoy "heavenly pleasures" and even, according to some scriptural texts, to escape thereafter the cycle of birth and death. The scriptural sanction for widow burning, as we shall see, is dubious and precisely part of what was under contest in the debate over its prohibition.

The ignominy of *sati* does not, however, lie only in the cruelty of the practice. It rests equally and inextricably in the place accorded to the outlawing of *sati* in the history of modern India. Historiography has constituted widow burning as the site upon which a charged battle was waged between colonial and countercolonial discourses. This was certainly the case. Yet equally salient, and neglected by this version, is the extent to which the suffering widow remained fundamentally marginal to a debate that was ostensibly about whether she should live or die.

This study sets out to critically investigate a particular discourse on women, culture, and Indian society that emerged at the turn of the nineteenth century and shaped discussions of widow burning. It does so by analyzing representations of *sati* and the debate over its legal prohibition among colonial officials, missionaries, and the indigenous male elite in Bengal in the period 1780–1833. My argument is that the debate

1

on *sati* was shaped by a specifically colonial discourse, which simultaneously privileged brahmanic scriptures as the locus of authentic tradition and constituted woman as site for the contestation of tradition. I examine the institutional and noninstitutional contexts in which this configuration of ideas developed, the processes that shaped it, and the modes in which it was variously deployed.

It is my contention that although *sati* became an alibi for the colonial civilizing mission on the one hand, and on the other hand, a significant occasion for indigenous autocritique, the women who burned were neither subjects nor even the primary objects of concern in the debate on its prohibition. They were, rather, the ground for a complex and competing set of struggles over Indian society and definitions of Hindu tradition. The debate, in which public opinion was mobilized in India and Britain alike, inaugurated a process whereby an exceptional and caste-specific practice was to emerge in the West as a potent signifier of the oppression of all Indian women, and thereby of the degradation of India as a whole. The indigenous legacy of this charge, which the practice carries down to the present day, is the way widow burning was to assume the exemplary status newly accorded to it, not merely in countercolonial discourse, but also in nationalist historiography. The latter has represented the prohibition of widow burning as signaling a new concern with women's rights, thereby enshrining central elements of the colonial narrative even while rewriting others.

## Colonialism and the Writing of Indian History

> *A major contradiction in our understanding of the* entire
> *Indian past is that this understanding derives largely from
> the interpretations of Indian history made in the last two
> hundred years. (emphasis mine)*[1]

This observation was made by Romila Thapar in the mid-1970s in the context of an examination of the way communalism has shaped the writing of Indian history.[2] Romila Thapar's essay predated the publication of Edward Said's *Orientalism,* a groundbreaking study of British and French colonial discourses on West Asia.[3] Said's text has inspired wide-ranging analyses of colonial discourses. While challenge to colonial forms of knowledge had been key to anticolonial struggle as well as analysis from the start, *Orientalism* inaugurated fresh, serious, and sustained consideration of the discursive dimensions of colonial expansion and rule.

Colonial discourse analysis is not so much a field as a critical reading strategy. "Discourse" signals a double focus: forms of knowledge and modes of description. Colonial discourses refer to the knowledges that developed alongside, mediated, and helped secure European conquest and domination, and to the rhetorical strategies that predominated in the representations of colonized peoples, societies, and cultures. Construed broadly, work within this rubric has examined the constitution of colonized society as an object of study essential to technologies of governance and state formation.[4] It has also documented how particular conceptions of history, community, identity, labor, and sexuality emerged under colonial domination, how colonial policy was shaped by them, and the shifts they represented from precolonial forms.[5] The relation of nationalist imaginings to colonial discourses has been an equally fertile field of analysis.[6]

The object of colonial discourse analysis has not, however, solely been the "Other" of the West. Part of what was at stake in the production of the colonized Other was the simultaneous construction of the Western Self, to whom the Other was variously an alter ego, underground self, and repository of irreducible cultural and/or racial difference. Insofar as the history of Western expansion is also the history of the European Enlightenment, such work has an implicitly comparative dimension and is an aspect of global history. Thus, even when such analysis has taken the West as its subject in both senses of that term, the West has been refracted through a different prism. Appearing in sharp relief is the importance of the Other to the Western sense of self, history, and culture: among other things the colony has served as a theater of social experimentation, an imaginary terrain in which to remap European social relations, and the place from which to mount a critique of metropolitan culture.[7]

As a reading strategy colonial discourse analysis has been deployed in a broad range of projects, though not always in the same way nor even to the same end. A number of conceptual difficulties have, however, been evident from the start, and some of these have become more pronounced as such work has proliferated. Among recurring weaknesses have been the limitations of conceiving of colonial relations in binary terms, the absence of attention to class and other differences among the colonized, the tendency to take the aggrandizing claims of colonial discourse at face value, and a frequent and astonishing marginalization of the Third World in the resoundingly Eurocentric ambit within which some of this criticism is grounded. These tendencies have led to a growing sense of frustration with, and concern regarding, the value and status of colonial discourse analysis.[8] It thus becomes important to clarify the presumptions that guide my own use of this framework in the case of India. By colonial discourse I mean the emergence of an interpretive apparatus for apprehending India that acquired specific kinds of force with the shift of the East India Company in the latter half of the eighteenth century from a mercantilist to a territorial power. The increasing assumption by the East India Company of such state functions as revenue collection and the administration of law necessitated an intensification of its knowledge of its new subjects. The ethnographic requirements of the colonial state paralleled the late-eighteenth-century orientalist "discovery" of India, and although the two cannot be conflated, there was an abiding relation between their analyses of Indian society and culture. Indeed, many of the orientalists were themselves employed in the colonial bureaucracy in one capacity or another.

What makes these discourses colonial is the specific historical conjuncture in which they emerge and circulate: the socioeconomic and political relations of colonial domination. It was these relations that mediated the discourse of modernity in India. There is, in other words, nothing *essentially* colonial about them. Furthermore, late-eighteenth-century discourses do not arise out of nowhere (the relation of European precolonial to colonial discourses would of course vary depending on the object of study); neither is a grid of analytic and cultural prejudices imperiously laid upon some putatively uninscribed landscape. Although some work in the West implicitly reproduces the high imperialist fantasy, propagated primarily for metropolitan consumption, that the colonized subject was imaged and hence realized at will, the actual history of colonialism tells a rather different story. As we shall see, colonial discourses emerged and prevailed in complex, dispersed, and contested relations of intersection, complementarity, and disjunction with a range of indigenous discourses. Put another way, colonial discourses existed not in determining but in determinate though shifting relations with indigenous discourses. Furthermore, both colonial and indigenous discourses were internally differentiated. For example, early-nineteenth-century colonial discourses were not only inflected by class, gender, and race, but may in addition be disaggregated into several constitutive strands — orientalism, romanticism, utilitarianism, protestantism, evangelism, and so on. Indigenous discourses were similarly heterogeneous. They were distinguished by, among other things, class, caste, gender, philosophico-religious worldviews such as brahmanism, vaishnavism, and Islamic rationalism, degree of implication in the colonial apparatus, and competing visions of how to negotiate the logic of colonial modernity.

The complexity and heterogeneity of both colonial and indigenous discourses underscore the serious limitations of theorizing the colonial encounter solely in terms of a self/other binary. To begin with, there were more than two contenders involved in the proceedings. For instance, although not a homogeneous group, taken as a whole, the Bengali *bhadralok,* a class that was itself thrown up by colonialism, sought to define itself through a process that simultaneously distinguished it both from the British colonialists and the indigenous *chottolok,* or lower orders, in the caste/class hierarchy.[9] Similarly, tensions between the discourses of colonial officials and missionaries, both in the metropole and in the colony, suggest that several factors determined the content and direction of missionary and official arguments. An analysis that privileges the self/other binary would perforce have to elide such complexities. It would err in converting a structuring element of colonial discourses, namely, the claim of a fundamental and constitutive difference between the European and the non-European, into a primary axis of analysis.

A binary analysis is, moreover, hardly up to the task to which it is being enlisted. It cannot fully grasp the implications of one of the fundamental conditions of the emergence of colonial discourse in the Indian context, namely, the colonial state's uneven penetration into indigenous society. As Ranajit Guha has argued, the colonial state in India achieved dominance not hegemony.[10] The question confronted by any investigation of colonial representations, then, is in what ways, to what extent, and among which sectors of society such discourses became dominant. This returns us to an ongoing discussion within Indian historiography as to the kind of social, economic, and ideological restructuring facilitated or inaugurated by colonial domination. Did colonialism represent a total transformation, an abrupt caesura? Did it, by contrast, merely undertake the kind of minimal realignment of social forces necessary to enable colonial extraction, leaving most of society relatively undisturbed?[11] Or did it entail decisive albeit differential shifts in socioeconomic and ideological relations, reconstellating in the process the mutually consolidating systems of caste, class, and patriarchy? Recent work has by and large tended toward this last position, and my own research supports such a conclusion.[12]

Critical attention to the discursive legacies of colonialism for nineteenth- and twentieth-century India has served to challenge and severely compromise the modernization narrative which, in its liberal or Marxist variants, has hitherto dominated the historiography of India. This critique has pointed to the unquestioned acceptance by this literature of the content of such categories as tradition and modernity. The story of colonial modernity is accordingly being rewritten through a process of historical specification. Here, it no longer appears, as in the colonial purview, as a potentially liberating project though one doomed to failure by the intractability of a backward indigenous culture. Nor is it, as in the nationalist version, a heroic epic in which the nation is posited as a universally desired and fully realized telos. Colonial and postcolonial modernity emerge, rather, as contradictory forms of existence constituted by multiple paradoxes: hard-won gains and painful losses, fresh forms of individual and collective empowerment, and new principles of social division. It would seem that even as colonial modernity opened up a structure of opportunities, it simultaneously inaugurated its own logic of discrimination and submission.

Although there are several strands within the current revision of the historiography on colonialism and nationalism, signal contributions have been made by the distinct yet overlapping projects of subalternist and feminist historians. Taken as a whole, the new scholarship has equally contested the cherished fictions of colonialism and nationalism. In many cases, the latter has constituted the burden of such critique. This is perhaps not surprising, given the crises of the 1980s in which regional movements, upper-caste violence, and Hindu majoritarianism have unequivocally shattered the founding myths of India as a secular and democratic nation whose federal political structure is capable of orchestrating a unity out of diversity.

The simultaneous critique of both colonialism and nationalism makes it misleading to assimilate this scholarship into some generalized "postcolonial writing back against the West." Such a description, not uncommon in the Anglo-American academy, would only grasp part of what is at stake in these interrogations. At the same time, it is also important to challenge neo-nationalist certainty that colonial discourses can easily be sequestered within the nineteenth and early twentieth centuries. For one thing, nationalist ideology secularizes and domesticates the rationality of colonial modernity.[13] A postcolonial critique of the former is, then, in part also a critique of the latter.

The project of historical specification also requires us to attend to the differential trajectories of colonial discourses in the Third World and in the First. For in the metropolis, where many of the chickens of empire have come home to roost, high-colonialist discourse can be found to give form and content to contemporary racist ideology, often with little or no rearticulation. Continuities between colonial and postcolonial discourses in the First World are thus of a different order than in the ex-colony. A genealogy of social and political discourses in contemporary Britain, for example, would involve analyzing the specific ambiguity in that context of the "post" in postcolonial. Additionally, it would require tracing the redeployment of colonial discourses in the effort to manage the crisis of a post-Empire, post–Cold War, multiracial Britain. It is within this conjuncture that British analysis of the discursive legacy of colonialism is grounded.[14]

The current crises of the national in both Britain and India are related in complex though different ways to the colonial pasts and recessionary presents of both societies. It is only by theorizing the specificities of their struggles with their respective pasts (the intersections as well as the disjunctions) that we can begin to grasp history in its proper dispersion. The questions of which pasts serve as resources for which presents, when, and why are key to such analysis. The issues that animate this book straddle Britain and India, the past as well as the present. Despite the multivalence of its concerns, however, this study is primarily a feminist investigation of early-nineteenth-century Bengal and an intervention in Indian historiography. It is in that sense an instance of postnationalist feminist historiography. At the same time, in its attention to the micropolitics of missionary and colonial accounts, it is equally an example of postcolonial or postorientalist feminist historiography. Though related, the designations—postcolonial and postnationalist—allude to different historical and semantic registers, and I will at various times be engaging one or the other more explicitly. As a result, aspects of this text will be more or less pertinent to the afterlives of colonial discourses in India and/or Britain and the West more generally. To cite one such contrast, missionary discourses will be found to resonate more strongly with current Western representations of India, while the contemporary legacy of *bhadralok* conceptions of gender and culture will be more readily apprehended in context of Indian political debates.

## Overview of Chapters

My analysis begins, in chapter 1, with the documents of the colonial bureaucracy. These include administrative and judicial proceedings, police records, official circulars, the legal opinions of pundits appointed to the court to interpret brahmanic scriptures, and the correspondence between the East India Company in Bengal and the Court of Directors to which it reported in London. After a brief discussion of the nature of the colonial state during the period under consideration, I examine the legislative history of *sati*, the process by which widow burning was constituted as an object of knowledge, and the understanding of Indian society that informed and shaped colonial policy. Officials, even when they agreed on the desirability of legislative prohibition, were divided on the political costs of intervening in what they construed as an inviolable aspect of Hindu tradition. This belief in the essentially religious character of *sati* persisted despite strong evidence to the contrary, as did a fundamental ambivalence toward the practice. Analyzing the interactions between colonial officials and the indigenous interpreters of scripture upon whom they relied exemplifies the power relations that structured the ethnographic project of the colonial state.

In chapter 2, I turn to an examination of the writings on *sati* of the indigenous male elite, the primary counterplayers in the debate on widow burning. Analysis of their discourse requires one to investigate the colonial context for the reconstellation of this class. Pamphlets, petitions to the East India Company, and newspaper reports addressed distinct though overlapping publics, and there is a specific cast to the primary focus of each. In general, pamphlets were more concerned with issues of scriptural interpretation, and petitions with questions of the legality or illegality of *sati* as it was actually practiced, while newspaper reports varied between matter-of-fact obituaries of the deceased males whose wives burned along with them, and contests over the details of specific incidents of *sati*. I read these sources in relation to each other, and in the context of official discourse, examining how they converged with, diverged from, and shaped each other. I also compare Rammohun Roy's post-1815 rhetoric in his publications on *sati* and related matters with his earlier published work. Rammohun's writing provides a rich template for tracing a set of critical shifts initiated by a specifically colonial discourse on India. This was to shape nineteenth-century elite consciousness in decisive ways, with particular consequences for women, and for the historiography of women, in modern India.

Chapters 3 and 4 are interlinked discussions of missionary discourse. Chapter 3 explores the functioning and reception of colonial discourse outside of an institutional apparatus and in a predominantly nonelite context. In it, I focus on analysis of the letters and diaries of the Baptist missionaries William Carey, Joshua Marshman, and William Ward. In particular, I examine their accounts of street preaching in and around the town of Serampore (Srirampur) where their mission was based. The fullest accounts of such itinerant preaching are available for the early years of missionary residence in India. They are thus invaluable sources for charting the development of missionary cognition of Indian society and culture. To the extent that they have recorded the responses of indigenous people to their sermons, these sources also provide a rich sense of subaltern engagement with and critique of their discourse.

Chapter 4 traces the consolidation of missionary discourse in the period after 1813, when evangelical activity was made legal in Bengal. In it, I move from the more "private" journals and letters to the texts written explicitly for publication, including scholarly monographs and evangelical fundraising literature. Comparative analysis of published with unpublished evangelical writings and of materials printed in India with those produced for a British audience shows how discursive elements were differently articulated and emphasized to serve varying objectives. Widow burning and the so-called degraded state of Hindu women were staples of evangelical literature in Britain, even though Carey, Marshman, and Ward had themselves paid little and infrequent attention to such matters in their journals and publications. Increasingly, however, in addressing British audiences, they also began to echo popular evangelical horror, while in India they eschewed such prose for arguments that continued to engage official and indigenous concerns.

Chapter 5 is a close reading of European eyewitness accounts of *sati*. I analyze how the narrative structure and focus of these descriptions is systematically shaped by a colonial discourse on *sati* and its participants. These narratives primarily represented *sati* as a religious ritual, evaded the physicality of the widow's suffering, and were most frequently structured around the twin poles of colonial horror of, and fascination with, widow burning. Reading these accounts against the grain and attending to the testimonials of widows they recorded, I challenge the notion of *sati* as a voluntary, religious practice of wifely devotion and clarify its material basis. I also foreground that which is marginalized in these descriptions: the agency of the widow and the materiality of her suffering.

## CHAPTER I

# Equivocations in
# the Name of Tradition

*The Official Debate on Widow Burning*

---

*[I]t is a fundamental principle of the British government to
allow the most complete toleration in matters of religion, to all
classes of its native subjects.*

G. Dowdeswell, Chief Secretary to
Government, December 5, 1812[1]

## Prologue:
## The Emergence of the Colonial State

---

The year 1765 is extremely significant to any consideration
of colonialism in India. For it was in that year that the East India Company concluded, in the language of Indian textbooks, the move from
being traders to becoming de facto rulers. No doubt the definitive status accorded to particular dates and events has been tempered by a
reconceptualization of history as a set of processes that are uneven, contingent, and contested, rather than an objective and objectifiable narrative of events. Even so, 1765 finalizes a crucial shift in the activities of
the British trading company in the landmass that later assumed the
name *India*.

The transition began with the British victory at the Battle of Plassey
in 1756, a battle initiated by the then Nawab of Bengal, Siraj-ud-Daula, in
an unsuccessful attempt to prohibit East India Company abuses of the
trading rights that it had enjoyed since the beginning of the eighteenth
century. The transition was sealed with the British defeat of his succes-

sor, Mir Qasim, who, though a collaborator in 1756, declared war on the East India Company, having concluded the untenability of its escalating demands and its systematic violation of trading agreements. As a consequence of the British victory at Buxar, the East India Company was granted, by the Mughal emperor, the right to collect revenue in the provinces of Bengal, Bihar, and Orissa and to administer law in the region.

The colonial state has received surprisingly little attention in Indian historiography. With the aid of recent scholarship, it is, however, possible to sketch in broad strokes the economic, political, demographic, and cultural context that shaped the nature of state institutions. At the most fundamental level, the East India Company encountered a society that was populous, an economy that was thriving, and political institutions that were well developed even if decentered and not integrated vertically. There was no possibility, then, of imposing an entirely new set of institutions.[2] Indeed, the British demand for Indian raw materials and goods in the mid-eighteenth century, and the absence of a complementary Indian market for British goods, made it imperative for the East India Company to adapt existing institutions and minimize disruption of trade and commerce. Only economic and political stability could guarantee the unfettered collection of revenues, which could then be used to purchase goods for import into Britain, providing thereby a mode of repatriating the legal and illegal revenues generated by the East India Company and its officials. It is no wonder, then, that the state "coveted regularity and tenure."[3]

Knowledge of colonized society was central to this endeavor and its systematization critical to the development of the colonial state. The centrality of the power/knowledge nexus to the project of the modern nation-state, so ably analyzed by Michel Foucault, has served to focus serious attention on its relation in the colonies.[4] In India, as elsewhere, the state initiated projects of enumeration and classification. The specificity of the colonial situation, however, crucially shaped its technologies of rule. Given its interest in maximizing revenues from the land, the East India Company immediately became involved in gathering and codifying information about land, its produce, and the rights in them of producers, proprietors, and the state. In this it was entirely dependent, at least in the beginning, on indigenous informants, who were not always willing to share their knowledge. This fact, Ranajit Guha has argued, produced untold anxiety about "native chicanery" and generated that potent mix of fear and contempt for the unknown that he characterizes as "the unmistakable sign of an ethnological encounter."[5] The colonial state's will to knowledge, unlike that of the metropolitan, required negotiating a radically different cognitive universe, one which it grasped only imperfectly and which it was never to wholly comprehend or subdue.

Colonialism was at its heart an encounter of incommensurable and differently freighted rationalities—a fact which by no means precluded compradorism or collusion. This, in conjunction with the reality that the colonial state, unlike the Mughal, remained alien and defined primarily by an extractive, appropriative relation to Indian society, has important implications for any analysis of it. It means first that the rhetoric of reform was a strategy of legitimation in a way different from the metropole. Unlike those excluded groups whom the European state genuinely hoped through its disciplinary regimes to thoroughly integrate as productive members of society, the colonial state's stake in the reformist rationalist project is evident only to the extent that it is compatible with the extractive principle: thus anxieties about "noninterference" recur throughout the debate on widow burning. It is this that I take to be the import of Sudipta Kaviraj's argument regarding the different stances adopted by the colonial state to what he describes as its three dissimilar and largely unrelated publics: the metropolitan British, the indigenous middle classes, and the indigenous masses. Kaviraj notes that the state adopts a tone of reasonableness toward opinion in Britain, establishes a dialogue through legislation and education with the indigenous middle classes who are its crucial intermediaries, and undertakes a monologue of force vis-à-vis the colonized masses who remain conceptually, if not physically, distant from it.[6] This differentiated strategy must be borne in mind in realistically sorting out the grand claims of colonial ideology and policy from the potential for their effects.

Recognition of the uneven reach of the colonial state and its Enlightenment rationality is central to scholarship as divergent as that of the Cambridge School on the one hand and the work of historians such as the Subaltern Studies Collective, Sumit Sarkar, and Sudipta Kaviraj on the other.[7] However, while the former's emphasis on continuities tends to sanitize colonialism, the purposive nature and violence of the colonial project are central to analyses of the latter group of scholars. The colonial state signals here neither an abrupt transformation nor a relatively benign continuity but is the effect of a complex mediation structured by relations of domination and subordination. For instance, Kaviraj argues that the precolonial state was a thin, rent-receiving, marginal entity located at the center of circles of community and caste. It operated through economic extraction, had no interest in actively intervening in day-to-day social processes, and its arrangements were structurally rather than legally enforced. Kaviraj goes on to note that the

British brought a highly symmetrical, centralized, and integrated structure to bear on this decentered totality.[8] One can draw on his observations to underscore the shift represented by the colonial state in the period under consideration here, 1780 to 1833. I would argue that it, too,
functioned primarily as a rent-receiving entity and was thin in relation
to the population it governed. It did seek to impose centralized systems,
law for instance, and certainly the logic of the international market affected the organization and social relations of production. The scope of
such efforts were, however, generally limited in this early phase, broad-
ening only after 1857.[9]

More importantly, throughout the colonial period, the state's power
was far more circumscribed in practice than on paper. The colonial state
did embody an intellectual threat, and in this, as Kaviraj has pointed out,
it differed from its predecessors, who represented political not civilizational challenges.[10] This threat was, however, only fully comprehended
by the intelligentsia formed in the crucible of colonial social relations.
It did not exert a uniform pressure on the body politic, for the colonial
state, in Guha's formulation, achieved dominance, not hegemony.[11]

Thus far, the state's quest for knowledge has been treated as though
it were instrumental in the narrow sense of the term. As we will see, this
was by no means the case. Knowledge of Indian people, philosophy, history, language, literature, and culture produced in the context of colonialism was neither synonymous with the project of ruling nor extric-
able from it. Likewise, the endeavors of individual European officials or
missionaries are neither reducible to the interests of the state nor entirely autonomous from it. As we engage the particularities of the discussions of widow burning, we would do well to remember the broader
context of colonial state formation and functioning which constitute
the backdrop to these events. Two of the issues raised here will recur
through the text: the variegated and differential workings of colonialism and the importance of disaggregating and specifying the domains
of its effects. More centrally, we will explore an issue largely neglected
until recently: gender as a site for reconstitutions of patriarchy and contestations of colonial power.

## The Official Debate on Widow Burning

The debate on *sati* spanned the approximate half century
between 1780 and 1833, the period of British expansion from its foothold

in Bengal, to its de facto control over much of the Indian subcontinent, either through direct or indirect rule. It was the first and in many ways the most sensationalized of the debates concerning social practices affecting indigenous women.[12] Colonial intervention in *sati* is frequently represented as the response of a Western, Christian sensibility horrified by a practice so cruel to women, particularly its tolerance in a *British* India. The abolition of *sati* in 1829, it is claimed, signaled the definitive rise of a new breed of colonial officials, the modernizing "anglicists" who, unlike their "orientalist" forerunners and colleagues, had no particular fascination with things Indian.[13]

This chapter will argue that this view of the official debate on *sati* is misleading in a number of ways. For one thing, as we shall see, the debate revolved primarily around the question of the political feasibility of abolition rather than the ethics of its toleration. Furthermore, posing a sharp opposition between officials for and against abolition tends to obscure what united their analysis of *sati* and of Indian society. In any case, the official mode of arguing against *sati* runs counter to such a representation of the debate. Rather than calling for the prohibition of *sati* as a cruel or barbaric act, as one might expect of a "true" modernizer, officials in favor of abolition were at pains to illustrate that such a move was entirely in keeping with the principle of religious tolerance. Contrary to the mythology that has overgrown the outlawing of *sati,* official strategy was to focus on its scriptural status and to insist that the prohibition of widow immolation was consonant with enforcing the truest principles of "Hindu" religion. Constituting the problem of *sati* primarily as a matter of scriptural tradition contributed greatly to the marginalization of widows, whose interests and suffering were, as will become evident, remarkably absent from these proceedings, calling into question its characterization as a debate on the status of indigenous women.

## *Sati:* A Legislative History

As a subject covered by criminal law, colonial policy on *sati* was formulated by the governor-general and his council, and officials at various levels of the criminal justice system in Bengal: magistrates, police officials, the provincial court (Nizamat Adalat) and the superior court (Sadar Nizamat Adalat). Also involved were the Court of Directors of the East India Company and, at the apex of the company hierarchy in London, the Privy Council. The city of Calcutta was beyond the purview of the legal discussions that exercised officials in the early nineteenth century. The city fell under the jurisdiction of British law and *sati* had been outlawed there by Sir John Anstruther, chief justice of the Calcutta Supreme Court, in 1798.

The criminal justice system in Bengal owed its basic structure to judicial reforms instituted by Warren Hastings soon after the East India Company's acquisition of the *diwani,* the right to collect revenues, in 1765. Hastings followed the Mughal practice of enforcing Islamic law in criminal cases as applicable to Hindus and Muslims alike. In the case of civil law issues that vitally affected family and property relations — marriage, divorce, inheritance, succession — Hastings, under an avowed policy of noninterference in native customs, established the principle of governing Hindus by Hindu law and Muslims by Islamic law. Hastings argued that the imposition of an alien legal system would be regarded as tyrannical by indigenous people, a view with which William Jones and Edmund Burke were later to concur. In relation to his work on the Parliamentary Select Committee's investigation into the administration of justice in Bengal (begun in 1781 and only concluded in 1795), Edmund Burke was to defend East India Company application of Hindu and Muslim law. This position was one with which utilitarians like Jeremy Bentham and James Mill disagreed in theory, though in practice, in relation to India, they were to take quite a different position. We will return to this later.

The judicial system implemented in Bengal also reflected the division in Britain between the bishops and the Crown Court, in which the former dealt with marriage, divorce, testaments, and religious worship under ecclesiastical law and the Crown Court with all other matters. The Calcutta Supreme Court was a combination of both a temporal and a religious court. Hastings's reforms thus extended to Bengal a system that prevailed in England, one, furthermore, that accorded with the East India Company's view of the place of religion in indigenous society. Additionally, the project of codifying law was intended to facilitate rule, ensure clarity as well as uniformity, and minimize the supposed prejudicial readings of indigenous interpreters of scripture, Hindu pundits, and Muslim *qazis.* Yet, while Islamic law could be generated from the Koran, no equivalent primary text existed on which a "Hindu" law could be based. Thus was begun a protracted process of invention, codification, and transformation, aspects of which we will examine in the specific instance of *sati.*[14]

Brahmin pundits were key participants in the process of codifying law and, by extension, in the debate on widow burning. Appointed to the civil courts to interpret scriptural law in civil cases, their input became critical, given that the debate was to turn on the question of whether or not widow immolation had a foundation in Hindu scriptures. Pundits were called upon to elaborate the scriptural position on all aspects of *sati*. Official knowledge of *sati* was dependent on these court pundits even though, as we will see, their responses were appropriated into a specifically colonial discourse on Indian society.

In addition to the *sadar* courts, which were initially in Murshidabad and later moved to Calcutta, provincial courts were established in the main towns of each administrative division. Twice a year these courts would travel as courts of circuit and adjudicate pending cases from the residence of the magistrate of each division. The magistrates, who were aided by assistants and *darogahs,* performed mainly police functions, although over time a number of judicial duties also devolved upon them.

The history of legislation on *sati* in the early nineteenth century is relatively uncomplicated.[15] In all, only four circulars were promulgated between the first recorded discussion of *sati*'s legality in February 1789 and its prohibition in December 1829. Official position on *sati* was first articulated in response to a clarification solicited by M. H. Brooke, collector of Shahabad District. In the absence of any instructions on the subject, Brooke had prohibited the burning of a widow and sought government approval for his decision. His action was commended but he was urged to use private influence rather than official authority in dissuading natives from *sati* on the grounds that "The public prohibition of a ceremony authorized by the tenets of the religion of the Hindus, and from the observance of which they have never yet been restricted by the ruling power would in all probability tend to increase rather than diminish their veneration for it." It was hoped that in the course of time natives would "discern the fallacy of the principles which have given rise to this practice, and that it will of itself gradually fall into disuse."[16] No support was cited for this claim of a religious sanction for *sati*. Eight years later, in May 1797, James Rattray, acting magistrate of Midnapore, wrote to notify Governor-General John Shore of his successful dissuasion of a widow from committing *sati*. He, too, received approval for using persuasion.[17]

The issue was raised once more in 1805 when J. R. Elphinstone, acting magistrate of the Zillah of Behar, reported his intervention in a case in which he alleged that an intoxicated twelve-year-old was being coerced onto the pyre. Like Brooke, Elphinstone requested instructions from the governor-general and council. The secretary of the government referred the issue to the Nizamat Adalat, asking how far and in what ways the practice of *sati* was founded in the scriptures. He added that if scriptural sanction precluded abolition, measures might be taken to prevent coercion and such abuses as the intoxication of widows.

The Nizamat Adalat in turn referred the matter to its pundit Ghanshyam Surmono (identified as Ghanshyam Sharma by A. F. Salahuddin Ahmed).[18] The pundit responded in March 1805 but not until April 29, 1813, some eight years later, was his exposition of the scriptural position on *sati* issued in the form of instructions to the district magistrates.[19] V. N. Datta attributes the reason for this delay to the departure of Governor-General Wellesley in 1805 and to unsettled political conditions in the years that followed.[20] More immediate grounds for the circular might be found in magistrate J. Wauchope's request for information on *sati*'s legality submitted to the Nizamat Adalat in August 1812.[21] We might also wonder whether the impending renewal of the charter in 1813, which would extend British parliamentary sanction for the East India Company's continued functioning as a monopoly trading company in India, was responsible for its prompt action at this time. British evangelists were bound to revive their attempts, unsuccessful during the debates that surrounded the renewal of the company's charter in 1793, to legalize evangelical activity in Bengal. Their campaign would be sure to bring attention to the East India Company's policies in the social realm, and officials must have been aware that any laxity on their part would be grist for the evangelical mill (see chapter 4).

Whatever the reasons, based on an official reading of Sharma's interpretation of the texts, the East India Company issued instructions declaring *sati* to be a practice founded in the religious beliefs of the Hindus. The 1813 circular clarified that the practice was intended to be voluntary and, if performed, was expected to ensure an afterlife together for the widow and her husband. It also stated that the widow who had taken a vow to commit *sati* was permitted to change her mind without loss of caste, providing she performed a penance. The preface to the instructions clarified that, given the scriptural status of *sati* and the government's commitment to the principle of religious tolerance, *sati* would be permitted "in those cases in which it is countenanced by their religion; and [prevented] in others in which it is by the same authority prohibited."[22] *Sati* was thus to be prohibited in all cases in which the widow was less than sixteen years of age, pregnant, intoxicated, or in any other way coerced. Magistrates were also instructed to transmit to the Nizamat Adalat details of each incident of the practice taking place in their jurisdiction, including any prohibitive measures they might have taken.

This April 29, 1813 circular laid the framework for official policy on *sati* until it was outlawed in 1829. Three more circulars were issued, but these merely refined existing legislation. There was to be only one attempt in 1817 to substantially widen the scope of East India Company regulation of *sati*. The effort was, however, shelved as inexpedient by Governor-General Hastings. Among the reasons offered for not further restricting *sati* were anxiety over a rise in the recorded incidence of the practice and differences of opinion among East India Company officials about the possible reasons for this increase. Hastings decided that "it would be inexpedient to promulgate the circular order . . . until the doubts which now exist in regard to the causes of the increased prevalence shall be removed."[23] Doubts on this score persisted and the circular languished in the files. Hastings's decision was to make him popular with the indigenous pro-*sati* lobby, whose approbation illustrates how official discussions were hardly internal to the bureaucracy.

Such circulars were usually prompted by the queries of district magistrates on specific points regarding what constituted a legal *sati*. The "legality" conferred by its supposedly scriptural origin had been established by the 1813 order. Such questions were forwarded by the Nizamat Adalat to its resident pundits requesting them to provide *vyawasthas* (legal opinions) in conformity with the scriptures. Thus a circular promulgated in September 1813 authorized *jogis* (a tribe of weavers supposedly the survivors of wandering mendicants) to bury widows with their deceased husbands, since the scriptures reportedly forbade burning in their case.[24]

Magistrates were similarly instructed on January 4, 1815, that women with children under three might commit *sati* only if arrangements had been made for the children's maintenance.[25] The Nizamat Adalat also specified that brahmin women could only burn through *sahamarana* (along with their husbands), while women of other castes were also permitted *anoomarana* (burning at a later date along with an article belonging to the husband). Finally, this circular instructed magistrates to submit an annual report of widows burnt in their districts to the Sadar Nizamat Adalat, specifying for each *sati* the name of the widow, her age, caste, the name and caste of her husband, the date of burning, and the police jurisdiction in which it occurred. An additional column was provided for recording any remarks that the magistrates thought deserving of attention.[26] In May 1822, in reviewing the immolation figures for 1821, the Nizamat Adalat decreed that information on the husband's profession and economic circumstances also be included for each *sati*.[27] Although no further instructions regarding the practice of *sati* were issued after 1815, the following years witnessed intense debate on the question of its abolition. Discussion was revived every year when the Nizamat Adalat analyzed the annual returns of *sati* and examined for each incident the conduct of district magistrates and police officers.

Official debate on *sati*'s abolition was structured by what was perceived as the tension between its desirability and its feasibility. Officials unanimously emphasized their desire to prohibit *sati*, even though they remained, as we shall see, deeply fascinated and ambivalent in relation to the practice. What divided them was their assessment of the feasibility or political costs of legal interdiction, concerns that illustrate how questions of the colonial state's own security overrode its commitment to reformist projects. Official fear of the consequences of prohibiting *sati* was tied to their analysis of *sati* as a religious practice and to their view of religion as a fundamental and structuring principle of Indian society. A third component was the official conception of indigenous people. They were believed to be unreflective practitioners of their faith but nonetheless jealous of it and prone to rebellion at the threat of its infringement. Official records themselves serve to contest this analysis of *sati* and Indian society and its people. Be that as it may, it was this discourse that shaped the debate. Discussion proceeded in terms of *sati*'s scriptural basis, and scriptural grounds were sought to justify state action.

The interpretive grid that colonial officials brought to bear in formulating policy on *sati* must be set in the broader context of European scholarly "discovery," in the late eighteenth and early nineteenth century, of the "Orient" and of Sanskrit as the root of what were henceforth to be known as Indo-European languages. Many of the most celebrated figures in the field, among them William Jones, H. T. Colebrooke, and H. H. Wilson, also served the East India Company in an official capacity. Frequently, their intellectual interest in the Orient had preceded their arrival in India, and many of them set out consciously to study law, linguistics, poetry, and philosophy, intending to contribute to the comparative study of human development. Their researches were often first presented to the Asiatic Society of Bengal, founded by Warren Hastings in 1784. In 1800, Governor-General Marquess Wellesley established the College of Fort William with the intention of training civil servants for the East India Company.[28] The Asiatic Society and the College of Fort William were two crucial sites where the intellectual aspirations of these scholar-administrators and the ethnographic requirements of the colonial state productively converged. Without wishing to reduce the complexity of this intellectual current, it must be noted that the privileging of brahmanic texts in the debate on *sati,* and the desire to ensure an authentic interpretation of them, is closely related to the veneration, within this scholarship, of Sanskrit, the language of the scriptures.

A dramatic increase in the incidence of *sati* lent urgency to the debate on widow burning. In the first three years of data collection, 1815 to 1818, the number of burnings nearly tripled, from 378 to 839. Although the figures declined after 1819–20, they never fell to the levels first recorded in 1815, but fluctuated between an annual incidence of 500 and 600. Over the years, the Nizamat Adalat proposed various explanations for this rise. Initially, it claimed that the increase might simply reflect more refined counting. In 1817–18, it was argued that the cholera epidemic that had ravaged Bengal might have contributed to increasing the number of widows immolated.

Some officials, however, proposed a more sinister explanation: that the government circular might have made people aware of more circumstances under which *sati* might be performed. Suspicion grew that the rise was somehow linked to government interposition. Walter Ewer, acting superintendent of police in the Lower Provinces, argued that "authorising a practice is not the way to effect its gradual abolition."[29] Courtney Smith, Nizamat Adalat judge, echoed Ewer's sentiment that government attention had given "a sort of interest and celebrity to the sacrifice." He recommended that all circulars be rescinded since they had a tendency "to modify, systematise or legalise the usage" and made it appear as though "a legal suttee was . . . better than an illegal one."[30] J. Pattle, Nizamat Adalat judge, even went so far as to suggest in 1819 that government orders might have produced "a mistaken spirit of jealousy and opposition."[31]

Not all officials agreed with Ewer, Smith, and Pattle. C. T. Sealy and A. B. Todd, for example, disagreed with Pattle's suggestion that the circulars were interventionist and had somehow stirred the flames of resistance. They claimed that the government was merely ensuring voluntariness of the practice, whereas prohibition would have constituted religious interference and as such was "an object which could never have been in contemplation of the ruling power."[32] Other officials asked for an even more rigorous enforcement of scriptural law as they saw it. For instance, in July 1828, W. Cracroft, magistrate of Dacca, recommended that only widows with pure caste status be permitted to perform *sati.* He suggested that such a rigorous interpretation of caste would dramatically reduce *sati* since few families, if any, would meet this standard.[33]

By contrast with those demanding a stricter enforcement of scripture, J. H. Harrington suggested in 1823 that these texts might be circumvented altogether. He proposed that *sati* need not be outlawed outright but that brahmin pundits and relatives involved in the event might be prosecuted as principals or accomplices in homicide.[34] Part of what was at stake here, as Gayatri Chakravorty Spivak has argued, was whether *sati* was to be conceived as legally punishable homicide or as ritually sanctioned suicide for women. The latter, as Spivak points out, was a position that could be sustained by certain (albeit questionable) readings of the *shastras* (sacred texts).[35] The distinction between legal and illegal widow burnings proposed by the 1813 circular had offered colonial officials one way to equivocate on the issue; Harrington's proposal of shifting the penalty from the widow and the practice to her family and to pundits was another.

Officials advocating further legislation were, however, in a minority. The general view was that in the context of a sustained high incidence of *sati*, anything short of total prohibition would be unwise. Yet this appeared to most officials to be out of the question. In the meantime, it was hoped that the spread of education, together with the opposition to *sati* from high-caste Hindus would serve to make the practice unpopular. There had been public indigenous discussions, both for and against *sati*, since 1818, when Rammohun Roy, who was to become the symbol of the native anti-*sati* lobby, published his first tract against the practice and unleashed fierce criticism from proponents of widow burning (see chapter 2).

Faith in the progressive influence of high-caste and better-educated Hindus was misplaced, for the practice was disproportionately high among this numerical minority. Official analysis of *sati* by caste for 1823, for instance, had revealed the following distribution of incidents: brahmin 234; kayasth 25; vaisya 14; sudra 292.[36] Benoy Bhusan Roy's analysis of caste data available in the *Parliamentary Papers* confirms that caste and social status were consistent indices of the incidence of widow burning in a given community. Although discernible among poor and lower caste families, *sati* was predominant among the brahmins, kayasths, vaidyas, sadgops, and kaibarthas. These groups accounted for 64 percent of recorded incidents between 1815 and 1827.[37] The regional distribution of *sati* also made it difficult to sustain the hope that a greater exposure to European influence would result in its declining popularity. Sixty-three percent of *sati*s between 1815 and 1828 were committed in the Calcutta Division, around Calcutta City, the seat of colonial power. This high figure for the environs of Calcutta may partly be the result of *sati*'s illegality in the city, which required residents to go beyond its boundaries to undertake the practice. The regionally skewed distribution of *sati* prompted some magistrates, like W. L. Melville in 1823, to propose abolition in certain districts.[38] Others used the regional variation as evidence that *sati* was a localized, secular phenomenon, not a universal, religious one.

Further, as we shall see below, Mrityunjay Vidyalankar, chief pundit of the Sadar Nizamat Adalat, had produced as early as 1817 a *vyawastha* pointing out that the scriptural sanction for *sati* was in fact ambiguous. In March 1824, the Court of Directors in London, drawing almost exclusively on official correspondence and Nizamat Adalat proceedings on *sati,* came to the conclusion that these papers were themselves replete with arguments on the basis of which abolition could be justified. In particular, the directors highlighted the following: the questionable scriptural status of *sati,* the violation of scriptural prescriptions in its performance, the inefficacy of current regulations, the support for abolition among Indians, the confidence of some magistrates that *sati* could be abolished safely, and the incompatibility of *sati* with principles of morality and reason. The Court of Directors, however, conceded that the final decision must rest with the authorities in India, since only they could evaluate the political consequences of such action.[39]

The March 1824 dispatch of the Court of Directors was the most detailed statement of their position on a policy vis-à-vis *sati*. The Court of Directors consistently equivocated on the question of abolition, hesitant to recommend any further action. (See plate 1 for a satirical representation from 1815 of East India Company policy on widow burning, highlighting its self-interested character.) It could not, however, entirely ignore the issue, which was kept alive in Britain through coverage in the evangelical and lay press of incidents of *sati,* statistics on widow immolations, and articles on the scriptural basis and feasibility of *sati*'s prohibition (see chapters 4, 5). Material that appeared in the lay press in Britain differed from that of missionary periodicals, not in substance but primarily in tone. The stakes, however, were often quite different. For instance, while evangelical journals like the *Missionary Register* publicized such practices as *sati* in order to generate support and funds for mission work, the *Oriental Herald*'s interest in *sati* was part of the opposition of its editor, James Silk Buckingham, to the East India Company's monopoly in India. Buckingham was a free trader who had been deported from India by the East India Company in 1823.[40]

In addition to press reports, public meetings on *sati* were held in Britain in 1823, 1827, and 1829, and petitions were presented to Parliament in 1827 and 1828.[41] For the most part, the British press, both lay and missionary, merely replayed arguments advanced in India, whether by East India Company officials, evangelists, or the indigenous male elite. British discussions of widow burning differed only in the sense that they began with the desirability of abolition and then proceeded to its feasibility, as against in India, where questions of practicality always came first. Pressure on the Court of Directors was also applied from some of the proprietors of the East India Company who, from time to time, initiated debate on the subject at East India House, the substance of which was published in the *Asiatic Journal*.[42]

British public interest notwithstanding, legislative prohibition came only on December 4, 1829.[43] The course of caution encouraged by the Court of Directors and preferred by the East India Company bureaucracy in India delayed legislative action, even though a numerically small but important indigenous lobby against *sati* had been in evidence since 1818 (see chapter 2). Further, from 1827 onward the press in India had regularly questioned government policy while reporting on incidents of immolation. The failure of the East India Company to intervene sooner in prohibiting *sati* has led Iqbal Singh to describe its policy as one of *"laissez brûler"* while V. N. Datta has described the administration's stance as one of "allowing things to take their own course."[44] Legislation, when it finally came, was not based on fresh information or dramatically altered circumstances. William Bentinck, the governor-general at the time of abolition, did gather intelligence from military personnel regarding the legislation's potential for producing disquiet among the armed forces. There was, in addition, a perceived sense of the political stability of the East India Company, a point explicitly addressed in Bentinck's minute on *sati* of November 8, 1829: "now that we are supreme, my opinion is decidedly in favor of an open, avowed and general prohibition, resting altogether upon the moral goodness of the act and our power to enforce [it]."[45]

*Sati,* either by burning or burial, was outlawed and made punishable by the criminal courts. *Zamindars* and *talukdars* were made responsible for immediate communication to the police of intention to perform *sati,* any lapse being made punishable by a fine or imprisonment. The Nizamat Adalat was authorized to impose the death sentence on active participants in *sati* if the crime was considered gruesome enough to render them unworthy of mercy.[46] It is not known to what extent the legislative act succeeded in putting out the flaming pyres. Statistics were no longer collected, although in the year after abolition the *Samachar Chundrika,* organ of the pro-*sati* lobby, carried reports of women who, they claimed, had burnt in defiance of government orders. The veracity of such newspaper reports was challenged by the *Sambad Kaumudi* and the *Samachar Darpan,* both supporters of abolition (see chapter 2). The government refused to be drawn into further discussion on the question. Referring the petition of those protesting the prohibition of *sati* to the Privy Council in England, it continued to maintain that its action had managed to combine faithfulness to Hindu scripture with principles of justice.[47]

The 1829 regulation concludes the most celebrated and public phase in the legislative career of *sati* in British India. However, the matter did not end there. As Vasudha Dhagamwar has pointed out, the draft of the Indian Penal Code prepared under T. B. Macauley between 1835 and 1838 included the category of "voluntary culpable homicide by consent," which was said to apply when a person above twelve years of age "suffers death or takes the risk of death by his own choice."[48] Consent was said to be valid only if there was an absence of coercion, intoxication, passion, derangement, or deception and if no material facts were concealed. In 1846, the Third Law Commissioners, in speculating on the provision for "voluntary culpable homicide by consent," concluded that it must have been introduced "because of the need to allow for the practice of *sati.*"[49] This provision, which once again made provision for the permissibility of "voluntary" *sati,* was subsequently modified and incorporated into the Indian Penal Code of 1860. The effective reintroduction of the permissibility of *sati* through the notion of "voluntary culpable homicide by consent" suggests that the process of transformation of *sati* from ritual to crime, to use Spivak's terminology, was far from complete.[50] "Voluntary culpable homicide by consent" reinstates the earlier distinction between legal and illegal widow burnings, simultaneously accommodating some burnings as "ritual" and penalizing others as "crime." This is a little-known postscript to the drama of "abolition." Although excised from the official narrative, it is testimony to the persistent ambivalence of colonial officials towards *sati,* and fatally unravels their claims to have definitively prohibited the practice.

## Official Discourse and Its Assumptions

As the legislative history of *sati* in the period leading up to the 1829 regulation suggests, the question of abolition was marked by official insistence on its scriptural status. Whatever their views on the feasibility of abolition, all colonial officials shared to a greater or lesser degree three interdependent ideas: the centrality of religion, the submission of the indigenous populace to its dictates, and the religious basis of *sati*. Those against abolition argued that prohibition of *sati* was likely to incite native resistance. As the Nizamat Adalat put it: "Such a measure would, in all probability, excite a considerable degree of alarm and dissatisfaction in the minds of the Hindoo inhabitants of these provinces."[51] Officials in favor of abolition also developed arguments reflecting these assumptions about Indian society. For example, Judge E. Watson's case for the feasibility of abolition rested on the precedent of Regulation 8 (1799), which, by declaring female infanticide, child sacrifice, and the burial of lepers to be capital offenses, had, in his view, similarly violated religious principles. It is in this sense that officials on both sides of the debate shared the same universe of discourse.

Walter Ewer's letter to W. B. Bayley, secretary to the government in the Judicial Department, written in November 1818, sums up the arguments of officials over the years.[52] Ewer, superintendent of police in the Lower Provinces, proposed that the contemporary practice of *sati* bore little resemblance to its scriptural model, which he defined as a voluntary act of devotion carried out for the spiritual benefit of the widow and the deceased. In reality, he argued, widows were coerced, and *sati* was performed for the material gain of surviving relatives. Ewer suggested that relatives might be motivated by the desire to spare themselves the expense of maintaining the widow and the irritation of her legal right over the family estate. Ewer is here referring to the provisions under Dayabhaga Law prevailing in Bengal which gave the widow limited rights over her husband's property upon his death.

"Hungry brahmins" greedy for the money due to them for officiating such occasions were also said to apply pressure on the widow by extolling the virtues and rewards of *sati*. Even if the widow succeeded in resisting the combined force of relatives and pundits, Ewer held that she would not be spared by the crowd. According to him, "the entire population will turn out to assist in dragging her to the bank of the river, and in keeping her down on the pile" (227). For the crowd, *sati* was said to offer the lure of a spectacle characterized by "[n]one of the holy exultation that formerly accompanied the departure of a martyr, but all the savage merriment which, in our days, accompanies a boxing match or a full-bait" (227).[53]

Ewer thus concludes that "the widow is scarcely ever a free agent at the performance of the suttee" (227). According to Ewer, scriptural transgressions, such as the coercion of widows or the performance of *sati* for material gain, could be the result of ignorance of scriptures, or might reflect conscious design on the part of relatives and pundits. In the former case, *sati* could be abolished without provoking indigenous outrage; in the latter, *sati* could not be considered a sacred act and could be safely prohibited.

Ewer's inference of the safety of abolition from instances of individuals acting by design suggests that, in his view, when Hindus acted "consciously" they could not, by definition, be acting "religiously." "Religious" action is, in this perspective, synonymous with passive, unquestioning obedience. If the widow is thus construed as a victim of pundits and relatives, they in turn are seen by Ewer to act in two mutually exclusive ways: either "consciously," that is, "irreligiously," or "passively," that is, "religiously." Hence Ewer nowhere suggests that pundits and relatives could manipulate religion to their own ends. As for the widow, Ewer submitted that, left to herself, she would "turn with natural instinct and horror from the thought of suttee" (227). However, in his opinion, given the widow's ignorance and weak mental and physical capacity, it took little persuasion to turn any apprehension into a reluctant consent.

Having demonstrated that the actual practice bears no resemblance to a "religious" rite, Ewer goes on to question the assumption of a scriptural sanction for *sati*. He points to the heterogeneity of the scriptures on the issue, demonstrating that Manu, conceived by East India Company officials as the "parent of Hindoo jurisprudence," did not even mention *sati* but, instead, glorified ascetic widowhood. It is important to note that what unites both the "temporal" and "scriptural" aspects of Ewer's arguments is the privileging of religion and the assumption of a complete native submission to its force.

This analysis was shared by others. E. Molony, acting magistrate of Burdwan, similarly emphasized that the decision of widows to commit *sati* stems not "from their having reasoned themselves into a conviction of the purity of the act itself, as from a kind of infatuation produced by the absurdities poured into their ears by ignorant brahmins."[54] For Molony, as for Ewer, the widow is always a victim and the pundit always corrupt. Molony, like Ewer, also conceded the possibility of a "good" *sati,* one that is voluntary and the product of reason, but only in the abstract. In reality, the widows were presumed to be uneducated and incapable of both reason and independent action.

The accent on "will" in the analysis of Ewer and Molony signals the ambivalence which lies at the heart of the official attitude to *sati,* placing them squarely within earlier Western responses to widow burning, which, Arvind Sharma argues, have been a mixture of pity, eulogy, and critique.[55] It suggests that within the avowed disapproval of the practice, there operated notions of "good" and "bad" *sati.* Good *sati*s were those that were seen to be true to an official reading of the scriptures. It was this kind of reasoning that informed the 1813 circular which defined *sati* as legal providing it met certain criteria, chief among which was that it be voluntary. The Nizamat Adalat accordingly instructed magistrates to pay close attention to the demeanor of the widow as she approached the pyre, so that officials could intercept at the first intimation of coercion. As a result, magistrates in the annual returns on *sati* recorded such remarks as the following: the widow burnt "in conformity to Shaster,"[56] "she burnt herself on the funeral pile of her husband, of her own free will,"[57] and "when it was learnt that she was neither pregnant, nor instigated, she was allowed to burn."[58]

Such acceptance of "good" *sati*s is also evident in the suggestions of J. H. Harrington and C. B. Elliot that the widow should be left free to commit *sati,* and that legislation should punish brahmins and others who assisted or unduly influenced her. They argued that this would prevent coercion, with the additional merit that, as Elliot put it, "No law obligatory on the consciences of the Hindoos will be infringed, and the women desirous of manifesting the excess of their conjugal love will be left at liberty to do so."[59] Official tolerance, if not approval, of *sati* as long as it was seen to be an act of free will was also reflected in a "non-horrified" announcement of two *sati*s in the *Calcutta Government Gazette* in 1827, at a time when it was officially maintained that fear of political repercussions was the only reason for tolerating widow immolation. It described the widow as "having abandoned with cheerfulness and her own free will, this perishable frame," and as "having burnt herself with him in their presence with a swelling heart and a smiling countenance."[60] However, many officials conceded the possibility of such voluntary *sati*s only in the abstract and insisted, like Ewer, that widows were, in actuality, incapable of consenting and must therefore be protected from pundits and crowds alike.

Analysis of official discourse makes it evident that arguments in favor of prohibiting *sati* were not primarily concerned with its cruelty or barbarity, although many officials did maintain that *sati* was reprehensible even as an act of volition. It is also clear that officials in favor of legislative prohibition were not, as has been generally conceived, interventionists contemptuous of aspects of indigenous culture, advocating change in the name of progress or Christian principles. On the contrary, officials in favor of abolition argued that such action was in fact consistent with upholding indigenous tradition. And indeed this was how the regenerating mission of colonization was conceptualized by officials: not as the imposition of a new Christian moral order but as the recuperation and enforcement of the truths of indigenous tradition. C. B. Elliot, joint magistrate of Bellah, expressed this sentiment when he suggested that the preamble to the *sati* regulation should appeal to scriptural authority for abolition, through apposite quotations from the Hindu texts. In his opinion, this would, "remove the evil from the less learned, who would thus be led to lament the ignorance in which they have hitherto been held enslaved by their bigoted priests, and at the same time to rejoice in the mercy and wisdom of a government which blends humanity with justice, and consults at once the interests and prejudices of its subjects, by recalling them from practices revolting, and pronounced erroneous even by their own authorities."[61]

Official conception of colonial subjects held the majority to be ignorant of their "religion." Religion was equated with scripture. Knowledge of the scriptures was held to be the monopoly of brahmin pundits. As Bernard Cohn has also argued, however, their knowledge was conceived as corrupt and self-serving.[62] The civilizing mission of colonization was thus seen to lie in protecting the "weak" against the "artful," in giving back to the natives the truths of their own "little read and less understood Shaster."[63]

The arguments of officials in favor of abolition were thus developed within the ambit of brahmanic scriptures. The pros and cons of *sati* were systematically debated as doctrinal considerations. In employing the scriptures to support their views, officials were dependent on the *vyawasthas* of court pundits whose exegesis of the texts made them accessible to colonial officials. *Vyawasthas* were the written responses of pundits to questions put to them by colonial officials on various aspects of *sati*. However, as I discuss below, officials interpreted *vyawasthas* in particular ways such that the concept of *sati* produced by official discourse was specifically colonial.

As noted already, official discourse on *sati* was grounded in three interrelated assumptions about Indian society: the hegemony of brahmanic scriptures, unreflective indigenous obedience to these texts, and the religious nature of *sati*. (I use the term *hegemony* loosely here to indicate the way in which colonial officials assumed brahmanic scriptures to be normative and prescriptive texts that organized social behavior and provided, as it were, the master narrative of "Hindu" civilization.) These assumptions shaped the nature and process of British intervention in outlawing the practice. Those in favor of abolition stressed its "material" aspects (such as the family's desire to be rid of the financial burden of supporting the widow) and thus the safety of intervention, while those opposed to prohibition emphasized its "religious" character and thus the dangers of intercession.

However, a close reading attentive both to the nature of evidence advanced for these ideas as well as to the social relations of their production makes it possible to contest official discourse. To begin with, the insistence on textual hegemony is challenged by the enormous regional variation in the mode of committing *sati*. The *vyawasthas* of pundits had elaborated differences by village and district, even by caste and occupation, in the performance of *sati:* "In certain villages of Burdwan, a district in Bengal, the following ceremonies are observed"; or "In some villages situated in Benares, the following practices obtain among the widows of merchants and other traders."[64] Local influence predominated in every aspect of *sati*. For instance, the pundits pointed out, "She then proceeds to the place of sacrifice . . . having previously worshipped the peculiar deities of the city or village."[65] In the context of local variations in the practice of widow burning, court pundits stated, "The ceremonies practically observed, differ as to the various tribes and districts."[66] Colonial officials acknowledged these differences and instructed magistrates to allow natives "to follow the established authority and usage of the province in which they reside."[67] However, such diversity was regarded as "peripheral" to the "central" principle of textual hegemony.

Similarly, regional variation in the incidence of *sati* did not serve to challenge official assumptions regarding the hegemony of religion, even though it did count as evidence of a material basis for *sati*. Colonial officials did not completely ignore the fact of such variation. The 1813 circular had recognized that in some districts *sati* had almost entirely ceased, while in others it was confined almost exclusively to certain castes. Despite this, officials decided to continue tolerating it, since they believed that, in most provinces, "all castes of Hindoos would be extremely tenacious of its continuance."[68] Whatever the justification for concluding this in 1813, such insistence was hardly tenable once systematic data collection was begun in 1815. For it quickly became apparent, as noted above, that 66 percent of widow burnings took place between the area surrounding Calcutta City and the Shahabad, Ghazipur, and Sarun districts. This indicates either that *sati* was not solely a religious practice as officials maintained or that religion was not hegemonic — another colonial assumption — or both. Officials, however, continued to insist on their analysis, interpreting regional variation to imply that although "material" factors might be at play, *sati* was primarily a religious practice. Therefore, as late as 1827, with eleven years of data at hand, W. B. Bayley could continue to be puzzled by what he called "anomalies" in the annual reports of widow immolation. He wrote to the court seeking an explanation "in regard to the following extraordinary discrepancies in the results exhibited in the present statement. In the district of Backergunge 63 instances of suttee are reported, and in the adjacent district of Dacca Telalpore only 2."[69] These could only be "extraordinary discrepancies" because Bayley, like other officials, continued to maintain that *sati* was religious and that "religion" had uniformly powerful influence in native life.

Equally reductive, and indeed more troubling in its effects, is the representation of the widow. Official discourse on *sati* constructs the widow as a perennial victim. The *Parliamentary Papers* contain both accounts of widows resisting immolation and reports of women apparently willing to leap into the pyre. Representations of women's resistance to *sati,* however, stress not their resistance but the barbarity of Hindu males in their coercion. As for incidents in which the widow appears to proceed voluntarily, these function as evidence of her subjection to religion. The widow nowhere appears as a subject-in-action, negotiating, capitulating, accommodating, resisting. Instead, she is cast as eternal victim: either a pathetically beaten down and coerced creature or a heroic person, selflessly entering the raging flames unmindful of pain. What distinguishes the two is the question of her consent.

This binary and reductive conception of the widow forecloses the possibility of a complex female agency. The point here is not that historical accuracy requires us to concede that some widows appeared to go willingly. For one thing, we have no independent access to the widows' subjective states outside of colonial representations of them. The meaning of consent in a patriarchal context is, in any case, hard to assess. What is striking, though, as will be explored in a close reading of European eyewitness accounts (see chapter 5), is the extent to which this binary representation in fact serves to attenuate the widow's struggle at the pyre. Certainly, there is evidence in many of these descriptions that the widow's actions and statements were the effect of multiple factors and calculations. Such evidence could have precluded a bipolar conception of the widow. It fails to do so, however, because in the final analysis, the discourse on *sati* posited tradition and religion (what we today would call "culture") as having the force of nature: as determining but not it-self subject to negotiation. This conception effectively assigned widows the position of being always already victimized, as if to say, "They know not what they do; they cannot know what they do; they must be saved. Ergo the civilising mission."[70]

Official representations further reinforced such a view of the widow by "infantalizing" the typical *sati*. The widow is quite often described as a "tender child." Here again, statistics on *sati* compiled by officials between 1815 and 1829 challenge such a conclusion. For instance, Benoy Bhusan Roy's analysis of the age distribution of widows who died in *sati* reveals that young women, between eleven and twenty, accounted for less than 5 percent of all burnings. The majority of widows who burned, 60 percent, were over forty-one.[71]

It is not the widow alone who is represented as passive, for all colonial subjects, male and female, are portrayed as finally subordinated to religion. The Nizamat Adalat stated this view quite dramatically in the context of discussing the Hindu practice of burying lepers. Reviewing a case that had come to their notice, court officials exclaimed, "no example can be of any avail. Their motives were above all human control."[72] We have here a classic instance of what Ronald Inden has described as one consequence of the essentialism of indology: the displacement of human agency onto constructs like Hinduism, which become thereby the substantialized agents of history.[73] Nineteenth-century indology, it would seem, posits the inverse of Althusser's dictum: determination not in the last, but in the first instance.

## Production of Official Knowledge on *Sati*: Interaction and Interrogation

Information about *sati* was generated at the instance, or rather insistence, of colonial officials posing questions to pundits resident at the courts. The pundits were instructed to respond with "a reply in conformity with the Shastras."[74] The exchanges between colonial officials and pundits constitute a rich corpus for unraveling the workings of colonial power and specifying the status of the discourse of court pundits. I examine below one, particularly significant, interaction.

As noted earlier, it was in 1805 that the question of scriptural sanction for *sati* was first put to the pundits of the Nizamat Adalat. Specifically they were asked "whether a woman is enjoined by the Shaster voluntarily to burn herself with the body of her husband, or is prohibited; and what are the conditions prescribed by the Shaster on such occasions?"[75]

The pundit responded: "Having duly considered the question proposed by the court, I now answer it to the best of my knowledge:—every woman of the four castes (brahmin, khetry, bues, and soodur) is permitted to burn herself with the body of her husband, provided she has not infant children, nor is pregnant, nor in a state of uncleanness, nor under the age of puberty; or in any of which cases she is not allowed to burn herself with her husband's body."[76]

The pundit clarified that women with infant children could burn provided they made arrangements for the care of such infants. Further, he added that coercion, overt or subtle, was forbidden. In support of his opinion, he quoted the following texts:

This rests upon the authority of Anjira, Vijasa and Vrihaspati Mooni. There are three millions and a half of hairs upon the human body, and every woman who burns herself with the body of her husband, will reside with him in heaven during a like number of years.

In the same manner, as a snake-catcher drags a snake from his hole, so does a woman who burns herself, draw her husband out of hell; and she afterwards resides with him in heaven.

The exceptions above cited, respecting women in a state of pregnancy or uncleanness, and adolescence, were communicated by Oorub and others to the mother of Sagar Raja.[77]

The question posed to the pundit was whether *sati* was enjoined by the scriptural texts. The pundit responded that the texts did not enjoin but merely permitted *sati* in certain instances, drawing on quotes which spoke of the rewards *sati* would bring to widows and their husbands. That the scriptures permit *sati* can only be inferred from the above passages. Nevertheless, based on this response, the Nizamat Adalat concluded: "The practice, generally speaking, being thus recognised and *encouraged* by the doctrines of the Hindoo religion, it appears evident that the course which the British government should follow, according to the principle of religious tolerance . . . is to allow the practice in those cases in which it is countenanced by their religion; and to prevent it in others in which it is by the same authority prohibited" (emphasis mine).[78]

Two moves have been made in reaching this conclusion. The pundit claims that he has answered the question "to the best of my knowledge." However, his response is treated as an altogether authoritative one. Further, permission by inference is transformed into scriptural recognition and encouragement of *sati*. Colonial policy on *sati* was formulated on the understanding produced by this interaction, for this encounter generated the circular that framed official policy on *sati* until abolition. The statement itself was also repeatedly recalled by officials arguing against abolition. Certainly the permissibility of *sati* was less ambiguous elsewhere in the texts, though the practice was nowhere required by them (see chapter 2). However, at issue here is not the scriptural accuracy of the pundit's response so much as the logic at work in official interpretations of *vyawasthas*.[79]

This example embodies many of the key principles by which a body of information about *sati* was generated. Questions to pundits were intended to establish clarity on all aspects of *sati*. Thus in 1813 court pundits were asked to specify the precise meaning of the phrase "of tender years" in their *vyawastha* which claimed that a woman with a child "of tender years" was not permitted *sati*. Clarification was sought by officials as to the age of the child and whether or not the child had to be weaned before its mother could commit *sati*.[80]

Pundits were required to comb the scriptures and produce unambiguous textual support for their responses. Inferential conclusions or recourse to customary practice were only acceptable where explicit documentation was unavailable, even though pundits at the Sadar Diwani Adalat had claimed in the context of producing inferential scriptural support for the burial of *jogis,* that the texts themselves gave due weight to custom: "The long established usages peculiar to a country, tribe or family are to be respected; otherwise people will be distressed."[81] Despite this, officials continued to privilege scripture over custom, claiming faithfulness to the texts in doing so. It was in this context that Acting Magistrate B. B. Gardiner appealed to the higher court in October 1813 for a clarification of the modes of burning appropriate for various castes, since the pundit at his court had referred only to customary evidence in his response to the question.[82] The pundits at the superior court produced a *vyawastha* supported by scriptural evidence. Their *vyawastha* was forwarded to Gardiner by officials at the Nizamat Adalat with a reprimand to the district court pundit for having "referred to the custom of a country, upon a point expressly provided for by law."[83]

Official insistence on clarity was crucial to enabling the constitution of "legal" and "illegal" *satis*. Through such continual and intensive questioning, criteria for an officially sanctioned *sati* were generated. As noted previously, *sati* had to be voluntary. Brahmin women were permitted only *sahamarana,* burning with the husband's corpse. Non-brahmin women could burn through *sahamarana* or *anoomarana. Sati* was forbidden to women under sixteen and to women with infants less than three years old. Women of the *jogi* tribe were permitted to bury themselves.

Although scriptural authority was claimed for this model, a careful reading of the *Parliamentary Papers* suggests that such authority was dubious. For example, while officials treated *vyawasthas* as truthful exegeses of the scriptures in an absolute sense, it is clear from reading them that the pundits issuing them believed them to be interpretive. Pundits attested to the interpretive nature of their *vyawasthas* in a number of ways. *Vyawastha*s were often prefaced with such declarations as "Having inspected the paper drawn up by the chief judge of this court we proceed to furnish a reply *to the best of our ability*" (emphasis mine).[84] They also characterized their replies as textual readings: "The authorities for the above opinion are as follows."[85] The interpretive character of the *vyawasthas* was also evident from the way in which the scriptures were used: "In the above sentence by using the words 'she who ascends,' the author *must have had in contemplation* those who declined to do so" (emphasis mine);[86] or "From the above quoted passages of the Mitateshura *it would appear that* this was an act fit for all women to perform" (emphasis mine).[87] *Vyawastha*s claimed to pronounce neither scriptural truth nor the only possible response to a given question.

In part, the corpus of texts designated "the scriptures" made any claim to a definitive interpretation difficult to maintain. The scriptures were an enormous body of texts composed at different times. They included the *srutis,* or Vedas, the *dharmashastras,* or *smritis,* and the commentaries. The Vedas are believed to be transcriptions of the revealed word of God. There are four Vedas: RgVeda, Yajur Veda, SamaVeda, and AtharvaVeda. Each text was subdivided into four parts: Samhita or Mantra, Brahmanas (priestly texts), Aranyakas (forest books), and Upanishads (esoteric philosophical texts). The *smritis* were mnemonic and historico-social texts. The principal *smritis* are products of named and thus "historical" subjects: Manu, Yajnavalkya, and Narada. The commentaries and digests were treatises interpreting and expounding the *shastras* and mainly produced between the eleventh and eighteenth centuries. Different commentaries were held to be authoritative in different regions.

The fact that the texts were authored at different periods accounted for their heterogeneity on many points, not least of which was the scriptural position on *sati*. Two pundits could thus issue divergent *vyawasthas* on the same point, and quote different texts or different passages from the same text to support their statements. The explicitly interpretive character and contextual nature of these *vyawasthas* illustrates a general feature of the status of *srutis* and *smritis* within the Hindu tradition. As Arvind Sharma puts it, "The principle that though moral laws are eternal, their actual application is mutable is important for understanding Hinduism."[88] Different norms of conduct were held appropriate for different historical periods, which was characteristic of a system "which tends to be definitional without being definitive."[89] Colonial officials, however, misperceived the status and interpretations of these texts, regarding them rather as prescriptive and normative. It is interesting to note in this context that the dictionary definition of *vyawastha* captures its shifting meanings in the colonial period, bearing the double sense of interpretation and legal statute. In Sir Monier Williams's Sanskrit-English dictionary, for instance, *vyawastha* is defined variously as "settlement," "decision," "statute," "rule," "law," "legal decision," an opinion applied to the written extracts from codes of law, and the adjustment of contradictory passages in different codes.

The transactions between pundits and colonial officials mark one site of the conflict between competing rationalities that is a hallmark of colonialism. Drawing on Sudipta Kaviraj and Ranajit Guha's work, we may argue that what we see here is an encounter between two notions of historicity, authorship, and textuality. In his analysis of Bankimchandra's *Krishnacaritra,* Kaviraj has argued that a number of significant differences are to be found between precolonial and colonial-rationalist conceptions of these terms.[90] In a similar vein, Guha has underlined the contrast in colonial and precolonial understandings of the past and its relation to the present. According to Guha, contrary to the Enlightenment notion of the past as diachronic, teleological, and bearing upon the present (a conception that is evident in the logic of official questioning of pundits), the past in precolonial times was seen to be "made up of discrete moments recovered synchronically as the occasion required."[91] Guha's point meshes with Kaviraj's argument that change in the Hindu tradition prior to the nineteenth century had been achieved surreptitiously, through subtle alterations and successive shiftings of the narrative center of gravity. Taking the example of Krishna, Kaviraj argues that changes were frequently effected through the addition of new episodes in the story of his life. Such additions and transformations, he claims, were not seen to contradict older texts but to contribute to the issues at hand, for instance the idea of God. The author was regarded not as a text's creator but as its instrument, and his talent was seen to reside in the erasure of his individuality. Finally, the fixing of an idea or utterance in textual form, according to Kaviraj, ensured nothing more than its recurrence in relevant discourse. It offered no certainty of constancy of meaning or even of memory.

When read against this backdrop, the explicitly interpretive cast of *vyawasthas,* the pundits' disregard of chronology and of the citation and evidentiary protocols demanded of them by officials, and their apparent lack of concern about textual contradictions become a good deal more intelligible. What appeared to officials to be the random and indiscriminate use of scriptural fragments and the mixing of various kinds of evidence turns out to be the enactment of a different kind of textual practice. This conception of textuality was, however, incompatible with the project of the colonial state which sought to develop an exact science of ruling, which was, in turn, dependent on precise knowledges. It could brook neither ambiguity of meaning nor disregard for precedent in its drive for a uniformly applicable law. At the same time, for reasons already stated, India was no tabula rasa for colonial writing technologies. Officials were constrained to engage the discourse of pundits, and they accordingly developed strategies for handling the heterogeneity of pundits' *vyawasthas.*

In general, the older the text the greater was assumed to be its stature. Thus *vyawasthas* citing *srutis* or *smritis* were treated more seriously than those that referred to more recent texts (see chapter 2). Over and above this general principle, officials sometimes recognized diversity, as in the determination and enforcement of the appropriate modes of burning for brahmin and non-brahmin women. At other times they acknowledged textual complexity but for practical reasons did not seek to "resolve" it, as in the considered tolerance of regional variation in the mode of conducting *sati*—whether the widow's body was placed to the left or right of the corpse, the direction of the pyre, and so on.

A third response was to marginalize certain *vyawasthas.* A telling example of such marginalization was the fate of Mrityunjay Vidyalankar's *vyawastha,* relegated to the appendix of the Nizamat Adalat proceedings of 1817, with no more than a mention in the main text. Vidyalankar appears to have written his *vyawastha* after becoming pundit of the Supreme Court in July 1816. Vidyalankar's examination of the texts served to systematically call into question the colonial rationale for a scriptural sanction for *sati*. It problematized, among other things, the status of *sati* as an act of virtue, since it was a practice undertaken not in the spirit of selfless absorption in the divine but with an end to reward. Although Vidyalankar was soon to become vocal in his advocacy of *sati,* his *vya-wastha* contained sufficient scriptural justification for its prohibition. It was, however, ignored. (Interestingly, Vidyalankar's *vyawastha* precedes the first pamphlet on widow burning, published in 1818 by Rammohun Roy, symbol of the indigenous anti-*sati* lobby.)

Such continual reinscription of *sati* into a scriptural tradition despite evidence to the contrary points to the specificity of meanings imposed by official reading of the *vyawasthas,* and thereby to the production of a colonial conception of *sati.* The shift in the status of the *vyawastha* from contextual opinion to impersonal law is also analogous to a process that Paul Ricoeur, in another context, has called "textualization."[92] It disassociated opinions from their original contexts, not just fixing their meaning in law but also generalizing their application to society at large. In the case at hand, the generation of law from brahmanic scriptures extended a more restrictive high-caste law to women to whom it had not previously applied.[93]

If the construct of *sati* thus produced is specifically colonial, it can also be argued that "religion" in this discourse emerges as that part of culture which colonial power chooses not to interdict. If for some reason it was decided to prohibit a practice coded "religious," official strategy was to discount its claim to being "religious" through privileging a reading of the texts that would undermine such a conclusion. In the end this was the process followed in relation to *sati.* The scriptural basis for *sati* had been dubious from the start, and in the period after 1818, Rammohun Roy and other indigenous anti-*sati* campaigners had provided enough scriptural evidence for the abolition of *sati.* Prohibition, however, came much later when officials deemed it "feasible."

In the meantime, official policy, whatever its claim to noninterference, endeavored to enforce this colonial conception of a "scripturally authentic" *sati* through scrutiny of the details of its practice. Official presence was required at each *sati.* Magistrates were asked to tabulate data on each case: personal data on the widow, date, place, time, and mode of burning. They were also given explicit instructions to "not allow the most minute particular to escape observation."[94] Such details ensured that no shastric infraction, however small, whether on the part of the participants or of the functionaries policing the proceedings, could escape the official eye. Thus we have instances of the Nizamat Adalat criticizing officers for infringing the letter of the law in what were seen to be overzealous attempts to prevent burnings.[95] So much for official arguments that *sati* was horrid and its toleration merely strategic!

Detail was important to such a "penal mapping of the social body."[96] Magistrates were compelled to record details and were reprimanded for reports "totally destitute of remark."[97] The consistency of the Nizamat Adalat judges on this score drew the approval of the governor-general and his council, who commended them in 1820 on the "minuteness with which the Nizamat Adaulut have entered on the examination of the returns from the several districts."[98] No doubt the governor-general's praise was partly a recognition of how attention to such detail also functioned to police those employed at various levels of the colonial bureaucracy.

Whatever the official claims to religious noninterference, the process by which knowledge of *sati* was produced was specifically "colonial" and its attempted vigilant enforcement thoroughly interventionist. As the examples above indicate, despite the involvement of brahmin pundits, the privilege of the final authoritative interpretation of their *vyawasthas* lay with colonial officials. For it was the Nizamat Adalat judges and the governor-general and his council who determined which *vyawasthas* were "essential" and which "peripheral." The authority of the pundits was problematic. The fact of being native simultaneously privileged and devalued them as reliable sources. The pundits were essential to "unlocking" the scriptures for officials. But they were also believed by officials to be the "devious minority" against which it was the mission of colonization to protect the "simple majority."

Colonial distrust of brahmin pundits was related to the anti-Catholic temper of post-Reformation Britain. The polemic against Rome had two linked aspects.[99] Firstly, the infallibility of the church and papacy was called into question. The Catholic Church and its priests were accused of keeping the Bible from the people, who were in consequence held to be left in a state of superstitious ignorance. Secondly, the axiomatic supremacy of scripture was counterposed to the fallibility of the papacy. This no doubt predisposed colonial officials to finding the brahmin pundits untrustworthy. In addition, it strengthened their resolve to turn to the scriptures in order to minimize the perceived potential for their corrupt manipulation by these pundits.

One can see how a number of factors converged in the official privileging of brahmanic scriptures as the source of law. Ideas prevalent in late-eighteenth-century Britain about the best means to protect the populace from undue priestly domination intersected with a particular perception of Indian society as organized by religion. As we have seen, officials presumed that religious practices derived from scripture and that social practices derived from religion. Thus in their view, by founding law in these texts, they were simply enforcing tradition, not in any way transforming it. Further, as noted earlier, the turn to brahmanic texts must be placed in the context of the discovery of the antiquity of Sanskrit, and its recognition as the root of many European languages. Finally, the generation of law from brahmanic scripture was related to the practical needs of the colonial state for unambiguous law that could have general application. It is thus that they sought to systematize and codify law based on the scriptures. This process not merely eroded custom but also extended brahmanic law, previously applicable only to a high-caste numerical minority, to the rest of society.

It has often been argued that the prohibition of widow burning signals the demise of a sympathetic orientalism and the rise of the derision of anglicist utilitarians like James Mill, whose *The History of British India* was published in 1817.[100] This distinction, however, is not one sustainable in analysis of the debate on *sati*. There is no specifically anglicist or utilitarian voice to be heard. Indeed, it is important to note that even the most vigorous reformers in Britain opted for caution, if not reluctance, when it came to the colonies. Certainly, Jeremy Bentham was critical of what he saw as the East India Company's defense of native custom, which, in his view, smacked of veneration of antiquity for its own sake. Likewise, Mill regarded the implementation of indigenous law as an aspect of the mercantilist and extractive character of the East India Company and its monopoly privileges. Despite these philosophical objections, however, the positions they took in practice were distinctly conservative. Thus Mill's recommendation in 1810 simply reiterated the position the East India Company had pursued since 1772. He argued the importance of using Hindu institutions in effecting reform: "You might thus have a perfect code of laws, with such modifications as not to shock the prejudices and manners of the people, and with all the authority which the Brahmenical character and the most sacred names could attach to it."[101] This was precisely what existing policy had set out to achieve. Similarly, Bentham, in a letter to Rammohun Roy written in 1828, recommended that he "singly, or in conjunction with other enlightened philanthropists, [make] an offer to Government" to design an institution for prisoners and paupers that would implement this scheme of a Panopticon. Bentham suggested that the inmates of such an institution be classified and separated along religious and caste lines.[102]

The metropolitan career of utilitarianism was thus not continuous with its trajectory in the colony, where radical thought often met its limit point and even turned into its opposite. The colonial state was fundamentally defined by its appropriative relationship to indigenous society, and only those reforms were contemplated that in no way interrupted the logic of accumulation. Romantics and utilitarians may have represented sharply opposed currents in British society, but when it came to India, their difference lay not so much in how they analyzed Indian society, which in its broad features was remarkably similar. Rather, where they diverged was in their evaluation of it. The shift from orientalist praise to anglicist condemnation was thus primarily a transformation in attitude.

Such was the discursive terrain and scope of the official debate on the prohibition of widow immolation. Many of the themes that have emerged here will resurface in following chapters, in which I will consider the discourses of those other players in the drama that surrounded *sati:* the indigenous male elite and missionaries. It is to the former that we now turn.

## CHAPTER 2

# Abstract Disquisitions

## Bhadralok *and the Normative Violence of* Sati

---

*The Bengal Renaissance is primarily associated with the
great name of Rammohun Ray (1774–1833). It was he who
heralded the movement by his forthright criticism of traditional
Hinduism. The spread of Western education, the development of
commercial activity and the Christian missionary propaganda,
had produced a great impact on Hindu society. Rammohun
initiated a powerful movement for social and religious reform.
Age-old traditions, beliefs and rituals which were never
challenged before were for the first time attacked from within.*

A. F. Salahuddin Ahmed, "The Bengal
Renaissance and the Muslim Community"[1]

*In all countries and especially in India, social reform consists
chiefly in doing away with the disabilities or sufferings incident
to difference of sex or accident of birth or in other words social
reformers have chiefly to fight with the spirit of caste and its evils
and the subjection of women to the selfish interests and pleasures
or supposed interests of the male sex.*

Ramananda Chatterjee, *Rammohun Roy
and Modern India*[2]

## Prologue:
## The *Bhadralok* and the "Renaissance"

---

The "Bengal Renaissance" is perhaps the most widely
written about but, until lately, most misunderstood dimension of nineteenth-century Indian history. Primarily the story of elite male social reformers, writ large in the historiography as the autobiography of the

new urban middle classes, or *bhadralok* (respectable folk), it has been narrativized as a series of encounters between "tradition" and "modernity," as a battle between forces of obscurantism and agents of progressive reform. In this, the debate over the legality of widow burning occupies a special position. It serves to inaugurate the "renaissance," and the positions of early-nineteenth-century Calcutta intelligentsia on widow burning have, in this literature, frequently served as an index of their conservative or reformist proclivities.[3]

The *bhadralok* designates the social elite that emerged out of the economic transformations—the ruins as well as the opportunities—wrought by East India Company land reform and trade policies. It was an internally differentiated group, heterogeneous in its caste composition (though kayasths, vaidyas, and brahmins predominated) as well as in the routes through which individual members had achieved and/or consolidated their socioeconomic status.[4] It was thus a mix of old and new elites and included those with a continuing major interest in land as well as those who combined land ownership with commercial investments. The emergence of the *bhadralok* was directly tied to the introduction of private property in land and to the Permanent Settlement of 1793.[5] In a bid to ensure the regularity of revenue collection and maximize these amounts, the East India Company decided to recognize as "owners" *zamindars* who, under the Mughals, had been more properly tax collectors in a context in which there prevailed multiple, graded, and overlapping rights in land. It was hoped that the "incentive" of "ownership" would turn these men into improving gentry, eager to extend and intensify cultivation. Initial overassessments of land revenue had disastrous consequences. Depletion of agricultural reserves contributed to a famine in 1770 reportedly destroying one-third of the population of Bengal. This prompted the East India Company, under what came to be known as the Permanent Settlement, to place a ceiling on the revenues appropriated by it. It was hoped that this would shore up the *zamindars,* and restore social stability undermined by the disruptions caused by initial years of excessive levies. The social and economic consequences of this policy in realigning the prevailing system of complex, and regionally differentiated, customary rights and tenurial structures has been the subject of great and ongoing debate.[6]

Historians have argued that the conditions which accounted for the emergence of the bourgeoisie were to fundamentally shape the nature of this class and thus of the Bengal Renaissance.[7] For instance, it has been pointed out that this class did not develop "organically" but was, in effect, a creature of colonial dispensation.[8] The *bhadralok* were the middlemen of the East India Company's revenue and commercial transactions, the classic comprador class, benefiting from opportunities afforded by colonial rule, but ultimately constrained by the conditions of colonial subjugation. The economic and political context of colonialism meant that their empowerment as landlords did not enable their emulation of the improving English gentry as East India Company officials had hoped. On the contrary, they were to become a rentier social class divorced from the productive economic functions that had characterized their English counterparts. This was partly because the rise of these landed elites turned not on technological innovations, but proceeded on the backs of a peasantry made vulnerable both by the loss of their customary rights in land and by new laws which strengthened landlord control over peasant labor. At the same time, land continued to attract those whose fortunes were made through trading or money lending but who had relatively few avenues for productive investment in the commercial sector.

Land was not only coveted as a way of consolidating social standing. It was also a valuable asset, given the growing export market in opium and indigo. This development, along with the high unemployment caused by the destruction of the textile industry, increased both the vulnerability of the peasantry and the pressure on land. Indigo had replaced Indian textiles, which were subject to prohibitive duties, as a mode of remitting money to England. The export of opium and indigo was primarily controlled by English Agency Houses operating through Indian middlemen, since Europeans could not legally own land. These English merchants represented free-trade interests and were critical of the East India Company's monopoly privileges. The situation offered the *bhadralok* additional prospects for investment, an option that was to be eliminated with the rise of free-trade imperialism in 1833. Although there is disagreement regarding the extent to which India was deindustrialized in the early nineteenth century,[9] it is agreed that the needs of the Indian economy were increasingly and devastatingly subordinated to those of the metropole and to the logic of the import-export mechanism.

Any reconsideration of the nineteenth century is simultaneously a historiographical intervention and a meditation, oblique or otherwise, on the nature of "modernity" in contemporary India. This is so because, in the nineteenth century, "history" became the ground both of colonial domination and resistance.[10] The historiography on this period is, then, part of the genealogy of Indian "modernity," key to the self-representation of the contemporary nation-state and the ideological formation of its middle-class citizenry. It is thus that this literature is suffused with so much hope and despair, pride and acute disappointment. Those constructed as the forebears of "modernity" are berated or eulogized not simply because they are "our" forerunners, but because, in an important sense, their concerns echo contemporary predicaments.

One way in which Marxist historians have sought to understand the "failure" of the *bhadralok* in the early nineteenth century—their practically unanimous support of British colonization and the limitation of critique to specific policies, their preoccupation with issues like widow burning that affected only a small portion of upper-caste women, their virtual silence on caste oppression and the immiseration produced by the destruction of the textile and handicraft industries—is by situating them within the peculiar conditions of their emergence in the colonial context. Their failure is related to the fact that colonialism did not enable, in the words of one critic, the transition to a "full-blooded bourgeois modernity, but [to] a weak and distorted caricature of the same." [11] The objective conditions of their existence, the forms of land management, industry, and trade practiced by and available to them were, it is argued, not "properly bourgeois." [12] As a consequence, bourgeois liberal values are said to have been "theoretically espoused [but] . . . bereft of material content and a genuine social base." [13]

Teleology and economism compromise this otherwise valuable framework for illuminating the character and limitations of the reform efforts of the *bhadralok* in such matters as widow burning. This argument confers on "the productive principle" a magical propensity to transform social relations. The theoretical difficulty with this position is that it appears to take as an article of faith the universalizing claims of capital regarding its capacities to create the world in its own image, to inexorably bring liberal European values in its wake. Empirical analyses represent individual *banians, zamindars,* and businessmen as adjusting to, negotiating, and manipulating the changing economic and political context of the late eighteenth and early nineteenth century, reconstituting their practices in accordance with the new regime. However, at the theoretical level they are still conceived, in the manner of their European counterparts, as the bearers of an emergent and "universal" bourgeois consciousness.

One consequence of such economism has been the tendency to expect conservatism from those with a predominance of investments in landholdings and, by the same token, progressive positions from those with primary investments in the commercial sector. This division of the Calcutta intelligentsia into those representing the feudal past (conservatives) and those embodying, if only in embryonic form, the capitalist future (reformers and radicals) does not, however, stand up to scrutiny.[14] These figures took a bewildering array of positions that are, from the Marxist perspective, inconsistent. Let us consider here the cases of Rammohun Roy and Radhakanta Deb, both Calcutta *bhadralok* and symbols, respectively, of the anti-*sati* and pro-*sati* lobbies. Rammohun Roy's economic position was founded initially in money lending and in speculation in East India Company securities, and then consolidated through the purchase and management of land. Radhakanta Deb also owed his position as a wealthy landholder to the East India Company. His family's rise to prominence can be traced to his grandfather Nabakrishna Deb's appointment as East India Company interpreter, a position that enabled him to build a fortune through revenue farming, commissions on revenue collection, and so on.

While Rammohun Roy's critique of *sati* and Radhakanta Deb's espousal of widow burning have positioned them respectively as "progressive" and "conservative" members of Calcutta *bhadralok,* their stands on other issues cannot be neatly enfolded into these categories. For instance, Radhakanta Deb was pro-*sati* and anti–free trade, but also pro-English education and actively involved in a range of educational endeavors (for instance, the founding of the Hindu College, 1816, Calcutta School Book Society, 1817, and Agricultural and Horticultural Society, 1819). While his approval of *sati* placed him in the camp of social conservatives, widow burning was not practiced in his family, unlike the case with Rammohun.[15] The latter campaigned against *sati* and argued passionately against rituals but never forsook many high-caste practices, even going so far as to take a brahmin cook with him when he left for England in 1830. Similarly, while at first glance Radhakanta Deb's anti–free trade position appears to confirm his conservatism, free trade was to prove to be disastrous for the Indian economy. From the vantage point of the present, Rammohun's defense of it seems misguided, indeed a classic instance of a colonial intellectual's theoretical espousal of the abstract principles of liberalism — in this instance utilitarianism — in the face of mounting evidence of their disastrous consequences for the colonies.[16]

It is the argument of this chapter that berating the Bengali *bhadralok* for their failure to assume their "historic" mission, attributing specific beliefs to a residual feudalism and ensuing deficiencies to the tragedy of colonial underdevelopment, runs the risk of eliding under the label of "backwardness" or "traditionalism" the *modernity* of what was taking place in the context of nineteenth-century social reform. For, as will become abundantly clear, both advocates and opponents of *sati* were engaged in a thoroughly modern process. Both sides, even those representing themselves as the champions of tradition, were, in fact, elaborating their visions of modernity. What we have here is not so much a duel between tradition and modernity, in which, as in the framework above, the *content* of these terms is assumed, but a battle between competing versions of modernity. This premise does not require consistency from participants, whether between their position on different issues, or between the nature of their wealth and their stands on social and economic matters. It directs us instead to the terms and contours of the discussion on widow burning and, in the process, challenges the commonplaces of historiographical wisdom regarding the debate.

In this chapter, analysis will begin with a close reading of the texts of critics and defenders of widow burning. A range of documents — pamphlets, petitions, newspapers — will be examined to indicate the nature, scope, and chief concerns of participants. These texts will then be read against each other, against official discourse, and finally, in light of the historiography on social reform. This will return us to the broader issues raised in this prologue.

## The *Bhadralok* and Widow Burning

It is perhaps not a coincidence that 1818, which marked the emergence of the vernacular press in Bengal, was also the year which inaugurated public debate on widow burning among the indigenous male elite.[17] While there is no reason to suppose that the issue had not been discussed privately in social or intellectual gatherings in Calcutta, a number of events combine to suggest this year as initiating a more concerted public phase. During 1818, Rammohun published his first tract against *sati,* Hindu advocates of widow immolation petitioned the East India Company for removal of the restrictions that had been placed on the practice since 1813, and those against *sati* presented a counterpetition on the grounds of its illegality in "authorities considered most sacred." In addition, a letter to the editor of the *India Gazette* from Hariharananda, in referring to these developments, challenged supporters of *sati* to respond to Rammohun's critique and expressed "surprise and regret" at European tolerance of the practice.[18] The timing of these events was undoubtedly related to public awareness of disagreement among officials as to whether to rescind all circulars hitherto promulgated on widow burning, widen the scope of state intervention, or continue existing policy (see chapter 1).

These developments indicate the form that public discussions on *sati* were to take in the years that followed. Pamphlets, petitions, articles in newspapers and journals, and letters to the editor were the means most frequently employed by various sides in popularizing their views. There were, in addition, reports of incidents of widow burning. These were either detailed eyewitness descriptions or reports based on accounts of persons present at the immolation. Such detailed reports were mostly carried by the English-language papers (see chapter 5). The Bengali press, *Samachar Darpan* (published from 1818), *Sambad Kaumudi* (established 1821), and *Samachar Chundrika* (founded 1822) mainly carried news of *sati* in the context of the obituaries of men whose wives burnt with them. These were brief items giving particulars of date, place, time, and name of male deceased. The *Samachar Darpan* carried details of burning only occasionally, when the incident was deemed to be of an exceptional nature. For the most part, these reports were not accompanied by critical or approving commentaries on widow burning and contained little or no information about the widow. This was the case even with *Samachar Darpan,* published by the Baptist missionaries at Serampore. However, as we shall see below, Bengali newspapers did, from time to time, engage in battles over representation of incidents of *sati.*

The media employed in the debate suggest that all parties were cognizant of the value of print technology in constituting a critical, contestatory public domain. For given the specific way that *sati* had been constructed as a problem by East India Company officials, the contest over widow burning was situated precisely in the public arena even by those who insisted on its being a private affair and, as such, beyond governmental intervention. For instance, privately published indigenous pamphlets were simultaneously translated into English and widely circulated among the indigenous and British communities. Furthermore, the English-language press, both missionary and lay, reprinted or extracted indigenous pamphlets, petitions, and press reports on *sati.* (The press in Britain also frequently carried material on widow burning published in India.) Pamphlets, petitions, and the press were the chief modes of communication with the colonial state. These media lent themselves to a situation in which opponents and defenders of *sati* sought to address distinct and only partially overlapping constituencies, indigenous and European, nonofficial and official. And each was deployed in specific ways and privileged certain aspects of the discourse on *sati* over others.

My analysis of indigenous discourse begins by examining documents produced by either side in the aftermath of prohibition in December 1829: on the one side, Rammohun Roy's "Abstract of the arguments regarding the burning of widows considered as a religious rite," [19] and, on the other, the "Petition of the orthodox Hindu community of Calcutta against the Suttee Regulation." [20] In a debate marked by tedious repetition, these texts concisely summarize the main arguments of opponents and proponents of widow burning. These documents will then be situated within the much broader discussion that took place between 1818 and 1829. This corpus will enable us to grasp shifts in the discourse over this period, and the specificities as well as commonalities of the discourse of pamphlets, petitions, and newspapers.

Rammohun's discussion of *sati* in "Abstract" is grounded from the beginning in a deliberation of scripture. As he puts it, "The first point to be ascertained is, whether or not the practice of burning widows alive on the pile and with the corpse of their husbands, is imperatively enjoined by the Hindu religion?" (367).

Rammohun claims, in answer to his own rhetorical question, that "even the staunch advocates for Concremation must reluctantly give a negative reply," and he offers textual evidence from *Manusmriti:* "Manu in plain terms enjoins a widow to *continue till death* forgiving all injuries, performing austere duties, avoiding every sensual pleasure, and cheerfully practising the incomparable rules of virtue which have been followed by such women as were devoted to only one husband" (367–368). He corroborates this statement with one from *Yajnavalkya* regarding a widow's right to live with her natal or marital family on the death of her husband. Having established that *sati* is not incumbent on the widow, Rammohun deliberates which of the two options, *sati* or an ascetic life, is more meritorious. In this he draws on the Vedas whose authority, he claims, has priority over the *smriti*s: "From a desire during life, of future fruition, life ought not to be destroyed" (368). This most "pointed and decisive" statement counters, in his view, the claims of advocates of *sati* who also argue their case with reference to the Vedas, but by drawing on a passage that Rammohun finds abstract and open to multiple interpretations. The sentence in question is the following: "'O fire, let these women, with bodies anointed with clarified butter, eyes coloured with collyrium and void of tears, enter thee, the parent of water, that they may not be separated from their husbands, themselves sinless, and jewels amongst women'" (368–369). Rammohun points out that this passage nowhere enjoins women to commit *sati*. Secondly, he notes, "no allusion whatever is made in it to voluntary death by a widow *with the corpse of her husband*" (369). In any case, he adds, "the phrase 'these women' in the passage, literally implies women then present" (369). Finally, he concludes that the passage has been interpreted by some commentators as an allegory of the constellation of the moon's path in which butter signifies "the milky path," collyrium "the unoccupied space between one star and another," and husbands "the more splendid of the heavenly bodies." Allusions to ascending and entering the fire are understood as "the rise of the constellations through the south-east horizon, considered as the abode of fire" (369). Rammohun concludes, "Whatever may be the real purport of this passage, no-one ever ventured to give it an interpretation as *commanding* widows to burn themselves on the pile and with the corpse of their husbands" (369).[21]

Rammohun thereafter considers the *smriti* texts, which he designates as "next in authority to the *Vedas*" (369). This corpus is seen to be ordered hierarchically, with *Manu* heading the list as the text "whose authority supercedes that of other lawgivers" (369). Since *Manu* has already been shown to approve of ascetic widowhood, Rammohun turns his attention to those *smriti* texts like *Angira* and *Hareet* that do appear to place a positive value on *sati*. Rammohun notes a passage from *Angira* exalting a widow who commits *sati* as equal to Arundhati, but dismisses as inferior its recommendation of *sati*, since it is avowedly a "means to obtain future carnal fruition" (370). As such, it is assigned a low rung in the hierarchy of spiritual acts.

Having demonstrated that *sati* is not commanded by the scriptures and having argued that, even where it is presented as an option, it is of inferior virtue as an act undertaken to procure rewards, Rammohun concludes his tract by considering "whether or not *the mode of* concremation prescribed by *Hareet* and others was ever duly observed" (371). Rammohun points out that "these expounders of law" require the widow to voluntarily ascend the pyre and enter the flames. In his opinion, violation of either of these provisions "renders the act mere suicide, and implicates, in the guilt of female murder, those that assist in its perpetration" (372). Rammohun is here concerned with the question of the widow's will, an issue which had been central to official discussions of *sati*. He claims "no widow ever voluntarily *ascended* on and *entered* into the *flames* in the fulfilment of this rite" (372). No wonder, he says, that those in favor of *sati* have been "driven to the necessity of taking refuge in *usage,* as justifying both suicide and female murder, the most heinous of crimes" (372).

Where Rammohun challenges the scriptural sanction for widow burning, undermines its spiritual value, and argues that most immolations were involuntary, the pro-*sati* petition proposes a contrary view of the practice and its status, both in the scriptures and in reality.[22] The petition against the 1829 prohibition of *sati* argues:

Under the sanction of immemorial usage as well as precept, Hindoo widows perform of their own accord and pleasure, and for the benefit of their husband's soul and their own, the sacrifice of self immolation called suttee, which is not merely a sacred *duty* but a high privilege to her who sincerely believes in the doctrines of their religion; and we humbly submit that any interference with a persuasion of so high and self-annihilating a nature, is . . . an unjust and intolerant dictation in matters of conscience. (156)

Eulogy of widow burning is not, however, the petition's main focus. Rather, the petition seeks to demonstrate that the East India Company's criminalizing of *sati* is based on an erroneous reading of the scriptures. This is hardly surprising since, as we have seen, the official debate turned on the issue of *sati*'s scriptural grounding. The pro-*sati* argument does, however, differ in one other respect from that of Rammohun and most colonial officials: in the relatively greater weight it assigns to custom. The petition claims that "the Hindoo religion is founded, like all other religions, on usage as well as precept, and one when immemorial is held equally sacred with the other" (156). Thus while Rammohun valorizes scripture over custom, criticizing his opponents for "being driven to the necessity of taking refuge in *usage,*"[23] the pro-*sati* petitioners argue that the antiquity of Hinduism implies an equal status for both. Despite this claim, however, they proceed to present their case almost exclusively in terms of scripture.

The petitioners seek to undermine the credibility of scriptural interpreters held in esteem by the colonial administration, among them Rammohun, as well as the validity of their interpretations regarding the textual basis for the prohibition of *sati*. They charge the government with deriving its interpretations from apostates: "But we humbly submit that in a question so delicate as the interpretation of our sacred books, and the authority of our religious usages, none but pundits and brahmins, and teachers of holy lives, and known learning, ought to be consulted . . . not . . . men who have neither any faith nor care for the memory of their ancestors or their religion" (157). Pundits and brahmins are proposed as authoritative interpreters, and the differences of opinion between the pro- and anti-*sati* members of the debate are reduced to an opposition between believers and unbelievers.

The petition was signed by eight hundred persons and included pundits of the Government Sanskrit College, Supreme Court, Nizamat and Diwani Adalat. As we know, the claim that the government was dependent on unbelievers like Rammohun is without basis, since officials had relied primarily on pundits at the civil and criminal courts where many of the pro-*sati* signatories were employed.

The petition was accompanied by a document signed by 120 pundits presenting scriptural evidence in favor of *sati* or, in the words of the petition, "the legal points declaring the practice of suttee lawful and expedient" (159). The enclosure sets out the chief arguments of those advocating prohibition of widow burning—that asceticism has greater value than *sati*, that *sati* brings temporary rewards while ascetic widowhood holds the promise of permanent bliss, and that *Manu* recommends asceticism and has priority over other *smriti* texts since his text "is immediately originated from *Sruti*" (160)—and objects to each in turn.

In response to the suggestion that ascetic widowhood is more highly recommended than *sati*, the petition quotes *Manu* as cited in the *Nirnaya Sindhu:* "On the death of her husband, if, by chance, a woman is unable to perform concremation, nevertheless she should preserve the virtue required of widows" (160). Here, the petitioners claim, "the order of meaning has preference over that of reading": in other words, that ascetic widowhood is a secondary option and one intended for women unable to perform *sati* (161). Thus they conclude, patently stretching their case, "It appears from the Shastra that the first thing which a widow ought to do is to ascend the flaming pile" (161).

The second objection to *sati* as producing only temporary bliss is countered with the observation that asceticism is also a "gradual step for final beatitude" and that, while *sati* involves only "short term suffering" and delivers "heavenly blessings," ascetic widowhood subjects women to "labouring under austerities for a long time" (161). The greater "spiritual" value assigned to ascetic widowhood is thus contrasted negatively with what is seen as the prolonged material suffering it implies for widows.

Finally, the case is outlined for why the absence of a positive injunction to *sati* in *Manu* presents no particular problem for its scriptural status. First, it is pointed out that many acts currently performed in society, such as *Durga puja* or *dola jatra,* have no basis in *Manu* and yet are not believed to be inconsistent with scripture; indeed their nonperformance would be regarded as improper. It is interesting to note that although the petition begins with a general argument for regarding custom as equal in importance to scripture, this is the only point on which customary support is cited. In any case, the petition continues, the absence of *sati* in *Manu* cannot be construed as an argument against it. The *Dattaca Chandrika* is offered as positing the converse: that "nonprohibition constitutes sanction." Finally, the petition ingeniously proposes that if copies of the *Institutes of Manu* in Bengal neglect to mention *sati,* this cannot be supposed to be the case generally for, it argues, *"the text has been omitted by the mistake of the printers,* for the authors of the *Nirnaya Sindhu* and other works, which are most prevalent in Dravira and other countries, quoted the following text of Manu: 'A widow may either practice austerities or commit herself to the flame'" (162). A printing mistake is thus made accountable for the status of *sati* in *Manu*'s text in Bengal!

The petitioners conclude their case for regarding *sati* as a scriptural practice by returning to a consideration of interpretive principles. They suggest that the RgVedic mantra "let not these women be widowed," which is to be chanted at the time of concremation, implies that *sati* was conformable to *sruti* and propose that where *sruti* and *smriti* conflict, "the former has preference over the latter" (162). Thus they conclude that "it is unobjectionable that concremation, being enjoined by the *Sruti,* which is the most prevalent authority and original of all the *Smritis,* must be performed" (162). Where Rammohun prioritizes *Manu* as a founding text containing the whole sense of the Veda and insists that no code be approved which contradicts it, the pro-*sati* petition argues the absolute priority of *sruti* in every case, although within the *smriti* texts *Manu* is conceded a premier position.

A number of differences are immediately discernible between Rammohun's "Abstract" and the pro-*sati* petition. Some are a consequence of substantive disagreements about how the scriptures are to be interpreted; others are an effect of the difference between a pamphlet setting out to consider widow burning as a "religious rite" in the aftermath of legislative prohibition, and a petition protesting such governmental intervention. The petition was a plea that challenged the right of the government to legislate on widow burning, the validity of its reading of scriptures, and the credibility of the interpreters it had relied upon in coming to its conclusions. By contrast, Rammohun's pamphlet dispassionately stated its case. Even though the battle was hardly over—advocates of *sati* decided in July 1830 to appeal to the Privy Council to overturn the legislation of 1829—the pamphlet appeared neither concerned with dismantling pro-*sati* arguments nor with addressing the question of the appropriateness of East India Company intervention. No doubt this is partly because prohibition was an already accomplished fact. But it was also partly because neither side, in fact, was saying anything new. In the decade that had preceded prohibition, both lobbies had debated each other on virtually all of these issues in one forum or another.

The substantive philosophical issue that separated ideologues on either side of the debate was the value conferred on rituals by the scriptures. Rammohun Roy's critique of *sati* was part of his broader philosophical position that the ultimate goal of selfless absorption in the divine was to be pursued not through goal-oriented religious rites or practices like *sati,* but through contemplation and adoration of divinity. His argument against *sati* was thus of a piece with his critique of image worship and advocacy of monotheism. Accordingly, in Rammohun's view, *sati,* even when voluntary and, as such, faithful to the scriptures, was of decidedly inferior merit as an act undertaken to procure such rewards as the rescue of husband and wife from the cycle of rebirth. By contrast, ascetic widowhood recommended itself because it was believed to be motivated neither by the prospect of future reward, nor a desire to gratify the senses. The ascetic regime imposed on upper-caste widows involved a punishing denial of sensory pleasures. Widowhood was thus seen to hold the potential for selfless existence and for a life of sustained contemplation of the Supreme Being.

Rammohun's position on religious rites and idolatry brought him into conflict with a number of his contemporaries, including Kashinath Tarkavagish and Mrityunjay Vidyalankar. Rammohun and his adversaries engaged each other's positions in a series of publications and counterpublications from 1817 onward.[24] The key point of contention between him and his interlocutors was whether the performance of religious rites was necessary for communion with the divine. Vidyalankar had, in his official capacity as the pundit at the Supreme Court, provided the East India Company with an analysis of the ambiguous scriptural position and value of *sati* (see chapter 1). But while he had argued in his *vyawastha* that, in privileging acts performed without expectation of reward over goal-oriented ones, the scriptures implicitly accorded a low status to *sati,* he did not go on to conclude from this, as Rammohun had, that goal-oriented acts were thus to be deprecated. Vidyalankar believed instead, and this view was shared by many in favor of *sati,* that such practices were a prerequisite for obtaining divine knowledge. It was thus that Vidyalankar could furnish the East India Company with scriptural arguments regarding the questionable merit of *sati,* while remaining a staunch advocate of widow burning and of the practice of rituals in general. The value of scriptural study and religious ritual to attaining knowledge of the divine was also the subject of a day-long debate between Rammohun and Subramanya Sastri in December 1819 which was reportedly attended by prominent Calcutta *bhadralok,* including the pro-*sati* Radhakanta Deb.[25]

Rammohun's first and second pamphlets against widow burning (1818 and 1820), written in the form of a dialogue between an advocate and an opponent of *sati,* explicitly addressed the spiritual merits of *sati.*[26] The second pamphlet did so more elaborately than the first, given that Kashinath Tarkavagish in his 1819 response to Rammohun's first tract had taken a position analogous to Vidyalankar. Tarkavagish defends *sati* as a permissible and customary alternative sanctioned by the scriptures for those unable to pursue ascetic widowhood, and argues its necessity given women's incapacity for virtue or disinterested worship.[27] "It is therefore very improper that women who have never been conscious of so much as the meaning of Wisdom, shall . . . be desired to follow the system of sacred knowledge."[28] According to Tarkavagish, widows are likely to go astray by living unchastely or by living chastely but for the wrong reasons. In his view, burning represents the lesser of the two evils with the added advantage that through it a widow can rescue herself and husband and "get rid of her feminine sex."[29] Rammohun's second pamphlet sets out to refute these claims through more detailed textual exegesis. He cites a wide range of texts—Vedas, *smritis,* Puranas, and Itihasas (drawing extensively on the Bhagavad Gita)—to expose the weaknesses of a pro-*sati* position forced to concede the ambiguous status of widow burning. As the opponent of widow burning in Rammohun's second pamphlet puts it: "Angira, Harita, Vishnu and Vyasa, authorised widows to choose the alternative of Concremation, or of living as ascetics. . . . besides Manu, Yajnavalkya, Vashista, and several other lawgivers have prescried asceticism only. Why therefore, despising the authorities of Manu and others, do you persist in encouraging weak women to submit to murder, by holding out to them the temptations of future pleasures in heaven?"[30] Here, as in his stand on image worship,

Rammohun remains critical of what he describes as "superstitious practices which deform the Hindoo religion and have nothing to do with the pure spirit of its dictates."[31]

Although the bulk of Rammohun's second tract focuses on questions of scriptural interpretation, in his concluding section he addresses justification of widow burning based on woman's supposed innate incapacity for virtue and, by implication, her potential to disgrace her family. Stating that the advocate of *sati* was finally admitting his "true motive," Rammohun elaborates a remarkably sophisticated analysis of women's subordination. The opponent of widow burning sharply criticizes his adversary for imputing faults to women "not planted in their constitution by nature" and for then persuading others "to look down upon them as contemptible and mischievous creatures, whence they have been subjected to constant miseries." He also proposes that men have taken advantage of their greater physical strength to deny women "those excellent merits that they are entitled to by nature, and afterwards they are apt to say that women are naturally incapable of acquiring those merits."[32] He draws on women's conduct to argue that in resolve, virtue, and trustworthiness they are, if anything, superior to men. Iqbal Singh, Rammohun's biographer, goes so far as to say (and there is more than a grain of truth in his view) that implicit in Rammohun's position here "are most of the arguments that have since found universal currency in support of movements for the emancipation of women and their claims to equal rights with men."[33] I return to a fuller discussion of this section of the pamphlet at the end of this chapter.

The focus of Rammohun's and Tarkavagish's pamphlets suggests that these were discussions primarily internal to the *bhadralok* in Calcutta and its vicinity. In each text, the advocate and opponent of widow burning explicitly takes up, and seeks to demolish, the arguments of his adversary. The discussion proceeds substantively. The credibility or authenticity of participants is not in question, as it was to be in the pro-*sati* petition of 1830; there is merely disagreement over competing interpretations of scripture and of the place of custom. Thus Tarkavagish defends as customary the tying of widows to the pyre. His 1819 tract nowhere argues that *sati* was voluntary, a claim that was to become increasingly central to the pro-*sati* position. One argument, abandoned in later discussions, is the justification of *sati* on the grounds of women's incapacity for virtue and wisdom. The 1830 petition, for example, forsakes this proposition for advocacy on the grounds that burning involves less suffering than the rigors of widowhood. Although both the pro- and anti-*sati* pamphlets were translated into English, and the translation of Rammohun's "Second Conference" was dedicated to the wife of the governor-general, the marchioness of Hastings, these tracts were fundamentally situated within contemporary discussions on the place of ritual in religious worship. Accordingly, they are not concerned with the role of the East India Company, details of how *sati* is practiced, what might account for its prevalence, or what it might imply about indigenous society.

Such concerns were, however, expressed elsewhere in petitions to the East India Company such as that presented to Hastings by opponents of *sati* in 1818, in the period between Rammohun's first and second tracts. Not surprisingly, this text argues its case against *sati* quite differently. The petitioners were aware that officials were deliberating as to whether to repeal the orders in force since 1813, a possibility that pro-*sati* forces sought to encourage by means of a petition to the East India Company. Those opposing *sati* also submitted a representation to the government. Their petition begins by expressing alarm at the prospect that the 1813 orders, which had specified conditions in which burning was legal, might be repealed and suggests that those advocating such action "must either be ignorant of their own law, or amongst the more inhumane of any class of the community."[34] The petitioners state their wish to vindicate themselves from the implication that the pro-*sati* petition expressed the views of the majority, claiming that it represented only those "individuals who have been influenced to sign [it]" (115). Then, drawing on "their own knowledge . . . [and] the authority of credible eyewitnesses" the petition states:

cases have frequently occurred, where women have been induced by the persuasions of their next heirs, interested in their destruction, to burn themselves . . . that others, who have been induced by fear to retract a resolution, rashly expressed in the first moments of grief, of burning with their husbands, have been forced upon the pile, and there bound down with ropes, and pressed by green bamboos until consumed by the flames; that some, after flying from the flames, have been carried back by their relations and burnt to death. All these instances . . . are murders, according to every shastur, as well as to the common sense of all nations. (116)

The petition continues that widows had also burnt years after their husbands' death and with men who were not their husbands, that brahmin widows had died by *anoomarana*, and that "contrary to the dictates of nature and morality, as well as of law," pregnant women and women with young children have been known "to burn themselves with their deceased husbands" (116). According to the anti-*sati* petitioners, the translations of scripture made available by the government had secured texts from "interpolation or false exposition" and clarifies that these incidents were "instances of suicide" assisted by bystanders "in direct opposition to the shasturs of the Hindoo faith." To remove the restrictions currently placed on *sati*, would, in their view, be "an insult to the known humanity of the British nation" (116). After challenging advocates of widow burning on their claim of greater tolerance shown by Muslim rulers toward Hindu religion, the petition concludes by briefly stating the ambiguous scriptural status of *sati*.

What is striking about the 1819 anti-*sati* petition is that it is far more concerned with illegalities in the *practice* of widow burning in relation to the prevailing law than with the scriptural merits of *sati,* the focus of the pamphlet exchange between Rammohun and Tarkavagish. Scriptural issues are marginal in the petitions. This is equally true of the statement of appreciation addressed to William Bentinck, prepared in the wake of the prohibition of *sati,* in January 1830 and signed by three hundred residents of Calcutta.[35] The petition, reportedly drafted by Rammohun, was intended to counter the mobilizing efforts of the pro-*sati* lobby. It is concerned with how prohibition protects women and removes "the gross stigma hitherto attached to our character as wilful murderers of females, and zealous promoters of the practice of suicide."[36] It argues that *sati* originated in the jealousy of certain Hindu princes who, to ensure the faithfulness of their widows, "availed themselves of their arbitrary power, and under the cloak of religion, introduced the practice of burning widows alive."[37] The princes then sought to legitimize the practice "by quoting some passages from authorities of evidently inferior weight . . . as if they were offering female sacrifices in obedience to the dictates of the Shastras and not from the influence of jealousy."[38] This thesis is supported by reference to such practices as fastening women to the pyre and other measures that according to the petition violate the "language and spirit" of scriptures. Scriptural texts themselves, however, receive only passing mention.

Even though critique of widow burning turned on the disjunctions to be observed between scriptural precept and actual practice, it is striking to note that Rammohun's elaboration of the material basis of *sati* is not to be found in his writings on the subject. Rather, the link between widow burning and women's property rights is developed most fully in his "Brief Remarks Regarding Modern Encroachments on the Ancient

Rights of Females According to the Hindu Law of Inheritance."[39] According to him, ancient law givers—Yajnavalkya, Katyayana, Vyasa, among others—allowed mother and son equal share in the property bequeathed by the husband or father. Over time, however, such rights had been eroded so that widows were left at the mercy of sons and grandsons, and women without children were completely dependent on the generosity of the larger family. According to Rammohun, the weakness of women's property rights encouraged polygamy since no provision had to be made for the maintenance of women, and this in turn increased their social vulnerability. The distressing conditions in which many widows found themselves led them "to the horrible act of suicide."[40]

According to Rammohun, nineteenth-century Dayabhaga Law represented an erosion of women's ancient rights. He also held it accountable for the greater incidence of *sati* in Bengal relative to regions in which Mitakshara Law prevailed.[41] Dayabhaga Law gave widows limited rights over a husband's property upon his death. In doing so, it made the widow a potential obstacle to the designs of surviving relatives and thus susceptible to their schemes. Rammohun's argument that *sati* was related to women's property rights under Dayabhaga Law is now widely accepted.[42] The introduction of private property and the resulting market in land had altered the significance of a widow's rights. This point is given credence by a remark made by G. Forbes of the Calcutta Court of Circuit in August 1819. Forbes recommended prohibition of widow burning, adding, "[i]t may be worthy of remark that, there are no less than 57 civil suits, involving property amounting to four lacs of rupees, now pending in this court, in which Hindoo widow ladies are parties."[43]

Indigenous discourse for and against *sati* was dispersed across a variety of texts, their tenor and inflections shaped in part by the audience being addressed. As already noted, the simultaneous English translations provided by either side indicates that the audiences significantly overlapped. They should not, however, be conflated. In general, petitions to the government addressed the legality or illegality of *sati*. In them, opponents of widow burning emphasized its involuntary nature and only secondarily engaged questions of scripture, while proponents tended to integrate into a discussion of scripture, their claims regarding widow burning as a freely expressed and inalienable right of Hindus. By comparison, pamphlets on *sati* focused primarily on questions of scripture and turned only secondarily to the details of practice.

Contests over the details of practice are, however, to be found in the columns of the Bengali press, although even here they were more infrequent than one might expect. As stated earlier, coverage of widow burning in the Bengali press was mostly limited to obituaries — not, it should be noted, obituaries of women, but of the men whose wives burned with them. The major Bengali newspapers in this period were the *Samachar Darpan, Sambad Kaumudi,* and *Samachar Chundrika. Darpan,* nominally edited by Joshua Marshman, was in actuality run by the pundits employed by the Baptist Mission Press.[44] *Sambad Kaumudi* was a paper with which Rammohun Roy was closely associated. *Samachar Chundrika* was aligned with pro-*sati* forces. It is a regrettable fact that originals of the *Kaumudi* and *Chundrika* are unavailable for this period and that we must rely on English-language papers like *Bengal Hurkaru,* which regularly published a column of "Translations from the Native Press." Similarly, our access to *Samachar Darpan* from 1819 through much of the 1820s is limited to the extracts published in Brajendranath Bandhopadhyay's *Sambadpatra Sekaler Katha.*[45] Despite these constraints it is possible to examine the role played by the indigenous press and their representations of widow burning.

It is important to clarify from the outset that it would be misleading to designate *Darpan, Kaumudi,* and *Chundrika* as representing, respectively, the missionary, anti-*sati,* and pro-*sati* positions. These newspapers did not report on *sati* in a singular or consistent manner, and there were, in fact, a number of similarities in the ways each addressed the issue. Only occasionally did they challenge each other's representations or debate each other's claims. *Samachar Darpan* is perhaps most curious in this regard. For even while the Baptist missionaries were taking every opportunity to berate widow burning and all that it implied in the English *Friend of India,* the relative autonomy enjoyed by pundits at *Darpan* meant that their discourse diverged sharply from other mission publications and was far more akin to that of other indigenous papers.

The most common representations of widow burning tended to be matter-of-fact news items stating particulars of specific incidents. Such reports did not attempt to evaluate the incident in any way. The following are typical examples:

Sahamaran. Two weeks ago in Purbasthali village in Burdwan district, Syamsankar Bhattacharya died at the age of about fifty years. His forty year old wife mounted the burning pyre with him, and gave up her earthly life on the bank of the Ganga in Gopipur. They have left behind two sons and two daughters. (*Samachar Darpan,* July 7, 1821)[46]

Suttee—We learn that Gunesh Niabgush a man well versed in Sanskrit, Logic, and other sciences and who was about sixty five years of age and an inhabitant of Bansbaria died of severe fever on 15th instant. His widow without hesitation burnt herself on the Bank of the Hooghly river according to the usual custom of the Hindoos. (*Sambad Kaumudi,* May 22, 1824) [47]

Ramtonoo Doss of the Koyburto caste, inhabitant of Nandah . . . died on the 10th of shrabun, at his fiftieth year. The widow about forty years of age, burnt herself with the dead body of her husband on that day, leaving behind her four sons, all young men. (*Samachar Chundrika,* July 30, 1825) [48]

These reports are remarkably similar. They are limited to basic information about the event and appear to suggest that the unnamed women in question went willingly. Less frequent, though not rare, were reports that situated incidents within a slightly broader compass, suggesting, for example, the logic of the widow's action. Though evaluative, such contextualization was not always in the service of a critique or defense of the practice.

An old inhabitant of Saukherytelah, more than one hundred years of age, father of Ramjoy Dass having long been afflicted with an old malady (that being always the case at old age) and being very infirm died on Tuesday last the 18th Instant. His wife not willing to endure the distresses of a widow at that old age (she then being in her ninety-ninth year), burnt herself on the funeral pile of her husband. (*Samachar Darpan,* October 22, 1825) [49]

We are astonished to hear that Muddum Mohun Chuckroburthy, about fifteen years old, inhabitant of Twenty-four Pergunahs, having lately died, his widow, a little girl only twelve years of age, no longer willing to inhabit this transitory world, at the loss of her husband obstinately burnt herself on the funeral pyre. (*Sambad Kaumudi,* October 8, 1825) [50]

In a like vein, the *Samachar Chundrika* of June 12, 1826, reported the death of the widow of a brahmin *vakil* from 24 Pargannahs:

His widow thinking herself altogether worthless in the world . . . and anticipating the many distresses that she would have to suffer if she survived, declared her determination of immolating herself, and after having obtained the sanction of Government . . . burnt herself with the remains of her departed friend.[51]

Here *Darpan* and *Chundrika* note, without commentary, the material reasons that in their view prompted the widow in these cases, while *Kaumudi* offers a rationale that is more philosophical in orientation, death as an escape from the illusory and transitory state that is life. None of them in any way support their claims regarding the reasoning they attribute to the widow.

A third kind of representation was that which explicitly editorialized on widow burning, either within the account itself or in challenging another newspaper's report. In this category would fall items in the *Samachar Chundrika* that accentuated the voluntary nature of *sati* and portrayed the widow as the chief instigator, organizer, and beneficiary of her own praiseworthy destruction. Here is a report from *Chundrika* about a widow whose husband had died of cholera:

His chaste and virtuous widow only 22 years old, being resolved to burn herself with the dead body of her husband, immediately sent notices of her immolation to the Government, but permission being not easily brought her, she was obliged to wait for two days, and on the morning of the third day, after obtaining sanction she ordered a pile to be prepared, and resolutely mounting it, she ordered it to be set on fire, and thus burnt herself to the great surprise of spectators.[52]

In an obvious reference to this kind of account the *Sambad Kaumudi* made the following sarcastic observation in a case in which a widow had escaped from the pyre thanks to her family having been prevented from fastening her to it: "Had the men in the present case been able forcibly to accomplish the cremation of Veendhyuvasenee, we should most probably have been told of the suttee having 'ascended the heavens in company with her husband pleased in her mind, and with a satisfied conscience.'"[53] In general *Darpan* was given to neither rhetorical flourish nor polemic in its reporting of *sati*. Its tone was noncommital whether in noting that a widow had died "with the right observance of rules," or in its description of a failed attempt to dissuade the widow: "she paid no heed to them."[54]

The concerns familiar to us from pamphlets and petitions are largely absent from newspaper reports: questions of scripture, the credibility of particular interpreters and their readings of these texts, the voluntary or involuntary nature of *sati,* and so on. Such issues, however, surfaced in the contests over representation of *sati* that occasionally erupted between these papers. One such instance was the response in *Chundrika* to a March 5, 1822 report in *Kaumudi* in which the latter had noted what it described as "well-known" excesses in the custom of widow burning. A letter to the editor of *Chundrika* protested *Kaumudi's* assertions that "Widows who are pregnant . . . or have not arrived at years of maturity, are made to eat something that inebriates them, and then thrown upon the burning piles of their husbands." The writer Biprudoss asked the editor to corroborate the story, claiming that such statements were difficult to believe given the public nature of burnings and the ever observant magistrates "who never allow a woman to burn . . . before they have given the subject a serious and cool consideration, and found the woman to be devoid of all the passions, and to have a constant faith in her husband." He suggested that chaste women were usually disagreeable to those who were themselves unchaste and concluded by saying that without supporting evidence, it could only be supposed that the editor of *Kaumudi* was either an "Infidel, or one deprived of the use of his reason."[55] A second letter made the same point, asking, "Was this the result of the liveliness of his own imagination, or has he printed that story . . . tending to revile the manners and customs of his own country, merely to please some foreigners whose manners and customs are quite different from ours?"[56] Later that year, in May 1822, a letter to the *Chundrika*, hoping to silence "religious sceptics," cited scriptural "authorities" on *sati* in response to an exchange between English opponents and indigenous advocates of widow burning in the English paper *John Bull*. The writer noted that "the subject is now in discussion even in England" and that "it was altogether unbecoming of persons of a different faith to ridicule the faith of others" and such conduct "could only do mischief to the Government, and . . . [bring] misery to the people."[57]

Such exchanges were, however, unusual. Through most of the 1820s the indigenous press reported *sati* with minimal or no commentary, be it critical or adulatory. Not surprisingly, this changed dramatically in the period leading up to prohibition. The shift is discernible from the second half of 1829, as news of impending prohibition gained credibility. At this time, even the *Darpan* got into the fray in a three-way crossfire between it, *Kaumudi,* and *Chundrika*. *Chundrika*'s fears regarding prohibition were expressed in a piece that drew on a strategy more common to petitions. It challenged the credibility of those natives upon whom the East India Company was said to be relying in legislating against *sati*, natives who, it claimed, were Hindus in name only. The paper also insisted that despite the efforts of Englishmen to "dissuade the devoted wife by tempting and coaxing her, . . . no one could be convinced or prevented so far," adding, "What is more conclusive for us than this?"[58]

These arguments were challenged by *Darpan* and *Kaumudi* alike. *Darpan*'s reporting on *sati* is markedly more aggressive in this period, suggesting that the paper might have been more closely supervised by Baptists who had hitherto given pundits employed at the press a relatively free hand in its production. *Darpan* explicitly defended East India Company legislation against the criticisms of *Chundrika,* which, in turn, led the latter to wonder whether indigenous support for prohibition adduced by the former was not, like missionary claims of conversions, mere exaggeration.[59] *Chundrika* claimed that prohibition endangered religion: "Hindoo religion is now on its last legs."[60] It also insisted that legislation could not prevent Hindu widows from burning with their husbands. *Chundrika* was here partly responding to reports that heralded the success of legislative prohibition. Within ten days of the anti-*sati* promulgation, for example, the *Bengal Hurkaru* was reporting that twenty-one widows had been saved from death.[61] *Chundrika* alleged that women who had been so prevented had starved themselves to death or had "miraculously" died, claims whose veracity were contested by *Kaumudi* as well as *Darpan.*[62] Several reports in the *Kaumudi* described women who had initially appeared distraught at being prevented but had soon recovered from their apparent distress. In one case, the woman was placed in police custody to prevent the possibility that she might take her life. Although she had first refused food, according to *Kaumudi,* "After two days her hunger overcame her sorrow; and she with much importunity and distress requested some food which was brought to her immediately. From that time, she has remained contentedly with her family, and busied herself with the work of the house." The paper explained the widow's initial conduct as follows: "The loss of a husband is the heaviest of all afflictions; for the widow is at once cut off from every pleasure in food and all other things. Therefore in such privations they do not feel the preservation of life an object of desire."[63] *Kaumudi* reported several similar incidents to illustrate the success of prevention and undermine the veracity of *Chundrika's* claims regarding the defiant conduct of widows insistent on their own destruction.[64]

Such battles over *sati* and its prohibition continued to be waged in a sporadic fashion over the next three years, during which time the matter was kept alive by the foundation of a Dharma Sabha (society for righteousness) to challenge the law and defend the Hindu religion. The Sabha was founded by pro-*sati* Calcutta *bhadralok* in February 1830 and in July of that year undertook to appeal the regulation prohibiting widow burning to the Privy Council in England. This was the only recourse available to it, given that Governor-General Lord William Bentinck was not to be dissuaded from his decision. Francis Bathie was entrusted with undertaking its pro-*sati* mission in England. Those in favor of the regulation entrusted their case to Rammohun Roy who was also departing for England, but on behalf of the Mughal emperor. Between June 25 and July 11, 1832, the by now well-rehearsed arguments of either side were presented before the Privy Council, which upheld the 1829 regulation, laying to rest, at least for the time being, the question of *sati*'s legality.

Meanwhile, between 1829 and 1832, Bengali newspaper columns in Calcutta became forums for lively exchanges between *bhadralok* on both sides of the *sati* divide, with each seeking to satirize the other and claiming justice for its own position.

## Indigenous and Official Discourse: Specificities, Intersections, Disjunctions

So far, we have analyzed four sites of *bhadralok* discourse in the debate on *sati:* in the previous chapter, the *vyawasthas* of court pundits, and here, petitions, pamphlets, and newspaper accounts.[65] These sites are distinct in a number of ways. *Vyawasthas* were produced by pundits employed in the courts in response to the specific inquiries of magistrates and judges regarding the scriptural status of *sati*. They were requisitioned by East India Company officials as part of the formulation of colonial law. Petitions to the East India Company were also addressed to colonial officials. However, they originated from *bhadralok* interested in demonstrating the strength of their respective constituencies and essentially were arguments about the legality or illegality of widow burning. In them, opponents of *sati* argued their case primarily by means of a discussion of the micropolitics of the practice, and scriptural texts received only passing mention. Advocates of *sati,* by contrast, founded their claims to its legality principally in their reading of scripture. References to practice were limited to claims regarding the widow's eagerness to ensure her own demise for the sake of herself, husband, and family.

Relative to *vyawasthas* and petitions, pamphlets were primarily embedded in discussions internal to the *bhadralok* in which widow burning was part of a broader discussion regarding the place of ritual in religious practice. However, given ongoing official discussion of widow burning and the intersecting worlds of *bhadralok* and East India Company officials, the latter was undoubtedly one of the audiences being addressed, witness the near-simultaneous English translations made available by the authors. Pamphlets thus provided valuable material for officials, who were themselves divided on the issue, and served as important indices of indigenous sentiments on widow burning. Pamphlets tended on the whole to be concerned with scriptural issues, with little or no attention to questions of policy or the details of practice.

Finally, there were newspaper reports of incidents of widow burning. These were almost entirely autonomous of the preoccupations of official discourse, varying from the bare-bones, no-comment approach of obituaries of deceased men whose widows had burnt with them to reports that paused to speculate, if only minimally, on the event and on the motivation of the widow. Interestingly, when they did speculate about the widow's motives, they offered consistently secular reasons. This was true even of the most consistently pro-*sati Chundrika,* which explained specific incidents by reference to the harrowing prospects of widowhood, unlike petitions and pamphlets which, when defending widow burning, spoke of the lure of celestial regions. The occasional contests over *sati* observable in the Bengali press were related to periodic rumors of proposed legislation, as when it was suspected that Lord Hastings might intercede in the matter. As we have seen, this had led in 1818 and 1819 to representations to the governor-general from both sides in the controversy. Hastings's eventual failure to prohibit widow burning led to a resolution of approbation for his tolerance of religion from some Calcutta *bhadralok* in December 1822.[66] The pattern shifted definitively only in the second half of 1829, when news of impending prohibition turned newspaper columns into forums for debating first the appropriateness of intervention and, after December 4, 1829, the success of legislation.

Questions of focus and audience, however, only take us so far in understanding the dynamic, varying and evolving relations between *bhadralok* and official discourse. A more fruitful approach to the question is analysis of the discursive specificities of each. Take, for instance, the modalities of their deployment of scripture. In the previous chapter, for example, it became clear in examining the social relations of production of pundits' *vyawasthas* that there were competing notions of textuality at work. Officials required pundits to read scriptural texts in ways unfamiliar to them, privileging, as they did so, scripture over custom, explicit over ambiguous scriptural statements, and older texts over newer ones. These interpretive priorities were part of official assumption of *vyawasthas* as authoritative in a legal sense. By contrast, pundits invariably attested to the interpretive status of *vyawathas,* drew equally on scripture and custom, and, to the abiding frustration of colonial officials, did not strive for consistency in their readings. Over time, however, pundits' *vyawasthas* began to assume the form required of them, thus leading to the institutionalization and enforcement of a colonial discourse on scripture.

A similar process may be traced in the sites of *bhadralok* discourse examined in this chapter, although the absence of an employer-employee relation in shaping their production meant that such shifts were uneven and diffuse in their effects. They are nonetheless significant. Let us take the case of pamphlets, which occupy an interesting space between Bengali newspaper accounts, largely autonomous of official concerns, and petitions explicitly addressing officials. The issues that engage Rammohun, Tarkavagish, and Vidyalankar are only partly intelligible in terms of official or missionary rhetoric. Arguments regarding the place of ritual in religion had been raised by vaishnavism, which, since the fourteenth century, had also stressed direct communion with divinity, eschewing priests and idols as intermediaries. Likewise, the eighteenth-century Indo-Persianite culture which shaped Rammohun persuaded him of monotheism even before his encounter with English Unitarians. Discussion of such matters thus predated colonial critique, whose role was not to inaugurate it so much as give it fresh impetus. It thus comes as little surprise, for example, that a principled rejection of ritual cuts across Rammohun's writing, both prior to contact with the British and in the period after 1815, when he began engaging on this score *bhadralok,* officials, and missionaries alike.

There is, however, a striking contrast to be found in how Rammohun articulates social critique before and after his encounter with the British. The differences between the terms of his critique of idol worship in *Tuhfatul Muwahiddin* (1803–4) and his rhetoric against widow burning offer the sharpest instance of this shift. Sumit Sarkar has demonstrated how Rammohun's argument for monotheism in *Tuhfat* is developed rigorously in terms of the criterion of social comfort and of a concept of reason drawn from Islamic rationalism.[67] Sarkar argues that

[o]nly three basic tenets—common to all faiths and hence "natural" are retained: belief in a single Creator (proved by the argument from design), in the existence of the soul, and faith in an afterworld where rewards and punishments will be duly awarded—and even the two latter beliefs are found acceptable only on utilitarian grounds. Everything else—belief in

particular divinities . . . faith in divinely inspired prophets and miracles . . . "the hundreds of useless hardships and privations regarding eating and drinking, purity and impurity, auspiciousness and inauspiciousness" is blown up with relentless logic.[68]

Sarkar observes that Rammohun in *Tuhfat* comes "perilously close to the vanishing point of religion," a position he draws back from in his post-1815 arguments for monotheism, which are primarily grounded in a reinterpretation of the scriptures, especially the Upanishads.[69] As Sarkar puts it, "the claims of reason are now balanced and increasingly limited by Upanishadic authority as well as by a conservative use of the social comfort criterion."[70]

From my perspective, what is significant is that the shift in Rammohun's rhetoric parallels his increasing involvement with the British. It is known, for instance, that Rammohun did not know much English when writing *Tuhfat* in 1803–4. He was at the time employed by Thomas Woodforde in a private capacity at Murshidabad. In 1805 he is said to have formally entered East India Company service under John Digby. There is much controversy over the chronology of key events in Rammohun's life,[71] and, in any case, the chronological specification of "influence" is a complex matter. One can, however, agree with Rajat K. Ray that the "three main influences in Rammohun's thought — Persian, Vedantic and occidental — were imbibed by him successively, strictly in that chronological order."[72] To this I would add that although Rammohun may have encountered these systems of thought successively, their influence on him was not cumulative. Rather, Rammohun reinterpreted Persian and Vedantic philosophies in terms of the occidental. In other words, the move from a trenchant critique of religion derived from Islamic rationalism to a strategy arguing for social reform in terms of brahmanic scripture was, I would argue, related to the emerging dominance of an official Western discourse on India, a discourse of moral superiority that acknowledged India's greatness, but only in terms of its scriptural past. It was this past, one supposedly corrupted by the Muslim rulers who had preceded the East India Company, that British rule conceived itself as restoring. This logic had grounded official policy on *sati* in a discussion of brahmanic texts and insisted on a priority of scripture over custom, and older over recent texts.

Bentinck states this perspective succinctly in his defense of prohibition to pro-*sati* petitioners when he claims that the regulation, by enabling ascetic widowhood, only enforces that which was "commanded above other course in books usually considered of the highest authority . . . and stated to be adapted to a better state of society; such as by the Hindoos, is believed to have subsisted in former times."[73] He goes on to note that, by practicing ascetic widowhood, widows could be true both to the laws of government and to "the purest precepts of religion." Further, according to Bentinck, the widows would provide "an example to the existing generation of that good conduct which is supposed to have distinguished the earlier and better times of the Hindoo people."[74]

*Bhadralok* rhetoric on *sati* was not simply derivative of colonial discourse. We have seen how despite the glare of colonial scrutiny, Bengali newspapers continued, until the eve of prohibition, to treat widow burning as an everyday event in the life cycle of upper-caste Hindus. Elsewhere the traces of colonial discourse were clearly discernible. This is evident not simply in the turn to scripture in Rammohun's later writing, but also in the interpretive principles which both pro- and anti-*sati* *bhadralok* brought to bear more and more on scriptural texts. Understandably, these shifts are more evident in petitions to the East India Company than in the pamphlets of Rammohun and Tarkavagish, which continued to draw on a wide range of textual sources without, for the most part, striving to prioritize them according to antiquity or genre. As noted, pamphlets cited *srutis, smritis,* Puranas, and Itihasas.

Increasingly, however, the indigenous elite began to order the heterogeneous and unwieldy corpus designated "the scriptures" in a fashion similar to that of officials. They were ranked according to their antiquity in the following descending order: *sruti, smriti,* and commentaries. The *sruti* texts were placed at the apex since they were believed to be transcriptions of the revealed word of God. The pro-*sati* petition, for example, describes the *sruti* as "the most prevalent authority, and original of all the Smritis" (162). Next in line were the *smriti* texts supposed to have been written by particular sages. *Manu* is conceived as the most important among these. Thus Rammohun quotes approvingly Sir William Jones's description of *Manusmriti* as a "system of duties, religious and civil, and of law, in all its branches, which the Hindoos firmly believe to have been promulgated in the beginning of time by Menu, . . . a system so comprehensive and so minutely exact, that it may be considered as the institutes of Hindoo law."[75]

As we have seen, Ewer and East India Company officials also regarded *Manu* as "the parent of Hindoo Jurisprudence." The pro-*sati* petitioners are less vociferous about the founding status of *Manu,* for their argument in favor of *sati* was complicated by the text not having addressed the issue. However, they indirectly concede its importance to this debate by their great pains to prove that neglect of the issue by *Manu* does not compromise the stature of *sati,* even going so far as to suggest that the text outside Bengal does contain references to concremation. The problematic status of *Manu* for their perspective also prompts the pro-*sati* community to insist on the priority of *sruti* over *smriti* in case of conflict. By contrast, given the value of *Manu* to his position, Rammohun holds that it overrides *sruti,* although elsewhere, in his reformulation of Hinduism for instance, it is to the *sruti* texts—the Upanishads—that he turns.

*Bhadralok* and officials also concurred in assigning greater value to passages that were explicit in their references to *sati.* The more literal a passage, the more authoritative was its value as evidence. Thus, as we have seen, Rammohun rejects a passage from the RgVeda for being too abstract, while colonial officials reject the testimonies of pundits that were in their view based on mere inference. The pro-*sati* lobby is less committed to literalness since it does not serve them. Finally, scriptural evidence was consistently treated as superior to evidence based on custom or usage. In this context, officials ordered pundits to revise *vyawasthas* that depended on customary practice, Rammohun challenges pro-*sati* advocates for relying on that which he describes as "mere usage," and the pro-*sati* petition abandoned customary evidence even though it claimed an equivalence between scripture and usage.

To recapitulate, whatever their stands on the prohibition of *sati,* text-based arguments for and against widow burning were united in the view that scripture overrode custom, that explicit scriptural evidence had greater weight than evidence based on inference, and that, in general, the older the text the greater was its value. This privileging of the more ancient texts was tied to another discursive feature: the belief that Hindu society had fallen from a prior Golden Age. We have noted how official rhetoric conceived the prohibition of *sati* as a restorative act that returned to natives the "truths" of their own tradition. Rammohun also subscribed to the notion that nineteenth-century Indian society represented a decline from an earlier greatness, one which his reforms were intended to resuscitate. Indeed, Rammohun considered himself a restorer rather than a reformer, and specifically took exception to any description of him as the latter.[76] This stance explains his preference for the indirect agency of police over legislative prohibition, even though once the regulation was passed, he was to lend his energies to defend the law.[77] In thanking Bentinck for the legislative prohibition of *sati,*

Rammohun notes with satisfaction "that the heinous sin of cruelty to females may no longer be committed, and that the ancient and purest system of Hindu religion should not any longer be set at nought by the Hindus themselves."[78]

This notion of a fall from grace is also manifest in the claims made, by officials and by Rammohun, that the apparent scriptural legitimacy of *sati* was secured by tampering with the texts, or as Rammohun put it, by "interpolations and inventions, under the name of traditions." According to Rammohun this necessitated a return to the "original" texts, in this instance *Manu,* "the only safe rule to guard against endless corruptions, absurdities, and human caprices."[79] (Rammohun's argument here parallels his critique of Christian trinitarianism, advanced in his dialogue with the Baptist missionaries at Serampore and with Unitarians. Here also, Rammohun advocated a return to original Christian principles which he believed necessary to distinguish from the myths and superstitions that had accumulated around them.)[80] It can be argued that this desire to restore the so-called original texts contributed to the general neglect, in the debate on *sati,* of the commentaries written between the eleventh and eighteenth centuries. The theme of glorious past/degraded present is less prominent in the writings of the pro-*sati* lobby since their claim is that *sati* is part of the original canon and not an accretion. Even so, this idea of a fall grew to be crucial to nineteenth-century indigenous discourses across the political spectrum. It was to intersect with the idea that Britain rescued Hindu India from Islamic tyranny to produce specifically Hindu discourses of political and cultural regeneration.

The intersections and shared presumptions of *bhadralok* and official discourse represent shifts initiated by colonialism. As we have seen, such shifts were not total, and some were more immediately evident than others. For example, while at the beginning of the debate pundits were puzzled by the authority given their *vyawasthas* and the official conflation of scripture and law, by the end, such an equation was taken as given. The 1830 pro-*sati* petition, for example, describes the textual excerpts appended to it as "A translation of *a decision of the legal points* declaring the practice of suttee lawful and expedient" (159, emphasis mine). The *Asiatic Journal,* in reporting the submission of this petition to William Bentinck, remarks that it is "*accompanied by legal documents*" (emphasis mine).[81] The equation of scripture and law was thus complete. This privileging of upper-caste brahmanic scripture as tradition, and thus as the proper foundation of law, was to have far-reaching, long-term consequences, for women's property rights as well as, by the end of the nineteenth century, for the emergence of caste and communal consciousness. Equally significant, and perhaps more to the point here, was the way this discourse was to set the frame for debating, in the popular nineteenth-century turn of phrase, "the woman's question."

## Reconstituting Tradition, Constituting Woman

Colonial officials deliberated *sati* in terms of its status in religious texts. *Bhadralok,* on the other hand, drew on the scriptures most fully in pamphlets, to a lesser extent in petitions, and hardly at all in newspaper accounts of incidents of widow burning. The absence of recourse to scripture in the indigenous press is hardly surprising since here the writer is not seeking to make a case to colonial officials. When, however, the project was to state the argument for or against widow burning, it was to the scriptures, or rather various readings of them, that the *bhadralok* turned. This is clearly related to an official context in which *sati*'s status was premised on its scriptural and, thereby implicitly, its "traditional" and "legal" status. Given the parameters of the discourse, it is little wonder that the widow herself is marginal to its central concerns. The structure of the discourse precludes any other outcome. Instead, women become sites upon which various versions of scripture / tradition / law are elaborated and contested. It is thus that the alternatives to *sati* were also drawn from the scriptures. There is after all nothing necessarily logical or inevitable about ascetic widowhood as an alternative to *sati*. Why widowhood? Why *ascetic* widowhood? Why not an argument for widow remarriage?[82] Furthermore, given that both opponents and proponents of *sati* situated the practice in the context of the harrowing circumstances faced by upper-caste widows, it is striking that opponents of widow burning did not argue for the amelioration of the social conditions of widowhood. Instead, both sides naturalized widows' suffering and by implication the "option" of widow burning. Arguments simultaneously acknowledged and displaced the material basis of the practice, justifying widow burning as inflicting less pain.

If the debate centers not on women, but on questions of scriptural interpretation, what exactly *is* said about women and in what context? In Rammohun Roy's first pamphlet of 1818, discussion of the merits and demerits of *sati* gives way only at the very end to an oblique consideration of the widow as a person whose life is at stake. She appears in the context of the *sati* advocate's claim that immolation frees family and husband from the apprehension that the wife may go astray. Interestingly, the opponent of *sati* counters this fear of disgrace with another: "But is there not also a danger of a woman going astray during the lifetime of her husband, particularly when he resides for a long time in a distant country?" The advocate of *sati* disagrees, saying that a wife is under the husband's control as long as he is alive, but that "after his death that authority ceases, and she of course is divested of fear." The opponent of *sati* assuages this anxiety with the following assurance: "The Sastras which command that a wife should live under the control of her husband during his life, direct that on his death she shall live under the authority of her husband's family, or else under that of her parental relations; and the Sastras have authorised the ruler of the country to maintain the observance of this law. Therefore, the possibility of a woman's going astray cannot be more guarded against during the husband's life than it is after his death." [83]

In any case, the opponent of *sati* concludes, it is not control but wisdom and fear of God that effectively causes both men and women to abstain from improper conduct. While it may be unrealistic to expect from Rammohun Roy a full-scale critique of the desire to control women's sexuality, it is indeed disappointing that, confronted with this issue which is at the very heart of widow immolation, the opponent in this staged dialogue can only see fit to assure the advocate of *sati* that he has, in fact, nothing to fear; that effective mechanisms already exist for controlling women, thus precluding the need to burn them.

The physical suffering of widows on the pyre is addressed equally tangentially in response to the advocate's complaint that he is being accused of "want of feeling." The opponent concedes that advocates of *sati* may exhibit charity in other instances but not in *sati:* "by witnessing from your youth the voluntary burning of women amongst your elder relatives, your neighbours . . . and by observing the indifference manifested at the time when the women are writhing under the torture of the flames, habits of insensibility are produced." [84] Here again, the real suffering of women in *sati* is not posed as an issue in itself. It is mentioned only briefly and at the end of the pamphlet. The accent, moreover, is not on women but on the indifference and dullness produced in spectators from repeatedly witnessing such incidents. The pamphlet ends with the opponent of *sati* hoping that social practices will be brought in line with scriptural precepts, a development that, in his view, will have the advantage of effacing "the evils and disgrace brought on this country by the crime of female-murder."[85] This hope for a return to the good old textual days and for an end to the unwelcome attention brought by *sati* are a far cry indeed from the hopes and concerns that had compelled this writer in *Tuhfut*. Can there be any question that colonial discourse had cast its shadow across the pages of Rammohun's text? Furthermore, is there any doubt that the amelioration of male disgrace, and by extension that of the nation, is at greater stake than the alleviation of women's suffering?

The discussion of women is much sharper in Rammohun's second pamphlet,[86] a fact no doubt related to Tarkavagish's intervening riposte which, though primarily concerned with scripture, had suggested that women's incapacity for wisdom left widows ill-equipped to pursue a life of virtue.[87] Rammohun returns to this charge in the concluding section of his 1820 text, in order to challenge all those assumptions about women that served to justify *sati:* women's inferior understanding, lack of resolution, untrustworthiness, subjection to passions, and absence of virtue. Rammohun's strategy is fascinating in the ways it combines materialist explanations with claims about women's capacities, drawing on *sati* to illustrate precisely those qualities the absence of which, according to his opponents, legitimize the practice. This may appear to be a curious move in an argument against widow burning, but it illustrates the ambivalence toward *sati* that persisted even in this infamous and ardent opponent.

Rammohun begins by dismissing claims about women's so-called inferiority by pointing out that women are prohibited from education and then unfairly pronounced innately inferior. He then turns to the accusations that women are untrustworthy and lacking in resolve. Regarding the latter he has this to say: "You charge them with want of resolution, at which I feel exceedingly surprised: for we constantly perceive, in a country where the name of death makes the male shudder, that the female from her firmness of mind offers to burn herself with the corpse of her husband."[88] Here Rammohun seems to suggest that women undertaking *sati* exhibit heroism, that *sati* exemplifies women's strength of mind and character. In the very next paragraph, however, he draws on *sati* to challenge the idea of women's so-called untrustworthiness, making the claim, instead, for women's naiveté. In noting that men's deception of women far outweighs women's untrustworthiness, he states that women's trusting nature often leads them to be persuaded to immolate themselves. "One fault they have, it must be acknowledged; which is by considering others equally void of duplicity as themselves, to give their confidence too readily, from which they suffer much misery, even so far that some of them are misled to suffer themselves to be burnt to death."[89] I will return below to the issue of what enables this mobilization of *sati* in diametrically opposed ways.

Rammohun's defense of women in this section provocatively turns each of the advocate's accusations against itself. It does so, however, not by challenging the terms of the advocate's discussions so much as by suggesting, as in the earlier pamphlet, that his fears regarding women are unjustified. Thus the concern about women's "passion" is assuaged by contrasting polygamy and remarriage, prevalent among men, with the phenomenon of the wife who, at the death of her husband, either desires "to follow him, forsaking all worldly enjoyments, or remain[s] leading the austere life of an ascetic."[90] Similarly, advocates of *sati* are asked to reconsider their analysis of women as without virtue. The "proof" here is women's endurance of hardship. "The accusation of their want of virtuous knowledge is an injustice. Observe what pain, what slighting, what contempt, and what afflictions their virtue enables them to support!"[91] Far from women's lack of virtue "justifying" their ill-treatment, their ability to endure such suffering is seen to exemplify their virtue.

The issue of women's suffering arises in relation to a discussion of women's moral qualities. In this context it functions primarily as evidence of women's capacity for virtue. Although at the end of the pamphlet the opponent laments the want of compassion for women's suffering, the burden of his critique is not so much the injustice of their treatment as the unfairness of the conclusion that women lack virtue, given their capacities to endure hardship. It is also noteworthy that the implication of the opponent's position is that women have to be virtuous in order not to deserve *sati*.

Here again we may note how women and female suffering figure in the arguments against *sati* in ways that fail to focus on them per se. This tension is evident even in the writings of Rammohun, cast by historiography as the champion of women's rights. Although he suggests a material explanation for women's want of knowledge, and lambastes advocates for wanting "to condemn that sex to death merely from precaution,"[92] the burden of Rammohun's interventions lie elsewhere, in elaborating particular readings of the scriptures and contesting specific conclusions that advocates of *sati* have drawn about women.

Discursively, then, women remain a minor theme. Although it is ostensibly the question of whether they should live or die that inaugurates and sustains the debate, the materiality of their burning bodies and the anguish of their pain are remarkably absent from its purview. This is even more true of official discourse on widow burning. Bentinck's famous Minute on *sati,* for instance, makes not a single mention of the widow. The document focuses almost entirely on the safety of prohibition. Bentinck states at the outset that his conscience cannot "contemplate without horror" the "consignment, year after year, of hundreds of innocent victims to a cruel and untimely end."[93] Nevertheless, ending cruelty or the premature death of widows are not proposed as the objects of intervention. Instead, having assured readers that the measure will not provoke disquiet, Bentinck ends with the hope that prohibition will lead to a gradual dissociation of religious practice from murder (situating *sati* once again within "religion") and will "wash out a foul stain upon British Rule."[94] Indeed, the scriptural basis of *sati* and "embarrassment" over the British government's toleration of the practice were far more central to the East India Company's own discussions of prohibition than the fate of Hindu widows. The same was true of the petitions submitted to the British Parliament by British citizens against widow immolation.[95] *Bhadralok* for their part alternated between uncritical acceptance of *sati* and defense or critique of the practice in response to its vilification by colonial officials, the role of scripture being paramount in such contestatory literature.

The terms of the debate on *sati,* in particular the fundamental importance given to scripture, raise the following question: in what ways can it be regarded as an instance of "modernizing" discourse? It is clear that the discussion was not conducted along lines that are normally held to constitute the modern. It was not a secular discourse of reason positing a morality critical of outmoded practices and a new conception of individual rights. By contrast, the debate was a scriptural deliberation of the legitimacy of *sati* in which anti-*sati* officials and *bhadralok* were critical that in its contemporary form *sati* was not, in a sense, "outmoded enough," not true to its original form as a voluntary act of wifely devotion. Advocates of *sati,* of course, claimed the contrary. This so-called original *sati* was itself a myth but one that structured the discourse in important ways. It enabled even its opponents to accept the idea of *sati* in the abstract, while lamenting it in practice: whether because it was thought that women were inherently incapable of freely choosing their futures or because the "degraded" state of nineteenth-century Bengal was seen to have robbed them of their "true" capacities. As in the writings of Rammohun, the exemplary status accorded this original *sati* also underwrote representation of widow burning as emblematic both of women's courage and of their oppression, of their agency as well as their subordination.

The discussion of the rights of women as individuals is also strikingly absent in the debate, except insofar as it is posed indirectly in the context of the widow's will. As we have seen, except by advocates of *sati*, this will is conceded primarily in the abstract and only reluctantly, and by a few, in practice, thus justifying interventions on the widow's behalf, whether by the European official or the indigenous male social reformer. As such, it is closely allied to the division of *sati* into ideal versus actual burnings. Whatever the skepticism regarding the widow's subjecthood, however, this concern with individual will may itself be read as suggesting the modernity of this discourse.

But the discourse on *sati* was modern in another, more important, sense: it was underwritten and framed by a modern discourse on tradition. The shifts wrought by the colonial encounter between officials and *bhadralok* suggest that what we have here is not, as classic modernization theory would have it, a situation in which preexisting traditions are challenged by an emergent modern consciousness, but one in which both tradition and modernity as we know them are contemporaneously produced. The modernity of this discourse on tradition needs to be more fully recognized.

Here again the legacy is not a singular one, despite common ground between official and indigenous elite discourses. Officials posited tradition as a timeless and structuring principle of Indian society enacted in the everyday lives of indigenous people. To them, "tradition," interchangeable for the most part with "religion," was a sphere distinct from material life. This conception is evident in Ewer's arguments that when Indians acted religiously they acted passively, and in his legitimization of intervention in *sati*, given evidence for it as a material practice. (This view of tradition finds its clearest expression in descriptions of ideal type immolations, referring to no particular incident — see chapter 5.) It is also in this context that officials can speak of returning to natives the truth of traditions that had been interrupted by the "Islamic interlude." (The term "Islamic interlude" is of course misleading for a number of reasons, not least of which being that it conceives of Muslim rule as an interruption, nominates India as essentially Hindu, and that the term in fact designates a period spanning several centuries.)

The import of this discourse on tradition was not that it contained *bhadralok* perception of *sati* which, as we have stressed, varied between uncritical acceptance and elaborate defense or critique. It was, rather, in the way that a classical notion of tradition, one decidedly conceptual and divorced from the material density of the *bhadralok*'s immediate environment, was to seize their imagination, constitute their field of vision, and generate their maps for the future.[96] This turn to an idealized and rigorously upper-caste Hindu notion of tradition was to produce specific forms of self-empowerment and alienation among elite men and, as I will argue in the epilogue to this chapter, a paradoxical legacy for women in India.

This discourse on tradition also had implications for understanding widow burning. It produced analyses of *sati* in purely "cultural" terms that emptied it of both history and politics. It also effectively erased the agency of those involved in widow burning. These features are most clearly observable in official discourse, although indigenous representations of *sati* are also vulnerable on these counts when they draw on this conception of tradition. Not everyone involved in a *sati*, however, was seen to be equally subjected to the imperatives of culture. As we noted in Ewer's description in the previous chapter, family members, especially the males, and the pundits present at the pyre were given alternate subject positions. Family members were often seen to be acting in their own interest, pundits almost always so. Such interest is always coded as corrupt and to the detriment of the widow. Even so, within the general subjection of all indigenous people to "religion" or "tradition," men are offered some measure of will.

Not so the widow. Except in obituaries which simply note her death, marking it as neither suicide nor murder, representations of the widow cluster around two nodes. She is either a heroine, entering the raging flames of the pyre with no display of emotion, or an abject victim, thrown upon the heap and fastened to it by unscrupulous family members or pundits. We see such portrayals in official descriptions as well as in Rammohun's writings. These poles, "heroine" and "victim," preclude the possibility of a complex female subjectivity. Indeed, given the definition of tradition operative in the discourse on *sati*, the portrayal of the immolated widow as heroine merely rewrites her as victim of a higher order: not of man but of God (or religion). This representation of the widow makes her particularly susceptible to discourses of salvation, whether these are articulated by officials or the indigenous elite. It thus comes as no surprise that both offer to intercede on her behalf, to save her from "tradition," indeed even in its name.

Women, then, are not subjects in this discourse. Not only is precious little heard from them, but as I have suggested above, their agency is conceived in terms that are extremely reductive. (I return to this issue in chapter 5.) This does not imply, however, that women are the objects of this discourse: that this discourse is *about* them. On the contrary, I would argue that women are neither subjects nor objects but, rather, the ground of the discourse on *sati;* analysis of the arguments of participants very quickly indicates that women themselves are marginal to the debate. Instead, the question of women's status in Indian society posed by the prevalence of widow burning becomes the occasion for struggle between officials and the indigenous male elite.

Indeed, as the nineteenth century progresses, at a symbolic level the fate of women and the fate of the emerging nation become inextricably intertwined. Debates on women, whether in the context of *sati,* widow remarriage, or *zenanas* (separate women's quarters) were not merely about women, but were also instances in which the moral challenge of colonial rule was confronted and negotiated. In this process, women came to represent "tradition" for all participants: whether viewed as the weak, deluded creatures who must be reformed through legislation and education, or the valiant keepers of tradition who must be protected from statutory interventions and be permitted only certain kinds of instruction. For the British, rescuing women becomes part of the civilizing mission of colonization. For the indigenous male elite, protection of their status, or its reform, becomes an urgent necessity in maintaining the honor of the collective — religious or national. For all participants in nineteenth-century debates on social reform, women represent embarrassment or potential. And given the discursive construction of women as either abject victims or heroines, they frequently represent both shame *and* promise.[97]

Tradition was thus not the ground on which the status of woman was being contested. Rather, the reverse was true: women in fact became the site on which tradition was debated and reformulated. What was at stake was not women but tradition. Thus it is no wonder that even reading against the grain of a discourse ostensibly about whether women should survive their deceased husbands, one learns so little about them. To repeat an earlier formulation: neither subject nor object, but ground — such is the status of women in the discourse on *sati*.

Part of what enables this intimate interlocking of women and tradition is that this was a discourse of salvation: a recuperation of authenticity and purity, a vigorous protection of what were conceived as the weak and subordinated aspects of culture against their corrupt manipulation by the strong and dominant. We can see how easily this conception of tradition can intersect with one strand in patriarchal ideology, in which women are construed as pure, weak, and submissive, to produce a discourse in which both are intimately interwoven.

Contradictions and ironies abound and fortify each other. For ultimately, despite the focus on textual exegesis, the debate on *sati* was not about religion either. It was a secular debate on scripture, a contest over the legitimacy of particular readings, and an instrumental and purposive set of arguments about the spiritual merit of selfless actions performed without regard of reward. Interested men extolled the superior merits of disinterested action, arguing over whether women were intrinsically capable of such detachment. Both women and scripture became the modalities through which a new class identity was forged. They provided grounds for the cultural and ideological transformation that was necessary to the reconstellation of social relations in the colonial context. These processes mediated the realignment of the mutually consolidating systems of gender, caste, and class, and served both to contest colonial power and to refigure elite domination of subordinated social groups.

## Epilogue: From the "Bengal Renaissance" to "Colonial Rearticulations of Gender"[98]

We began this chapter with a brief critical consideration of the modernization framework within which the story of nineteenth-century social reform has hitherto been told. As a narrative for understanding the shifts initiated by colonialism, this perspective has recently come under severe pressure from scholars engaged in two kinds of revisionist efforts which are often, though not always, related: feminist projects that have reexamined the impact of colonial rule on women and on gender relations, and investigations that have attempted to historicize nineteenth-century colonial and indigenous discourses, and, in so doing, evaluate their gender, class, and caste content, as well as their universalist pretensions.[99] The emerging picture is mixed so far as women are concerned.

Many scholars, including Kumkum Sangari, Sudesh Vaid, Susie Tharu, K. Lalita, and Sumanta Banerjee, have argued that a peculiar and highly constricting blend of Victorian and brahmanic ideology of womanhood came to be privileged during the nineteenth century, one which moreover eroded many social and economic rights customarily enjoyed by middle- and low-caste women.[100] This scholarship has also suggested a more complex relation between *bhadralok* and social reform in the colonial period than that implied by modernization theory. Sangari and Vaid, for example, have pointed out how, in the colonial context, reform of the status of women became part of the self-definition of India's nascent bourgeoisie. And in a parallel argument Rosalind O'Hanlon has proposed that elite men, though disenfranchised politically, were reenfranchised as social critics of tradition.[101] It is becoming increasingly clear that social reform was the name for a process in which middle-class women gained limited advantages while the bulk of women were either excluded or actively lost out. Meanwhile, one effect of the increasing focus on women's "low status" that arose in the wake of colonial critique was a greater policing of women's behavior and the emergence of new forms of gender discrimination.

Women were neither passive nor silent in this process. Unlike the debate on *sati,* in which their contributions and responses are hard to reconstruct given available materials, women have bequeathed a rich and varied set of texts that record their view of subsequent events. These include prose, poetry, fiction, and autobiography.[102] Though predominantly the writings of middle-class and upper-caste literate women, such documents are nonetheless valuable. They record the hopes and anguish of women at the very heart of *bhadralok* reformist projects. The contours of these women's struggles did not always neatly converge with those of men even when they shared many of its presumptions.

The peculiar conditions under which the question of women's social and cultural status came to be part of the *bhadralok* agenda — as a defense against the civilizing discourse of a colonial power — has had implications for women in India. Unlike, for example, the development in Europe of an apparently universalist bourgeois discourse of rights (the gender and class specificities of which have in the past decade been compellingly documented by feminist scholarship), in India, as suggested above, *bhadralok* self-image was inextricably bound up with an *explicit* concern with the social status of women. If, however, European bourgeois discourse is only apparently ungendered, *bhadralok* rhetoric is often only superficially about women. Their impassioned discourse often amounted to an exercise in grandstanding through a meditation on tradition and modernity. It could combine cloying sentimentality and poetical flourish for the abstraction "woman" with a callous indifference for the condition of actual living and breathing women. It is within and against such constraints that the nineteenth-century *bhadramahila* (those most subjected to this discourse) sought to empower themselves and fashion their own agendas. Many were acutely conscious of the disjunctions of patriarchal discourse, and some even sharply satirized them.[103] The simple teleology of modernization theory can hardly grasp the complex paradoxes that constitute this story, let alone the contradictory legacy of colonial modernity for women in India.

## CHAPTER 3

# Missionaries and Subalterns

## Belaboring Tradition in the Marketplace

*I think it is impossible to convey to any person who never was in
that country, an adequate idea of the profound reverence in
which they hold their sacred books. But what is wonderful
[is that] they hear the divine authority of these books questioned
with patience and moderation, at all times and in all places.*

John Thomas, "Narrative of Himself
and his Labours in India"[1]

*Street preaching in Serampore is almost at an end. Nobody will
hear us.*

William Ward, Journal, October 31, 1802[2]

We move in this chapter from the elite world of *bhadralok*
and colonial officials to the streets and marketplaces of Calcutta's environs in which the Baptists began their evangelical experiment at the
turn of the nineteenth century. Evangelical writings represented a distinct and important dimension of European discourse on India, but one
that has received relatively little attention. The narration of this history
is begun here in two interlinked chapters. I start by analyzing Baptist
discourse in its emergent phase and proceed, in the following chapter,
to trace its consolidation, the shifts discernible over time, and the effect
of the context in which it was received on the tone and focus of Baptist
rhetoric.

William Carey, William Ward, and Joshua Marshman are key figures
in this history.[3] Their story begins with a pamphlet by William Carey

which had advocated the propriety of evangelical work, an argument that had led to the founding of the Baptist Missionary Society (BMS) in Kettering, England, in October 1792.[4] The beginnings of the mission were humble. The Churches of England and Scotland were indifferent to its endeavors. It was generally believed, in stark contrast to the mid-nineteenth century, that it was up to Christ to determine when, "the heathen" were to be "brought forth from the darkness." Despite the absence of institutional support, however, the BMS was soon followed by the establishment of other evangelical organizations, the London Missionary Society (1795) and the Church Missionary Society (1799).

The decision of the BMS to send William Carey to India was the fortuitous result of a letter followed by a visit from John Thomas, an English surgeon and resident of Bengal, seeking subscriptions for missionary work there. Thomas convinced the BMS of the prospects for evangelism in Bengal and on his return was accompanied by Carey and family. Carey was lucky that his arrival in Calcutta went unnoticed by East India Company officials. Missionary activity was illegal in British territory at this time and was to remain so until 1813. His discovery would most certainly have led to his deportation since he could not, as yet, claim a secular occupation. Carey was, however, less fortunate in his dealings with Thomas, who turned out to be an unstable character and in substantial debt to persons all over Calcutta. Leaving his untrustworthy companion, Carey decided to move out of the city to where the cost of living was more reasonable. He moved near Debhatta and then to Bandel, Maniktallah, and Nadia, where he and his family struggled under difficult conditions until March 1794 when he was offered a job as superintendent of George Udney's indigo factory at Malda. Udney was a supporter of evangelical work and also employed Thomas in a nearby village. Carey lived in Malda for the next five years on a modest but regular income, taking advantage of the seasonal nature of his employment to learn Bengali and begin preaching among the people. He was joined in 1796 by John Fountain.

This stable existence was brought to an end in 1799 by George Udney abandoning his failing indigo factory. Carey and Fountain had, in the meanwhile, received news that four more missionaries—William Ward, Joshua Marshman, William Grant, and Daniel Brunsdon—had set off for India. In preparation, Carey and Fountain purchased an indigo factory at Kidderpore and instructed the newcomers to declare themselves as their assistants. Contrary to Carey's advice, Ward and the others stated their true purpose and were about to be deported when they were invited by Colonel Ole Bie to found their mission in Serampore, a town sixteen miles north of Calcutta on the River Hughli, and under Danish control. After initial misgivings, Carey recognized the advantages of establishing a mission there.[5] He arrived in Serampore on January 9, 1800, and inaugurated the beginning of a lasting partnership with Ward and Marshman.[6] The contributions of Fountain, Grant, and Brunsdon were slight; all three died shortly after the founding of the mission at Serampore. As for John Thomas's role, it was that of a catalyst for the mission in India; he never became an official member of the BMS.

The Serampore trio, as Carey, Marshman, and Ward came to be known, are significant to the present project for a number of reasons. They were prodigious publishers of grammars of indigenous languages, translations of indigenous scriptures, phrase-books, periodicals, monographs, and popular tracts. As such, their work was an integral aspect of the burgeoning scholarship on the Orient. They have left behind a rich and varied set of materials invaluable to any investigation of European discourses on Indian society. They were also active in publicizing *sati*, being the first to undertake a survey of its incidence around Calcutta in 1803, twelve years before the East India Company instituted a similar procedure. Furthermore, William Ward repeatedly raised the issue of widow burning in the lectures and sermons he delivered during his visit to England in 1819–20; mission publications in India as well as Britain kept the issue alive during the 1820s. Finally, it was Carey who, in his capacity as the East India Company's Bengali translator, rendered from English to Bengali the 1829 proclamation that made *sati* a criminal offense, thus symbolically sealing the connection between the Serampore Baptists and the practice against which they had campaigned.

This chapter will draw on the more "private" writings of the Baptists—letters and journal entries. In chapter 4, the discussion will broaden to include the range of published missionary materials and to analysis of their relation to these journals as well as to each other. Of the three missionaries, Ward alone kept a regular diary (May 1799–October 1811). Carey and Marshman were less consistent, frequently using correspondence with family and with officials of the BMS to maintain a record of their experiences. The journals of the three missionaries were not strictly private, for edited highlights were printed first in the *Periodical Accounts* and later in the *Circular Letters* of the BMS. Even so, they contain initial impressions and experiences, and are marked by a degree of complexity and openness typical of any discourse in its emergent phase. Carey, Marshman, and Ward were still trying to comprehend the society to which they had journeyed, and their letters and journals make explicit the assumptions, desires, and failures that characterize their encounters with it. They may accordingly be conceived as registers of cognition in process. They present a sharp contrast to the reductiveness and numbing redundancy that are a feature of much of their later writing, particularly texts intended to raise funds. As such these early texts are important to a critical examination and reconstitution of missionary epistemology.

One especially significant feature of these letters and journals is the accounts they contain of the Baptists' attempts to preach their gospel. Such reports also frequently included the responses elicited by the evangelists from the predominantly subaltern audiences they addressed at street corners, temples, and markets.[7] These congregations were frequently perplexed by the burden of missionary discourse, which they challenged in ways that, in turn, frustrated the evangelists. The dialogues between the priests and their lively congregations give us a vivid and invaluable picture of that play of incommensurable logics so characteristic of the colonial encounter, especially in its early phase.

There were important differences in the contexts in which missionary and official discourse developed in Bengal. Official discourse, as we saw in chapter 1, emerged within an institutional setting, legal and administrative. Much of the debate on the legal prohibition of *sati* was concerned with questions of policing and law, involving East India Company administrators, magistrates, judges, and police officers. In analyzing their discourse, we turn to official papers: memoranda, legal instructions, the statistical tabulation of the incidence of *sati* in a given jurisdiction, Parliamentary Papers, and so on. Missionary discourse, on the other hand, traversed institutional and noninstitutional sites. It developed in heterogeneous contexts and is traceable through a broad range of documents: journals and letters, sermons, fundraising materials, newspaper articles, scholarly monographs.

This chapter examines a key noninstitutional site, that of street preaching, descriptions of which are available to us in missionary diaries and letters. The discussion here will be concerned not with *sati* but more generally with missionaries' analysis of Indian society, the place in it of scripture, and the relation evangelists posited between individuals and religion. Not surprisingly, these issues, central to official understanding of *sati,* were fundamental to the evangelical project and, as we will see in chapter 4, to missionary analysis of widow immolation. However, while East India Company interest in such matters was shaped by its function as a governing body, Baptist engagement was framed by a proselytizing mission. The former developed primarily as a politico-legal discourse (albeit with an unevenly asserted ethical component), the latter largely as a moral-ethical one. This distinction is not equally valid for all missionary material; in articles published in India, for example, the political and moral are more closely interwoven. Moral and ethical concerns are, however, foregrounded in letters and journals, the burden of which was to chart the personal triumphs and struggles of the evangelists in relation to what seemed to them to be a frustrating, often hostile, environment.

The insecure position of missionaries distinguishes them from colonial officials in Bengal. As noted above, missionary activity was illegal in East India Company territory until 1813, which is one reason why the invitation to settle in the Danish controlled town of Serampore was accepted by the Baptists. Serampore was seized by the British in 1801 but the missionaries were allowed to remain on the informal understanding that they would do nothing to stir indigenous protest. The efforts of Carey, Marshman, and Ward were accordingly dependent on the tolerance of East India Company officials.[8] The absence of political support for their enterprise also made them vulnerable to the indigenous communities in which they lived and preached. Their unsteady legal standing, and the fact that the missionaries had no authority over the native peoples they encountered, contrasts with the power that underwrote colonial bureaucracy and structured official relations with court pundits. The effects of this difference are manifest in the contrast between the interactions of missionaries and their native listener/interlocutors and those of judges and court pundits analyzed in chapter 1.

These important differences notwithstanding, missionaries and officials shared a great deal, especially with respect to their analysis of Indian society. Such commonalities are not surprising given that the two discourses did not develop in isolation from each other. The work of orientalists William Jones, H. T. Colebrooke, and Nathaniel Halhed was well known to Carey, Marshman, and Ward. Carey, for example, had turned to Halhed's Bengali grammar in learning the language. There developed a dense network of institutional and personal relationships between the Baptists, orientalist scholar/administrators, and other East India Company officials, at the center of which lay the College of Fort William, established in 1800 to train East India Company officials in the languages and customs of India.[9] The college drew equally

on the energies of the Asiatic Society (established in 1784) and the Serampore Mission. William Carey was hired as professor of Bengali at the
college in May 1801. This appointment tacitly secured East India Company acknowledgment if not circumscribed toleration of the Serampore
Mission, ensured a regular income for the Baptists, and made available
to them the resources of the indigenous scholars and British orientalists
employed there. In turn, the college and the Asiatic Society contracted
the Serampore Mission press to undertake the bulk of their printing.
The three institutions thus entered into a mutually beneficial partnership in the project of translation and publication of texts in Sanskrit and
other indigenous languages.[10]

## Baptist Accounts of Street Preaching: I

It was in the period between 1793 and 1804 that Carey,
Marshman, and Ward were most actively engaged in street preaching.
Before he moved to Serampore, Carey had preached in and around his
residence at Malda and at Madnabatti. With the setting up of the mission, preaching was conducted in the town of Serampore and in neighboring places. Missionaries also embarked from time to time on preaching journeys, traveling by boat and on foot, often staying away weeks at
a time. Of these journeys we have information mainly from Ward and
Marshman.

The direction of missionary activity gradually shifted with the establishment of the mission press at Serampore in 1800, and with the
appointment in the following year of William Carey as professor of Bengali at the College of Fort William in Calcutta. Carey's teaching commitments left him little time for preaching. Consequently, the richest
accounts from his pen are to be had for the period 1793–1800, before
his move to Serampore. Marshman and Ward continued preaching for a
few more years although their involvement, respectively in the mission
press and school, was to leave them little time for it.[11] In addition to
their individual commitments, Carey, Marshman, and Ward were also
involved with the project of translating Christian scriptures into various
indigenous languages and indigenous texts into English. As Marshman
remarked in a letter to Dr. John Ryland of the BMS, "the translation
forbids my itinerating, & will perhaps for some years."[12] These translations were undertaken by the missionaries partly for financial considera-

tions, as a way of funding themselves, and partly for evangelical purposes, as a means of spreading their message. Marshman clarifies this in his defense of secular activity:

How strange it seems for Missionaries to have so much of secular affairs to transact! . . . Yet is it less necessary? I sometimes examine myself on this head. Ah! were it neglected how soon w[ould] all our missionary efforts, printing, schools etc. be stopped. How soon s[hould] all of us engaged in the Mission, with our families, be compelled to return to England, unless indeed a few of us were detained in gaol as hostages for debt. These considerations convince me that in pouring instructions on the mind of a child, or balancing an acc[oun]t I am, as really employed in the cause of God, as when assisting in the translations of the word or preaching to the heathen the unsearchable riches of Christ.[13]

Carey, Marshman, and Ward also argued that native converts were in fact better placed to preach among the populace, both in terms of their fluency in Bengali and their familiarity with indigenous religion. It is not that itinerating ceased altogether. Rather, it was rarely undertaken, and the descriptions we have of these journeys are poor and consequently less useful. This partly seems to be the result of what Carey regards as "the sameness of one [conversation] to another."[14] Ward expresses a similar sentiment: "We go out everyday; but conversations being so much the same, I cannot think of detailing old words."[15]

Moreover, the Baptist approach to preaching also altered. Ward notes in his diary that the three realized that they were more successful in holding people's attention if they avoided engaging with Hinduism and Islam and focused instead on the life, death, and resurrection of Christ.[16] As we will see in the following section, it is missionary attacks on indigenous religion and society, and indigenous responses to such criticisms, that provide the basis for analyzing the nature, as well as grounds, for missionary claims regarding India. The "poverty" of later descriptions holds for all journal entries and letters, not just those that relate to preaching. For example, from 1804 on, Ward's diary merely lists the names of visitors to the mission, and notes progress on translations, fundraising, and conversions. On those rare instances when conversations with indigenous people are noted, missionaries are more likely to limit their accounts to summarizing their own arguments. Indigenous responses were rarely reported. These factors together underscore the importance of the early writings of Carey, Marshman, and Ward, and it is primarily with these that this chapter will be concerned.

In this, as in chapter 1, my analysis involves a narrative conceit. I begin by examining the strategies by which missionaries found congregations for themselves and the substance of their interactions on such occasions. This will provide us with elements of what might be called their dominant discourse on India. Simultaneously, the reported responses of congregations give us a sense of the relation of evangelical observations to their conclusions. In the second part, I analyze those elements, systematically marginalized by the dominant discourse of missionaries, which if conceded their proper place would make evangelical claims hard to sustain. The sequential presentation of the material is what constitutes the conceit, since dominant and marginalized aspects of missionary discourse are frequently present in the same text or journal fragment. As with any discursive analysis, the reader will have to wait until the end in order to grasp missionary discourse as the complex and contradictory entity that it was.

One of the first things that Carey notes soon after his arrival in India on November 11, 1793, is the safety of preaching and the ease with which a native congregation could be gathered: "The difficulty of preaching to the heathens, is I presume much less than has been imagined. I think from what I have seen [that] there would be very little danger of hurt in either heathen or mahometan countries."[17] Further, he states that a group of two hundred "listened with great seriousness"[18] and that the listeners are "very numerous, very inquisitive, and very attentive to the gospel."[19]

Getting an audience seemed to have posed less of a problem than the missionaries had imagined, given what they believed to be the fierce attachment of indigenous peoples to their religions. Communicating with them, though, was another matter altogether. Until he became conversant in Bengali, Carey was compelled to depend on indigenous intermediaries. Carey's first *munshi* was Ram Ram Basu, with whom he studied Bengali in the period 1793–96. As he writes to the BMS, "with the assistance of Moonshee, I am enabled to go out, especially on Lord's day, and preach to the natives."[20] In 1796 Ram Ram Basu was dismissed in favor of Golaknath Sharma. By the time Ward and Marshman arrived, Carey was himself in a position to initiate them into street preaching. They had, in addition, the assistance of William Carey's son Felix and of John Fountain. Ward notes in his journal that Marshman began preaching on his own in October 1800 and that he followed suit shortly thereafter, although he claims to still require the aid of Felix Carey.

The missionaries sought and found assemblies at markets, temples, and busy roadsides. Attracting a congregation and holding its attention in a public space involved considerable skill. Ward offers the fullest account of this complicated and often frustrating process.

There is a great deal of patience required in collecting a congregation together in this manner, and bearing with all their interruptions and wanderings. Suppose you were to stand at the corner of a street; a man passes; you ask him how he does, or where he is going? Sometimes he replies — sometimes he does not — sometimes he stays till you tell him your message, and then sets off. If he stay[s] another stops, and another, and then two more and so on. When you are in the middle of your sermon, half perhaps steer off — some more come — a brahman interrupts you. . . . Perhaps several are talking in the midst of a discourse about one particular sentence. I suppose Bro. C. has preached 100's of sermons to congregations such as these.[21]

Carey also notes the problems of preaching to a crowd that does not stand still. "The People are so moveable some going, and others coming, that often the congregation is quite changed before we have done."[22] He goes on to say that this requires them to repeat key criticisms of indigenous religions as well as important points from the gospel to ensure that all would have heard it.

The Baptist missionaries did not, however, always have to go in search of an audience. For instance, while at Malda, Carey had had a fairly consistent congregation of ninety laborers. Once established at Serampore, there was a regular group of worshippers including members of the mission, potential converts and visiting or neighboring Europeans. In addition, from time to time, various native and European inquirers would approach the missionaries, either individually or in groups, for information on the gospel. Thus Carey notes, while at Madnabatti, "Several of the Mahometans express a great desire to hear the word of God."[23] Similarly, Ward and Marshman write of the interest in the gospel among the residents of Jessore, Ghoshpara, and Lukhphool and their desire that missionaries come and preach to them. At other times missionaries were approached by persons seeking clarification on specific points regarding the gospel. Marshman tells of one such instance, when Aditya, described as "a rich native residing near Calcutta," visits Serampore along with a few "subtle men" believed to be brahmins to discuss the origin and meaning of sin.[24]

Baptist missionaries adopted a two-pronged approach to preaching: critical denunciation of indigenous religion and religious practices; and exhortation of the superior merits of Christ as the only savior from a sinful existence. On the face of it this strategy seems unsurprising, requiring little comment. Yet the specific ways in which the missionaries chose to challenge indigenous religious practice is fascinating in terms of what it suggests about their understanding of Hinduism and Islam, their view of the place of these religions in Indian society, and their conception of the relationship of native peoples to religion. Conversely, insofar as the missionaries report the reactions they elicited from the people among whom they preached, these writings also provide the basis for examining the extent to which the missionaries' ideas about indigenous society were shared by indigenous people and indeed borne out by their own accounts of preaching in Bengal.

Preaching was often carried out during festivals and at places of worship. In these settings one of the most common ploys for initiating dialogue was for the missionaries to ask those present a question about the religious practice in which they were engaged. The question, which was often directed at the priest or one who seemed learned to the missionaries, usually concerned the origin, meaning, and scriptural basis for a given practice. In a letter written to Reverend Andrew Fuller of the BMS in January 1795, Carey tells the following story:

I had occasion to go and preach to a company of people who were worshipping SAROSAUDI [Saraswati], the patroness of literature. The general opinion of the learned is, that the idols are only images, having no power in them; but that it is well pleasing for God to worship them in honour of the persons they represent, who they say, were eminent for virtue or goodness to men: The Brahmman however who attended this ceremony, told me plainly that *this image was God*. When I asked him, by what authority he did this? he answered, That the shasters commanded it. I enquired, What shasters? he said, The Bee Accoran [*vyakaran*], which I knew to be only a *grammar*. I was much drawn out in love to their souls, and was enabled to warn them against the devices of their teachers.[25]

The strategy followed by Carey here is typical. He first establishes the proper learned position on idols as mere representations. He then questions one of the brahmins at the temple on this point (it is unclear whether Carey is addressing the officiating brahmin priest or simply a brahmin worshipper) and demonstrates the latter's "ignorance" by pointing out how his claims about idols have no scriptural basis. The brahmin's reference to a grammar as the textual authority for his claim is seen to further confirm his ignorance. In this process Carey's superior knowledge of the texts has, in his own view, established his credibility.

He concludes with the observation that he was pleased to be able to warn the people against the wiles of the so-called learned.

Missionaries sought to demonstrate their own knowledge of indigenous scripture by interrogating natives about the scriptural authority for a given social practice. They tried to show that their audience was not properly "Hindu" or "Muslim," indeed did not have the requisite knowledge to be true to their professed faith. Below, Carey addresses Muslims at a bazaar at Maniktallah in this manner. The "we" here refers to Carey and to Ram Ram Basu who had accompanied him there.

A burial place, with a consecrated tomb, where offerings are daily made to the spirit of the departed person was near, some enquiries about the reason of their offerings were made, which led on to questions on their part; and then the Gospel and the Koran . . . became the subject of Conversation; they alleged the divine origin of the Koran; we enquired, have you ever seen or read it—the universal answer was no—but today a man came who pretended to have seen it—we asked him if he knew the beginning of every Chapter, for they all begin with these Words, "In the Name of God the Gracious and Merciful"—but he said no for it was written in Arabic, and no one could understand it—the Question now was then how can you obey it? and wherefore are you Mahometans?[26]

This strategy of quizzing indigenous people on the authenticity of their religious practices was common to all missionaries. Indigenous people were consistently asked, as in the instances above, to defend their practices and beliefs with reference to the scriptures. Quite often, as in the following incident, people were unable to provide a response acceptable to the missionaries. Here, Carey is reporting his exchange with a brahmin attending Saraswati *puja*. Pointing to the idol Carey asks why it was being worshipped:

he then said he did according to his faith; and that the Shaster commanded this. enquired What Shaster? he said Bee Accoran. I said that Shaster is only a Shanscrit grammar, and commands no such thing; have you read it? he acknowledged that he had not; then said I you can have no Faith about the Matter for faith is believing some Words, but this thing cannot speak; and the Shaster you have never read; he then said it was the custom of the country.[27]

In this account (strikingly similar to the one noted above), Carey goes on to question the brahmin's defense of the festival as customary with the argument that an appeal to custom per se was unacceptable since not all customs were defensible. The logic at work here is similar to that of East India Company officials in relation to court pundits. Missionaries sought to establish the validity of a given practice exclusively in relation to scriptural texts, challenging people on their ignorance if they were unable to provide appropriate textual support.

Such "ignorance" of scriptural texts seems to have been widespread. As Carey put it, "though their shasters abound in expressions of the evil of the heart, and the necessity of an entire change; yet not one in a thousand has ever seen or heard even *them*. Nay, I have found many Brahmmans so ignorant that they have never seen their *own shasters;* and many who are esteemed learned, do not know the difference between a *shanscrit grammar* and a religious book."[28] Muslims were deemed as ignorant as Hindus. Here is an extract from Ward recounting his experiences whilst accompanying Carey in preaching:

A Mussalman followed Brother Carey and talked of the Koran. He repeated some little, but when asked the meaning he said, "Nay, who can understand Arabic?"[29]

In the morning we saw in our walk a man sitting before a small mosque, with the Koran before him, and he reading in it most lustily. Brother C. asked him the meaning—"The meaning, Sahib, is another thing: I cannot tell that."[30]

According to missionaries such lack of knowledge was further reflected in the fact that many Muslim practices were actually "Hindu" in origin. Thus Carey says, "Tho' the Musselmen have no Cast, yet they imperceptibly adopted the Hindoo Notions about a Cast, and look upon themselves as a distinct one, in consequence of this they will neither eat nor drink with any but Musselmen."[31] Elsewhere he notes "that the Musselmens are as attentive to the imaginary cast, as the Hindoos are to theirs."[32] Similarly, regarding Muslim worship of the sun, Carey claims, "Mussalmans have so far Hindooized as to join in the idolatry."[33] It was not just Carey who found it significant that Muslims, as he phrased it, "intermix some pagan notions with the mahometan."[34] The secretaries of the BMS in England who carefully scrutinized his reports were also moved to question Carey on his remarks: "You speak of some Mahomedans as worshipping the Sun. Has not this an appearance of Paganism rather than of Mahomedanism?" Carey responds, "The Mahomedans by residing among the Hindoos, imbibe much of their idolatry. It is not a principle of Mahomedanism to worship the Sun or Moon: yet this is practised by many Mahomedans. They adore them as subordinate deities, and even fear the power of the Hindoo gods nearly as much as do the Hindoos themselves."[35] Evidently both Carey and the secretaries of the BMS regarded scriptural texts as the repositories of the truths of Hinduism and Islam.

Baptist missionaries counterposed native ignorance of scripture with their own mastery in other ways. For instance, Ward notes that in a discussion with native peoples, Carey sought to argue that the Kali Yug "was not according to their own shasters."[36] Here is a fuller account, also from Ward, of another incident in which Carey attempts the same argument.

Several people were at our house in the evening talking with Bro. C. Bro. C. asked—the principal Brahman, If there had been incarnations for the deliverance of mankind in other Joges [Yugs], why was it that in the Colley Joge [Kali Yug], when men were supposed to be most miserable, there was not one incarnation. He proves to the confusion of the Brahmans &c. that the Colley Joge, according to their own accounts must be past.[37]

Publicly demonstrating the lack of scriptural knowledge among the general populace served several functions. Missionaries believed that highlighting such ignorance would "shame" their audiences. In their view it demonstrated that indigenous people were unknowingly, and incorrectly, following practices that had no religious basis whatsoever. According to the missionaries, such ignorance facilitated domination of the masses by Hindu and Muslim priests. The missionaries were especially concerned with the former, whose insistence on exclusive access to Sanskrit scriptures was said to be a privilege they jealously guarded. Where the Baptists encountered brahmins equally ignorant of these texts, as in the occasions noted above, they warned the native people, as Carey did, "against the devices of their teachers."[38] Finally, Baptists believed that by exposing the ignorance of native people they exhibited their own mastery of religious texts. Their textual knowledge was intended to confirm for indigenous people the credibility of their mission to Bengal.

Leaving aside for the moment the question of how street congregations responded to missionary strategies and whether the evangelists were achieving their intended results, it is worth reflecting on what appears to have been a most curious approach adopted by the Baptists for denouncing indigenous practices. One might have expected them to argue that these practices were degraded *in and of themselves*. Instead, we find them *accusing* the people of not being true to scriptural precepts, something one might have expected them to appreciate rather than decry. Baptists insisted on the centrality of scripture to religious practice despite evidence of the unfamiliarity of these texts to most people, Hindu and Muslim. The absence of opponents able to engage in the debates initiated by the missionaries did not prompt them to reconsider their assumptions regarding the dominance of scripture in people's lives. Far from it: to the missionaries, ignorance of scripture merely confirmed native degradation.

Exposing the ignorance of the general populace may have been important, but nothing gave missionaries greater pleasure than undermining what they believed to be the revered and undeserved social status of brahmins. In a letter to his father soon after his arrival in India, Marshman described the position of brahmins thus:

The influence of the brahmans also is almost inconceivable to them who do not live within the light of it. They are Sacred, nay in some instances they are almost regarded as Deities. I have often seen people falling at their feet in the most profound reverence. If there are any who do not wish thus [to] respect them out of love, yet they stand in the greatest awe of them, not for their number, for perhaps they are not above a 20th part of the nation, nor indeed are they vested with any real power, but merely on account of their sanctity tho' perhaps there is not a set of worse men in the Earth.[39]

Carey shared Marshman's disgust of the reverence with which brahmins were said to be held since according to him it provided a major obstacle to the task of proselytizing. In a discussion of the difficulties with which missionaries had to contend, Carey includes under native superstitions, indigenous "veneration for the Brahmmans and implicit obedience to all their dictates." While acknowledging that not all brahmins are priests, Carey blames the scriptures for the esteem in which they are held, "because the shasters affirm that if a brahmman curses any one, the curse will infallibly take place."[40] Fear of reprisal, in his view, prevented complaints to the courts against them, so that brahmanic domination was impervious even to interception by civil authority. Elsewhere Carey dubs both Hindu and Muslim priests *"rulers of the darkness"* with whose "interested claims" the missionaries were compelled to contend.[41]

Given their belief in the power wielded by brahmins and the obstacle it thus represented to the evangelical project, missionaries did their best to "expose" the brahmins as frauds. Here, too, the scriptures generated the norm. The Baptists contrasted the brahmins they met with descriptions of them in the scriptures and defied them to live up to their textual counterparts. Carey thus challenges a brahmin to prevent the sun from setting, as brahmins were previously said to have done. There were undoubtedly brahmins who were well versed in the scriptures, but ignorance of these texts among the average member of this caste appears to have been common, representing for missionaries ready-made "evidence" against them. Take for instance the following episode in which Ward questions a brahmin on his right to wear the sacred thread, one of the distinguishing marks of his caste status: "A young brahman came after me. I stopped & asked him if he could read. He looked at the printing, but he could not read it. I then told him, that this poitou [sacred thread] bore false witness. It said that he was wise; but he was as ignorant as a sooder [sudra]."[42] This mode of evaluating what they encountered with reference to scriptures effectively placed missionaries in the curious position of "upholding" these texts, not to mention reproducing caste bigotry they attributed to brahmins alone. The authenticity of brahmins was measured in relation to whether their accomplishments and behavior reproduced scriptural prescriptions for their caste. Caste fundamentally shaped missionary attitudes and strategies in a given situation. Thus when the printers at the mission press presented a petition objecting to the insults to their Gods commonplace in the sermons to which they were subjected, Carey and Ward's predictable response was to challenge the brahmins *as brahmins* to defend their religion to the convert Petumber Singh: "Bro. Carey & I had a strong contention with tem in the printing office, & Bro. C. invited them to argue the point with Old Petumber . . . but they declined it; though Bro. C. told them that they were ten & he only one; that they were Brahmans & he only a Sooder."[43]

One is forced to conclude that the missionaries interpreted indigenous scriptural texts with the implicit and literal regard they insisted was characteristic of native people. Religious objects were treated in a similar fashion. For instance, the sacred thread worn by the brahmins inspired special awe among the missionaries, becoming for them a particularly charged icon of caste status and religious symbolism. This literalness in matters scriptural went as far as sharing the fear of retribution that they claimed was responsible for the privileged status of religion among indigenous people. Thus in the following incident, Ward can seem to tremble at the consequences of Komal desecrating his sacred thread, though Komal himself seems unperturbed:

Koomal told us a curious story. About 2 years since he was at a bad house with some companions. They went to sleep, but he continued awake. The oil light was going out. What was he [to] do; but taking a thread out of his poitou, he made a wicke with it; & this sacred poitou, which has always been an instrument of darkness; for once became the means of giving light. *Koomal in spite of the debtas still lives.* (emphasis mine)[44]

The same wonder for the sacred thread of the brahmins is evident in the following encounter when a brahmin agrees to sell Ward his thread for a rupee and Ward exclaims, "This is a more precious relick than any church of Rome could boast."[45]

The missionaries treated idols in an analogous manner. They would establish from worshippers whether an idol was regarded as God and then demand proof of its divinity, considering themselves triumphant if such proof could not be furnished.

I asked them if they had not a guardian God to their town, they said yes—Ramchanan, I asked is he a wooden one? or made of stone—they said who can tell what God is made of—said I what is the thing you worship made of—stone—well if it is God I cannot imagine it—now if the people of the town will agree to it I'll try whether he is God or not—I will bring a large hammer, and if I cannot break him to pieces you are right.[46]

There are, at the very least, two conceptions of God suggested by the response to Ward in this instance: an abstract notion that cannot be specified and a concrete idol which is distinct from the former. Such differences seem to have been lost on the Baptists whose only desire was to prove that the idol was not God, any more than many indigenous practices were "scriptural" or brahmins "authentic."

There is, then, evidence of a certain ambivalence in missionary writings. On the one hand, missionaries are at pains to demonstrate that idols are not God. Yet despite their critique of idolatry, Hindu images continue to inspire a certain wonder, as for instance, in Ward's reactions to one of the converts using part of a wooden idol for firewood.

Juggernaut [Jagannath] (the Lord of the world) was cut in two, & half of him was used in boiling the rice of his once devoted worshippers. To this very image these two had prostrated themselves, & they had performed his worship, & regarded him as a god. I hope to preach in this brother's house on Lord's Day, & if I can lay hold of the other half of Jaggernaut I will send him in triumph to Bristol.[47]

This sense of awe in the victory expressed by missionaries when "sacred" objects are treated as "secular" attests in a different way to the literalness with which missionaries treated matters and objects scriptural.

Literalness is, however, only one aspect of these accounts. The other related feature is the way these descriptions textualize social phenomena,
representing concrete, everyday and dynamic social practices as unreflective and ritualistic repetitions of some putative original enactment,
whether it be the opening of the Koran or prostrating before an idol.
"Tradition" in this discourse is the ceaseless and unself-conscious performance of such actions. Such a discourse on tradition is sustained by,
and in turn reproduces, a highly restrictive conception of indigenous
agency (see chapter 5). Textualized descriptions dominate the fundraising materials published by the mission. It is less frequent in their journals and letters but, as we have seen, not entirely absent.

Missionary strategy in preaching to Hindus and Muslims was not
merely a consequence of their analysis of indigenous society. It was also
an extension of protestant critique of Roman Catholicism. As noted in
chapter 1, protestants posited the axiomatic infallibility of scripture and
challenged the supremacy of the Catholic Church. The latter was accused of keeping people ignorant of the Bible, of insisting on the need
for priestly intercession between worshippers and God, and of "idolatrous" invocation of saints and angels. Evangelist strategy in relation to
doctrinal differences was to point to perceived inconsistencies in Roman
Catholicism through a largely literalist reading of the Bible.[48] Baptist
critique of the Hindus and Muslims they encountered, as we have seen,
shared many of these features. One may note the centrality accorded
to the Koran and Hindu scriptures, Baptist literalism in reading them,
and the abiding suspicion of brahmin pundits. Finally, there is the self-
evidence of the assumption of triumph every time the Baptists managed
to point out to their indigenous congregations perceived textual inconsistencies, contradictions in a comparison of text with social practice.

Missionary belaboring of scripture and of the inauthenticity of the
people they encountered did not rule out the self-righteous condemnation of indigenous religion more commonly associated with evangelism.
Indigenous scriptures were used against the natives to argue that Mo-
hammed and the various gods in the Hindu pantheon were vile and de-
spicable creatures.

I quoted them some accounts of the vile characters of their gods as recorded
in their Shastri, and said these cannot be Gods, . . . Narayan . . . appearing
in a female form excited very improper ideas in Seeb [Shiva] who was on
that account an old letcher, an old Goat and as full of abuse as a Billings-
gate Fish woman.[49]

Missionaries also spoke directly of their gospel in pointing out that embracing Christ was the only way to ensure salvation. Ultimately evangelical activity was about the promotion of Christianity. Missionary observations about indigenous religions were prefatory remarks primarily intended to highlight native "ignorance" and establish missionary credibility. However, these statements remain an integral part of missionary discourse.

Furthermore, much to the dismay of Carey, Marshman, and Ward, such opening remarks frequently constituted the sum total of a given sermon. Thus Ward notes that Carey "was obliged to say more on their system than he wished, and could only get but a little in of the Gospel. This is too often the case, but it will doubtless be very serviceable sooner or later."[50] Ward similarly criticizes a sermon of the convert Petumber Singh: "The old man had a tolerable congregation, but he talked rather too much against their gods, & too little about Jesus Christ."[51] The chagrin of the Baptist is, however, the historian's gain. For it is precisely all this "talking against" and about "their gods" and the responses that it elicited that enables one to read within and against the thrust of missionary descriptions of Bengal society at the turn of the nineteenth century.

## Baptist Accounts of Street Preaching: II

The preaching narratives of Carey, Marshman, and Ward clarify key features of dominant missionary discourse on India. These may be summarized as the centrality of brahmanic and Islamic texts, the social prominence of brahmins, and the general infatuation with religion of Hindus and Muslims. The assumption of textual hegemony—that all social practices derived from scripture—was not borne out by missionary reports. As we have seen, most people were not aware of the textual basis of social activity, even that which was coded "religious." Even if many social practices could be traced to scriptural precepts, it was not a text-based conception of religion that mediated expression of one's faith. Many of those identified by missionaries as brahmins, believed by them to be jealous protectors of Sanskrit texts, appear to have been equally ignorant of them. Such evidence, however, failed to challenge dominant missionary assumptions. Instead of forcing a reconsideration of their analysis, it appears to have been regarded as further proof of indigenous degradation. In a classic expression of what Edward Said has termed "the flexible positional superiority" of Westerners in relation to the Orient, it was not European knowledge but natives who were seen to be in need of revision.[52]

The assumption of a passive relation of indigenous people to things "religious" is contested by missionaries' own accounts of the active participation of congregations. The attentiveness and willingness of people to give missionaries a hearing has already been noted. But members of the congregation did not just listen. They spoke back—to the missionaries and to each other—producing exchanges the missionaries could not always control. Carey writes of such an experience, "A congregation gathered around me, and I felt much enlarged in talking with them. They heard with much attention, which is generally manifested by their answering almost every sentence by some observation upon it to one another. Their observations are sometimes so clamorous, that I have found it necessary to forbid them, and at other times to desist till the noise has subsided."[53] Carey is similarly forced to concede, vis-à-vis his Madnabatti congregation, that he may be misled by the lack of converts into believing the people to be "more ignorant than they are in reality," for he says, "I find many of them able to explain my meaning when I speak to those who never heard the word, and who in consequence are not able to comprehend my intention."[54] Ward also notes the way in which the congregation often got involved in discussion: "In the evening Brother Carey had a congregation disposed to quarrel amongst themselves, about what was the truth."[55]

Carey and Ward also mention a few instances in which individual listeners came to their aid by helping them to make their point. "One man indeed helped him [Carey] to show that the worship of the debtas was the worship of the devil, for that they had tempted men to sin."[56] At another time, Ward mentions that his fellow missionary, "Bro. Fountain, in a very hot contest with some brahmans was helped by a Brahman."[57] In addition, missionaries were of course assisted by those who evinced an interest in conversion to Christianity. But their assistance must be placed in a different category, motivated as it was by their inclinations in favor of the Christian gospel.

The spontaneous and lively engagement of ordinary congregations indicates the existence of a certain liberality of public religious discourse, a tradition within which people could locate missionary preaching. I will return to this below. This is confirmed by the willingness of people to engage with the preachers, a fact noted with satisfaction and surprise by the missionaries. Further, such hearing was often obtained at temples. As Carey observes in a 1795 letter, "I have repeated opportunities of discoursing with the Hindoos . . . for their idolatrous feasts very frequently occur, and I can often go into the places where the idols are, and oppose them to their faces, and the faces of all their defenders." [58] Ward also frequently mentions that "I went & stood on the temple steps, & got a great crowd around me." [59] It is clear from the accounts of the missionaries themselves that temples were not jealously guarded sacred spots, as they were wont to represent in their fundraising material, but social spaces that were used alternately for secular and religious purposes. While there might have been strictures around the use of the more venerated sites, the ordinary village or town temple was a multipurpose space, routinely providing shelter for travelers, including Carey, Marshman, and Ward.

If the writings of Baptist missionaries presented thus far merely imply that their oft-repeated claims about Indian society might be misguided, they can be found to be arguing this very point in their periodic protestations to the East India Company regarding the safety of evangelical work. For instance, during the controversy in 1807 over one of their pamphlets criticized for containing material offensive to Muslims, the missionaries defended themselves to the East India Company with the argument that although they regretted the remarks in question, they expected no trouble to ensue. They claimed that indigenous people were either indifferent to "things of this nature" or else remarkably open-minded. Regarding the latter they observed that "the natives . . . indulge in literary and religious discussions to an almost unbounded degree. . . . in numerous instances discussion has been desired by their native teachers, and approved by the multitude, even when it has ended to the disadvantage of their spiritual guides." [60] Missionaries explicitly acknowledged the openness of indigenous people on religious issues, but only when it suited them. To a careful reader, though, such statements merely confirm what is already evident in their accounts of preaching.

It is important, however, not to overstate the case. Congregations were not always hospitable. The missionaries were also challenged by their listeners. Indigenous people resisted missionary attempts to preach to them in a number of ways. Carey notes in dismay, "Often the name of Christ alone is sufficient to make a dozen of our hearers file off at once and sometimes to produce the most vile, blasphemous, insulting and malicious opposition from those who hear us." [61]

Missionaries were also taunted: "In the morning a native asked

Bro. C. who had been trying to get people together but could not, why he came, as he saw nobody whatever minded what he said." Ward similarly records, "In a late conversation with a brahman, Bro. M. was asked, If God had sent us to this country, as we said, how was it that three of our number were dead already."[62] Further, the tracts distributed by the missionaries were sometimes refused and at other times thrown away: "& many out of ill-will have torn them in pieces & scattered them thro' the streets."[63]

Spurning missionaries was one kind of response. Another was to refuse the absolutist terms of evangelism by adopting, for example, a relativist position. Indigenous people found unintelligible the missionaries' claims regarding the supremacy of their faith. They responded with the counter notion that each people had their own beliefs. Thus Carey remarks that in response to his questioning of the divine origin of the Hindu Shastras and the Muslim Koran, he received the reply "that God had created both Hindoos and Mussulmen, and had given them different ways to life."[64] Carey gets the same response to a question he put to another congregation regarding the way to salvation: "Every people have their own shasters, and their own kind of holiness; attend to the proper work recommended by the shasters of your own country."[65]

The missionaries were frustrated by this kind of relativism for its premise made inadmissible any of their arguments regarding the special claims of Christ. They continued to insist that adopting the Bible would give converts the certainty of salvation, an insistence that did not always elicit the response they desired. For, as one member of a congregation once asked, "'if the gospel be the way of life, how is it that we never heard it before.' I answered, 'God formerly suffered all nations to walk in their own ways; but now commandeth all men every where to repent.'" Carey's explanation did not satisfy his listener, however, who retorts, "'Indeed . . . I think God ought to repent for not sending the gospel sooner to us.'" The suggestion that God might be unjust offends Carey, who then proceeds to devote the rest of his sermon to arguing "that God had never done injustice to men!"[66] A similar failure of communication is evident in another incident in which Carey's audience, after listening to his exhortations regarding hell, compare it to the plight of prisoners at Dinajpur jail. Carey of course fiercely contests this notion since according to him death would release a prisoner from jail, while in his view there could be no escape from hell.[67]

Missionary obsession with the essentially sinful nature of human beings was completely incomprehensible to their Bengali congregations.

The Baptists were continuously preoccupied with sin; their own sinfulness and that of others around them. The missionaries' journals are full
of entries deploring the state of their souls and imploring Christ to re-
deem them from this condition. They sought to convey some of the in-
tensity of their desire for salvation to their congregations who were, in
their view, in even greater need of deliverance. Such confessions were
puzzling to their listeners, and as the following interaction reported by
Carey reveals, could easily rebound on the preachers.

"I am a sinner, and I know that there are only two places for mankind after
death, heaven and hell; but I cannot bear the torments of hell; what must
I do? and what must you all do?" They enquired, of what sin I had been
guilty? I told them, "Many; but particularly that my heart was impregnated
with sin; as pride, envy, wrath, and the like." They said, I must forsake sin;
I said, "Will this make amends for my past guilt? Suppose a man guilty of
murder was to live a peaceable life always afterwards, will that expiate his
guilt?" I believe they really thought that I had murdered somebody, and
that the guilt of murder lay heavy on my mind; for they asked if I wanted to
know what was a proper atonement for murder?[68]

One can see how a dialogue initiated by Carey to "awaken" natives to
their own degradation turns into one in which Carey appears to indict
himself and is in turn questioned by the congregation about past mis-
demeanors. This is further evidence, if indeed such is required, that in-
terchanges between missionaries and native people were truly dialogical
and not always in ways that missionaries could control. The indigenous
people the Baptists encountered responded to them with what was essentially their own discourse, one that did not share the premises of the
missionaries own and which, when it engaged with the evangelists, did
so on its own terms.

    One aspect of subaltern discourse that especially frustrated mission-
aries was its refusal to conceive of the spiritual and material as distinct
realms of life in which the former was at all times to have priority. The
"spiritual" discourse of missionaries was frequently interrupted by the
"worldly" concerns of their congregation. Here are two incidents from
Ward's journal that capture moments in which the missionaries were interrupted midstream:

[One man] asked why we came, and said if we could employ the natives
as carpenters, blacksmiths, &c. it would be very well, but that *they did not
want* our holiness.[69]

An old man, who was drunk, was rather rough with Brother C. on Lord's
Day morning while he was talking to the natives. He said—You English

have taken the whole country and now you want the people to receive your religion. They would be great fools if they did.[70]

This second quote is an unusual entry and represents the most explicit critique of imperialism recorded in the journals and letters of Carey, Marshman, and Ward. Concerns about subsistence were, however, a frequent, indeed recurring, theme among those to whom the Baptists preached.

It is also very common for them to say, "We have no God but our bellies." One day some dancing bramins came to me, and I asked them, why they pursued so vile an employment? They answered, "For our bellies."[71]

In the morning Brother Carey had a hearer who said he was a poor man, he worked all day, & when he got home he went to sleep. This was the way he spent his life: those who could read might attend to the shasters.[72]

A brahmin from Chandranagar, said to be a businessman, similarly makes the point that lying and cheating may be sinful but that they were endemic to his profession. Ward writes, "He said he could not sell a rupee's worth of things without lying; & if he became holy as I talked, how was his . . . business to go forward. I appealed to the people, & exposed his wickedness."[73]

Missionaries were disheartened by the refusal to privilege the spiritual domain. For the consistent braiding of the material and the spiritual undercut the possibility that people might be provoked into conversion by a growing sense of their own depravity. Evangelical frustration was only further heightened when indigenous concern for material survival was mixed with relativism. Here is Ward's response: "I was astonished at the ignorance & worldy-mindedness of this man. He had not one thought higher than his belly; & about his future state he said it must be as God pleased; all religions were the same."[74]

It is abundantly clear from the journals of Carey, Marshman, and Ward that their encounter with India was marked by a fundamental cognitive failure to acknowledge the consequences of apprehending society as it actually existed. Like East India Company officials, missionaries appear to have been possessed by the image of a textual India, in which brahmanic texts were the fount and origin of all sociality and where the rhythm of life was determined by the precepts of an all-legislating scripture. In this conception Hindu scriptures accorded individuals a fixed place in a social structure which was presided over by the priestly caste of brahmins and in which each person was handed a script to guide his or her unquestioning passage upon this earth. It was, of course, a profoundly conservative vision and one at considerable odds with the social and cultural context of late-eighteenth- and early-nineteenth-century Bengal.

From the fourteenth century on, this region had been transformed by lower-caste movements with roots in both vaishnava Hinduism and sufi Islam attacking idol worship, brahmanism and caste regulations, and advocating monotheism, the equality of individuals, and devotion, or *bhakti,* as the surest means to God. The cumulative impact of these periodic movements was to progressively weaken brahmanism and to make heterodoxy the rule, rather than the exception, among Hindus and Muslims alike.[75] Some idea of the extent of the disjunction between evangelical claims about Bengal society and the more complex reality the missionaries encountered may be had from a brief consideration of key themes in eighteenth-century folk literature and culture. I draw here on Sumanta Banerjee's fine analysis of rural folk forms and their subsequent transformation in the urban colonial setting of Calcutta. Banerjee argues that two parallel traditions existed in rural Bengal although there was, until the mid-nineteenth century, no firm separation between a high and low culture. One was a classical tradition patronized by local courts, whose poets turned to their immediate and lofty environment for inspiration and imagery and used a heavily Sanskritized Bengali. The other was a folk tradition which drew both its rhetoric and language from the world of the common peasant. One of the contrasting features between the two traditions was the way in which folk culture domesticated Hindu gods and goddesses (they tended to be elevated in classical forms) and endowed them with the virtues as well as failings of ordinary mortals: "Verbal desecration of high falutin and mystical theories . . . or the coupling of serious myths with their earthy, abusive parodies of gods . . . were an important part of Bengali folklore. They offered a sort of non-official, extra-ecclesiastical version of the world seen by the lower orders."[76] Songs, rhymes, and poetical narrative, even when their protagonists were Krishna or Kali, became occasions for reflecting on contemporary social developments. There was, in short, no division between sacred and secular concerns. Equally, the themes, motifs, and language reflected the shared universe of Hindus and Muslims in late-eighteenth-century Bengal. Arabic and Persian words (which had become an integral part of colloquial Bengali through trade) were to be found in the compositions of both communities, whose poets wrote verses for those Muslim *pirs* and Hindu gods they worshipped in common.[77]

Into this heterodox and permissive atmosphere enter the missionaries with a proselytizing and civilizing mission. While elements of their critique of society, such as of idol worship and of caste, might have resonated with contemporary indigenous challenges to both, missionaries failed to produce the conversions to Christianity for which they had hoped, quite possibly because the broader framework of evangelical discourse, with its concern with sin and the superiority of Christ, was alien to those to whom they preached. This becomes clear in Carey, Marshman, and Ward's failure to win to their cause the low-caste "rebels," as they saw them, in the Nadia-Murshidabad region. For, notwithstanding their textual view, the three were well acquainted with the monotheistic anticaste movements in Bengal. Regarding the people at Lukhphool, Ward says,

Our friends here are inveterate foes of the brahmins. It seems that formerly some fakier or Fakiers wandered about, being esteemed very holy people, & declaimed against the systems of the Hindoos & Mussulmans, that there was but one God, the father of all, who alone was to be worshipped; sin was to be forsaken, & a further revelation expected. These sentiments many thousands seem to have embraced. . . . our friends at this place are made up of all casts. The goroo or principal is an oldish man, named Neloo, formerly a weaver.[78]

Members of these sects also sent deputations to Serampore with questions about Christianity.

This morning four more people came a journey of four days to enquire about the way of life. Three of them are Mussulmans, that is they were born amongst Mussulmans; but I believe they are to be classed among a pretty numerous body of people, Hindus and Mussulmans, who neither worship the debtas nor mind Mahomet. They are in a state of doubt, believing in one God, supposing it wrong to gratify the grosser vices; but mixing with all they believe many prejudices of both the Hindoos & Mussulmans.[79]

The Baptists kept up contact with such groups in Ghoshpara, Jessore, and other places but found that they were not eager to convert.

I was at first too sanguine in my hopes, & a little mistaken in them. Seeing them make & converse together so freely & speak so contemptuously of cast I thought they must have rejected it, & hearing them so heartily despise Mahometanism, idolatry & brahmanism and listen to the Gospel, I was ready to hope they were not far from the Kingdom of God. However I see all this may exist & the carnal heart remain unchanged; We almost fear that they like many Protestants whose chief Religion is hatred of Popery, have far more hatred to error than love to truth.[80]

Elsewhere Marshman laments, "I fear they sigh more for a deliverance from . . . tyranny than . . . [from] sin."[81] Missionary knowledge of these anticaste movements was not slight. Not only did they investigate the possibility of sending a missionary to settle among these sects, but Ward's writings became and remain an important source of information on these groups.[82]

Given this context, missionary failure to take cognizance of the complexity of indigenous relation to religion appears quite astonishing. One may put it down to the initial phase of contact in which an analysis of India acquired through the representations of fellow European traders, travelers, and evangelists was in the process of coming to terms with the teeming actuality of Bengali society, but then, as we shall see, this analysis persisted well beyond this period. One could also suggest that the missionaries were merely evincing the ferocious elitism that according to Ranajit Guha presumes the absence of rationality in all subaltern action.[83]

Specific failures may also be attributed to misunderstandings. For instance, it seems apparent that when indigenous people referred to the *shastras,* they did so in order to speak broadly of a way of life or common set of beliefs. They were not necessarily speaking, as were the evangelists, of specific scriptural texts. This is why individuals could claim shastric authority for a given practice but, when pressed, be able to name only the grammars commonly used as teaching tools in village schools.[84] Missionaries do not appear to have entertained the possibility that the circulation of textual discourse was independent of the circulation of texts; that, for example, poetic and dramatic texts like the *Ramayana* had been widely popularized by storytellers, poets, and musicians. Even if they were to have acknowledged this, however, it is unclear what difference it might have made, for they held nontextual knowledge to be illegitimate.

Finally, one could posit a pragmatic reason for their analysis of Indian society and its people. The insistence on the hegemonic hold of Hinduism and Islam presented missionaries with a perfect alibi for a poor record of conversions. This propositon is amply supported by the prominence of representations of India in the published materials of the Baptists, especially those intended to raise funds for mission work, as a land of frenzied superstition (see chapter 4). It is interesting that even in the journals and letters where this kind of writing is rare, when it does appear, it is usually in the context of discussing the financial status of the mission or the number of successful conversions.

A discourse that separated the spiritual from the material was one which gave a form of perpetual structural advantage to the evangelists, while simultaneously placing indigenous people in a bind. Within it, spirituality implied infatuation, while worldliness represented a kind of corrupt self-interest that moved indigenous people beyond the pale of salvation (by Christ in missionary discourse and by colonization as in official discourse). This division intersected with a particular conception of tradition as timeless determinant to reduce the individual to nothing more than tradition's signature.

A narrowly pragmatic or intentionalist reading would, however, be inappropriate. Carey, Marshman, and Ward did not consciously scheme to invent a discourse that would authorize their view of the world. They were drawing on the discursive repertoires that were available to them and probably did not apprehend the contradictions in their discourse *as* contradictions. Like any other ideological system, missionary discourse could accommodate contrary and competing evidence. In this instance, necessary adjustments were enabled through the belief that natives were ignorant of their own traditions, through faith in the inherent superiority of European knowledge, and through the treatment as "exceptional" of material that challenged "rules" of their own making.

# Of Missionaries, Officials, Subalterns, and *Bhadralok*

Missionary discourse on India shared key premises with official conceptions of indigenous society regarding scriptural texts, indigenous subjectivity, and domination by brahmins. Their deployment of these ideas, for instance their respective modes of privileging scripture, illuminates the intersection as well as specificity of each discourse. Missionaries used scriptural texts in a number of ways: as a mode of comprehending India, as a means of asserting their textual knowledge over the "ignorance" of indigenous people, and as proof of the spiritual degradation and fallen state of contemporary society. In addition, the Baptists initiated the translation of brahmanic scriptures, a project with both scholarly and financial dimensions. Indigenous scriptures thus provided the material basis as well as some of the ideological content of missionary discourse on India.

Officials also regarded brahmanic scriptures as the most authentic source books on India. This belief, given the function of the East India Company, resulted in these texts becoming the sources of civil law, a more far-reaching consequence than their use by missionaries in preaching and sermonizing. It was for this reason that brahmin pundits and Muslim *qazis*, assumed to be knowledgeable about the scriptures, were employed in courts to interpret the law. Needless to say, their "expertise" was always in doubt and officials challenged them to defend their reading of the texts in ways that were similar to missionaries' quizzing of their subaltern audiences. Since the scriptures were made the sources of law, officials were more invested than missionaries in insisting on particular interpretations of them. But both officials and missionaries agreed on the importance of scripture and its absolute precedence over custom.

Officials and missionaries also shared a marked ambivalence toward indigenous "textual" culture. Official ambivalence was evident, for instance, in the 1813 circular on *sati*, which despite its professed aversion to widow burning, ensured that it would be practiced in a manner consistent with their reading of the scriptures. Missionaries expressed their ambivalence most clearly in their awe of indigenous idols and other objects of a "sacred" nature, and in their critical but mournful response to the discrepancies they noted between scripture and society. This ambivalence placed both officials and missionaries in the ironic position of appearing to uphold the very traditions which officials claimed to tolerate strictly for political reasons and whose destruction was supposedly integral to the evangelical enterprise.

This relation of complementarity between officials and missionaries provides a striking counterpoint to the contrast discernible between subaltern and *bhadralok* discourses. The irreverent refusal of these street audiences to take on the terms of the missionaries' critique of contemporary society, in contrast to the *bhadralok*'s increasing engagement with official rhetoric, points to the differing relations of these two groups to the ideological project of colonialism. The argument here must proceed carefully: the preaching narratives analyzed in this chapter cover a period (1793–1804) during which even the *bhadralok* remained impervious to the civilizational challenge proposed by European colonization. (Indeed, it was in 1803–4 that Rammohun was to pen *Tuhfut.*) That threat was perceived slowly and only fully from the latter half of the second decade of the nineteenth century. The subsequent trajectory of the *bhadralok,* however, bears out what we see here. This class would endeavor to separate itself from European and subaltern alike, and colonial discourse would provide it with some of the elements for doing so. Thus the Hindu elite would eschew their Indo-Islamic heritage, privilege shastric traditions, and turn their backs on a vital heterodox folk culture, contributing thereby to the subsequent growth of caste and communal consciousness.

In a sense these differential responses are an effect of the structural locations of each group. If the peasants, artisans, weavers, and others encountered by the missionaries seemed indifferent to them, this is partly because, as Ranajit Guha has argued, the objective conditions of subaltern existence generate a predominantly local worldview or orientation.[85] Unlike East India Company officials or local landlords and revenue collectors, the missionaries were not oppressive agents in the lives of most people. Nor had their message acquired the power to liberate those oppressed in society. By contrast the education, employment, social location, and life experience of the *bhadralok* meant their intimate implication in the colonial apparatus. It is no wonder then that it was they who produced the most sustained negotiations with official and missionary discourse.

The preaching narratives of Carey, Marshman, and Ward are testimony to the collision of universes integral to colonial encounters. Given the general difficulties of communication under these conditions and the specific social context of Bengal at this time, it is perhaps not surprising to discover that the Baptists could boast of few converts — only thirty-one in their first ten years in the region. The power of their discourse in India was modest and derived mainly from its intersection with that of officials whose legal and educational policies were grounded in similar analysis of society. In Britain, on the other hand, evangelical discourse came into its own. Freed from any bureaucratic containment born of East India Company fear of the political consequences of "interfering in religion," evangelical propaganda blossomed. It created, enlisted, and sustained British domestic opinion on the basis of a reductive discourse on India which was contestable from within the missionaries' own accounts. Evangelists mobilized narratives of religious infatuation and cruel superstition, the likes of which are conspicuously absent in missionary journals, and argued that the unreflective indigenous subject could only be rescued by the enlightened agency of the evangelist. The writings of Carey, Marshman, and Ward provided grist for the propaganda mill, and Ward, in particular, actively produced such literature. This corpus will be the focus of the following chapter.

PLATES

Plate 1. *The Burning System Illustrated*, by Thomas Rowlandson, 1815, hand-colored engraving, 14.7 cm x 24 cm, India Office Library and Records, p. 2687. (*Dialogue:* This custom tho' shocking to humanity we still allow in consequence of the revenue it brings in, which is of importance! I have also private reasons for not suppressing the burning system immediately. / Why my Lord with a view to Oeconomy under existing circumstances it might be imprudent to press the measure at present; besides I think I feel also the private motives which activate your Lordship.) By permission of the British Library.

Plate 2. *The Rite of Sati*, by Bahadur Singh, Lucknow, c. 1780, tinted drawing on paper, 34.5 cm x 44 cm, India Office Library and Records, Add. Or 24. By permission of the British Library.

Plate 3. *A Suttee*, anonymous, c. 1800, *sati* scene 248, watercolor, British Drawings at the India Office Library, amateur artists. By permission of the British Library.

Plate 4. Untitled engraving of a *sati*, *Baptist Magazine*, February 1822, 83. By permission of the British Library.

Plate 5. *Burning a Hindoo Widow* (also listed as *The Suttee*), by James Peggs, engraving, in *India's Cries to British Humanity*, 3d ed. (London: Simpkin and Marshall, 1832), 213.

## CHAPTER 4

# Traveling Texts

## *The Consolidation of Missionary Discourse on India*

*My principal methodological devices for studying authority here are what can be called* strategic location, *which is a way of describing the author's position in a text with regard to the Oriental material he writes about, and* strategic formation, *which is a way of analyzing the relationship between texts and the way in which groups of texts, types of texts, even textual genres, acquire mass, density and referential power among themselves and thereafter in the culture at large.*

Edward Said, *Orientalism*[1]

Edward Said's concepts of "strategic location" and "strategic formation" are invaluable to the project of this chapter, which is to expand the horizon of analysis from the early journals of the Baptists to the subsequent trajectory of nineteenth-century evangelical discourse. We attend here, in particular, to the process and effects of the consolidation of missionary discourse in the period after 1813. The legalization of missionary activity in that year ensured Baptists in the colony a security of tenure that they had not previously enjoyed. Meanwhile in Britain, the 1813 debate over the renewal of the East India Company charter served to inaugurate a populist metropolitan discourse on India that gave new prominence to *sati* and to questions of women's status. These issues, which had not hitherto been foregrounded in the writings of the Serampore Baptists, were also increasingly represented in the materials published by them in India, although their arguments in this instance were tempered by the political and discursive context in Bengal.

121

"Tracking" and "excavation" are the terms that best capture the method used here in examining the travel of missionary texts between Britain and India, the relation of unpublished to published materials, and the publics addressed and constituted in each location. "Tracking" points to the diachronic dimension. "Excavation" suggests that which is implicit in any attempt to comprehend intertextual relations: the process of moving between differently sedimented materials and levels of textuality. Unlike in chapters 1 and 3, where the indigenous voices embedded in official sources and missionary preaching accounts have served as a counterpoint to official and missionary claims about Indian society, the tactic adopted here is akin to that employed in chapter 2. I read a range of missionary texts against one another, identifying how, over time, they intersect, diverge, or articulate with each other. In other words, the historicity of these texts has been sought primarily within the texts themselves.

The consolidation of missionary discourse is explored in a number of overlapping ways. I begin by comparing the first edition of William Ward's *Account of the Writings, Religion and Manners of the Hindoos,* published in Serampore in 1811, with the last edition of the same work, retitled *A View of the History, Literature and Mythology of the Hindoos,* published in London in 1822 before his death (both editions hereafter cited in text and referred to as *Hindoos*). I argue that the two editions are marked by differences which exemplify the discursive and political moments of their production and which may be summarized as expressing the shift of the text from one resembling a miscellany to one approximating an ethnography. Second, I examine how Ward's writing, specifically his *Hindoos,* is appropriated in an increasingly reductive manner by evangelists in Britain during the debate in 1813 on the renewal of the East India Company charter and in the years following. Third, I document how Ward's own discourse consolidates in a similarly reductive direction in the period between the two editions, contrasting his journal and 1811 *Hindoos* with the speeches he delivered during his visit to Britain in 1819–20, the substance of which was published in an epistolary form as *Farewell Letters.* Finally, I compare evangelical discourse on *sati* in Britain with missionary writings published primarily for circulation in India. The production and selective appropriation of Ward's *Hindoos* and the representation and deployment of *sati* will serve as the twin strands of analysis.

Ward's *Hindoos* serves the present project in a number of ways. The text became an important source of information on Hindu religion and society in Britain. Not only did the work go through at least eight editions between 1811 and 1822,[2] it was also repeatedly drawn upon by evangelical and other publications, Baptist and otherwise.[3] One can trace which aspects of Ward's work received greatest attention in Britain and what might have accounted for certain inclusions and exclusions. In addition, the range and richness of Ward's corpus — journals, letters, fundraising literature, "scholarly" monograph — makes possible the kind of intertextual reading developed here. It enables us to compare the two editions with each other, the book with other writings by Ward, and, in turn, the appropriation of Ward in other texts.

Analysis of the shifts in Ward's rhetoric and of the modalities of its appropriation illuminates, in a general sense, the processes by which discourses are consolidated. We can explore how elements which are at first diffuse gradually become fully articulated, and can identify the textual strategies that produce this effect. We can also clarify how discourse is never a seamless web, but carries within it features that can potentially disrupt its claims although such disruptions are contingent on desire and power. Finally, from the multiple expressions of any given discourse, we can isolate the narrow, strategic deployments of some of its aspects in, for instance, fundraising efforts, which attempted to configure discursive elements to specific ends.

## Ward's *Hindoos*

Ward's *Hindoos* may be located in what Mary Louise Pratt has described as the informational tradition of a broadly construed travel writing, the purpose of which was "to incorporate a particular reality into a series of interlocking information orders" — aesthetic, geographic, mineralogical, and ethnographic among others.[4] According to Pratt, such writing typically represented itself as "natural," effacing the contexts and conditions of its production. This is true of Ward's *Hindoos*.

There is precious little available in Ward's journal or elsewhere describing his process in writing this text. It would appear from his letter of 1809 to Andrew Fuller of the Baptist Missionary Society (BMS) that he had been working on *Hindoos* since at least 1803.

I have been for the last five or six years employed in a work on *the religion and manners of the Hindoos*. It has been my desire to render it the most authentic and complete account that has been given on the subject. I have had the assistance of Brother Carey in every proof-sheet; and his opinion and mine is in almost every particular the same. He and Brother Marshman think the work would be read in England.[5]

Ward's claim is corroborated by an entry in his journal in 1802 in which he notes that he had persuaded a potential convert "to give me a little knowledge of Hindoostanee, & an account of Hindoo manners."[6] The following year there is a similar entry about his having asked the servant of one Mr. Hasted to give him an account of "the manners and customs" of the people in Rajmall hills.[7]

The idea of a book in progress becomes explicit in his journal in 1806. In February and March of that year there are frequent references to work on the project. On February 9, 1806, he notes, "Yesterday I was at Calcutta writing with the head Shanscrit pundit [Mrityunjay Vidyalankar] of the [Fort William] College. I am anxious to get from him an intelligible and genuine account of the Hindoo Philosophy."[8] This is followed by several similar entries, "Yesterday I was at Calcutta writing an account of the Hindoo Philosophy with the Head Pundit of the College";[9] "This morning I went down to Calcutta to write with the head pandit."[10] On March 25, 1806, Ward even writes of putting the "first form of the Hindoo Religion, Manners & customs to press."[11] The status of the work is unclear, however, for later that year he claims that he has refrained from accepting an advance subscription for the book "till the work is in greater forwardness."[12]

Apart from a stray entry the following year in which Ward remarks, "My first volume is finished at press. I now see that it will make 3 vols,"[13] no more mention is made of the work until December 1810: "I went down to [Calcutta] this evening to be ready to call on Mr. Edmonstone, the Secretary to Government with a copy of my Book, now completed, & to obtain leave to publish it. He is unable to see me till Saturday morning."[14]

The East India Company's approval came a month later on January 8, 1811: "This day the permission of Government to publish my book was received."[15] Ward's last journal entry pertaining to his book is recorded on March 17, 1811. In it he mentions that the governor-general, Lord Minto, had been presented with a copy of his book but had yet to acknowledge receipt of it.[16]

This is as much as is available from Ward's diary of the conditions of production of his text. (In any case Ward does not appear to have maintained a regular journal after October 1811.) Unlike official memoranda, through which one may reconstitute the processes by which official knowledge was generated in a given instance (see chapter 1), or preaching narratives, in which the reports of dialogues with indigenous people also provide grounds for documenting missionary discourse (see chapter 3), the information here is frustratingly limited. One would like to know, for example, the processes by which the text constituted such domains as "philosophy," "history," "customs," "mythology," or "literature"; how Ward proceeded to gather information; who aided him in his task, apart from Carey, Marshman, the head pundit Mrityunjay Vidyalankar, and the two others specifically mentioned in his diary; and how he negotiated conflicting information he might have received from different sources. One could compile a long list of questions such as these, but it would be to no purpose. The available material simply does not enable us to explore them.

If journals and other sources cannot be read for such "answers," there are other ways to make the text yield its historicity. Following Hayden White, we can attempt to read the context from the very surface of the text.[17] Take for instance the language employed by Ward to describe his work with Vidyalankar at the College of Fort William. He describes it as "writing with." The words represent a partial truth. Ward was certainly "writing with" the pundit in the sense of actively collaborating with him. But, like any other author, he was also necessarily selecting, interpreting, evaluating, discarding, and framing the material given him by his native informant(s) and writing what was undoubtedly *his* text. Again the description "my book" is at once accurate and misleading. It was Ward's insofar as he had the power to determine its final form. But the possessive "my" also obscures the labor of those like the pundit whose knowledge made Ward's project possible.

The point here is not to reclaim Ward's text as that of the pundit, but to point to an area that remains to be adequately explored: the relation between indigenous *munshis* and pundits and the European scholar/ administrator/missionary. Important aspects of this issue have been addressed in two studies of the College of Fort William, a key institutional site for such collaboration. David Kopf has argued in his history of the College of Fort William that it facilitated cross-cultural exchange.[18] This characterization has been countered by S. K. Das as mistakenly benign since it fails to acknowledge the power relations between Europeans and Indians employed at the institution.[19] However, in lamenting the "contradiction" between the scholarly and administrative impulses that had led to the foundation of the College of Fort William, Das ends up positing scholarship as autonomous from history and politics, and forecloses questions regarding their imbrication in the colonial context.

A related issue is the linguistic competence of turn-of-the-century

European orientalists and their dependence, largely unacknowledged, on the labor of indigenous literati. M. A. Qayyum's analysis of the production of early Bengali grammars suggests that the linguistic capacities of Halhed, Carey, and Graves Chamney Haughton were uneven and much poorer than has been assumed or might be suggested by the translations and grammars attributed to them.[20] Ward candidly notes Baptist reliance on indigenous scholars in the context of the mission project of publishing grammars and dictionaries of indigenous languages: "The College has ordered 100 Mahratta Grammars which we lately printed, & 100 Mahratta Dictionaries to be printed. These works are by Bro. Carey; viz. *extracted out of a Mahratta pundit*" (emphasis mine).[21]

The verb "extracted," with its connotations of a purposive expropriation of raw material for use in another product, captures more accurately than "writing with" the overdetermined context in which European knowledge was produced in the colonies. It also signals the place of indigenous informants in such projects: that of *munshis* to colonial sahibs.[22] The recognition of the subordinate structural position of *munshis* and pundits should not be taken to imply they did not leave their own impress on the texts so produced.[23] The co-implication or tensions between their readings and those of the European orientalist or missionary is, however, a matter in need of further analysis.

The role of the indigenous informant or scholar was a thorny issue for the Baptists, particularly in relation to the missionary translation project. Carey, Marshman, and Ward embarked on an ambitious attempt to translate Christian scriptures into numerous indigenous languages, most of which were unknown to them. Indigenous translators were thus employed to undertake the work. The faithfulness of such translations has been a matter of controversy both during and after the lifetimes of the Serampore trio. Critics challenged the linguistic abilities of the Baptists and argued that many of their translations were unintelligible. Equally problematic to some evangelists was this dependence on non-Christian translators.

The Baptists defended themselves by claiming that every translation was verified by two pundits trained by Carey in the art of translation, and finally by Carey himself against the Sanskrit original, Sanskrit being conceived here as the parent language from which others were derived.[24] Quite apart from the authenticity of translations supervised by men who lacked knowledge of the languages being worked with, we see here the underlying presumption of the superiority of European over indigenous knowledge which alone could make such a procedure credible.[25] The Baptist defense also underscores the ambiguous status accorded indigenous people in such endeavors. Their knowledge, although crucial, was always subject to European revision. As in the treatment of court pundits (see chapter 1), they could be admitted as informants but never as authors. Perhaps the clearest illustration of the elision of the native implicit in such a process is a much reproduced portrait of William Carey in which he is seated at his desk beside a pundit. There is neither self-consciousness nor irony in the caption to the picture which simply reads "William Carey."[26]

The strategy employed in other chapters in which indigenous discourse served as a critical counterpoint to official and missionary representations is not available to us here, for the indigenous voices embedded in Ward's text cannot be separated from the weave of the author's narrative. How then to historicize the discourse of Ward's *Hindoos*? I do so here by means of considering the features that distinguish the 1811 edition from the one published in 1822. It should be clarified at the outset that the distinctions and shifts proposed between the two editions are not to be treated as absolute. Multivolume texts like Ward's, part of the colonial will to encyclopedic knowledge, cannot be subsumed under a single or totalizing descriptive schema. Rather, I suggest, the differences point to the general tendencies that mark each edition.

These tendencies are evident in the contrasts in tone and in the claims made in the preface to each edition. The brief preface to the 1811 edition is characterized by modesty. In the very first sentence, Ward claims that the volumes "contain imperfections, and that persons possessing more leisure, had they possessed his information, would have presented to the public a work more worthy of their approbation" (*Hindoos*, 1811, vol. 1, iii). Despite this, Ward continues, he hopes "that the materials here collected will be found to furnish a more correct and complete account of the Shastrus, Religion, Manners, and Customs of the Hindoos, than any thing which has hitherto been published on these subjects" (*Hindoos*, 1811, vol. 1, iii).

Ward describes his strategy in the work as "laying before the public simple facts": "The author is . . . aware, that an eloquent writer would have presented the matter contained in these volumes in a more pleasing form; and have added numerous reflections with the view of assisting the reader in forming his judgement. This, however, did not come within his plan, which was to confine himself to a collection of a large body of facts, and leave the reader to the impressions which they are calculated to make" (*Hindoos*, 1811, vol. 1, iv). Then, "without any further apology," Ward goes on to present, in summary form, the contents of each chapter.

Ward describes his work as a collection of facts presented to the reader with minimal editorializing in the hopes that readers may draw their own conclusions. No doubt the claim to such unmediated presentation of material is necessarily suspect, and, as Renato Rosaldo has suggested, such textual self-effacement can itself be an authoritative move.[27] Despite this caveat, there is a sense in which this is a reasonable description of the work, especially when it is compared to the 1822 edition. As we shall see below, the first edition reads most often like a compendium of information in which the data is only partially analyzed. The relationship between items, customs, and beliefs is minimally fleshed out, if at all. The burden of synthesizing the material, of extrapolating its larger social significance, falls to the reader.

The preface to the 1822 edition presents a sharp contrast. Here, Ward's claims about Indian society are confident, authoritative, and totalizing. The preface neither "defends" the work nor finds it necessary to summarize or discuss the material it contains. Its starting point is different: the work begins with an argument for Europe's civilizing mission in the East.

It must have been to accomplish some very important moral change in the Eastern world, that so vast an empire as is comprized in British India, containing nearly One Hundred Millions of people, should have been placed under the dominion of one of the smallest portions of the civilized world, and that at the other extremity of the globe. This opinion, which is entertained unquestionably by every enlightened philanthropist, is greatly strengthened, when we consider the long-degraded state of India. (*Hindoos*, 1822, vol. 1, xvii)

The rest of the preface then proceeds to illustrate this "long-degraded state" through delineating the debilitating social and moral consequences of "philosophical" as well as "popular" "Hindoo" beliefs and customs. Of the former kind of "Hindooism," according to Ward, all that was to be found in the present was mere "mimicry": "this part of the system, even in its outward forms, is completely lost" (*Hindoos*, 1822, vol. 1, xxii). Popular "Hindooism," on the other hand, was, in his view, even now flourishing.[28]

Ward describes how from youth, what he calls the "Hindoo" mind was taught reverence for gods, brahmins, and sacred texts, a conditioning that produced unreflective devotion. "The living scenery with which he is surrounded (all the world to him), forms a creation deriving its existence from these divine books; as far as his vision, or the faculty of hearing, or his powers of research extend, he perceives nothing but temples, gods, priests, services, and the profound homage of one hundred millions" (*Hindoos,* 1822, vol. 1, xxx).

According to Ward, idolatry, human sacrifice, self-torture, and self-immolation were among the consequences of such devotion. Ward focused at length on the consequences of such "superstition" for women in India. He argued that, in their case, mindless devotion was reinforced by lack of education, leading to practices like *sati* that annually destroyed hundreds of women or else turned them into "monsters" who destroyed their own children to fulfill religious vows. As we shall see in chapter 5, reports of women's testimonials at the pyre, many from missionary eyewitnesses, clarify beyond doubt that "religion" was not what had brought them to the pyre. Ward, however, advances his case against Hindu religion through descriptions of *sati* and East India Company figures on widow burning in Bengal. Is it peculiar, he asks, "that these females, to whom all knowledge is denied, should be more superstitious than the men? Can we be surprised at seeing them, under the influence of the demon of idolatry, destroying their children, casting themselves into the rivers, and perishing on the funeral pyres?" (*Hindoos,* 1822, vol. 1, xlix).

The preface ends with Ward appealing to women in Britain to rescue women in India "from the accumulated miseries to which they are subject" (*Hindoos,* 1822, vol. 1, l). Ward similarly points to the political stability of Britain's position in India to make a more general case for implementing social improvements. Civilizing interventions, he claims, would increase Britain's material prosperity: a civilized India would consume British manufactures to a greater extent "than she does at present, or will ever do, remaining uncivilized" (*Hindoos,* 1822, vol. 1, liii). The preface ends on a rousing note: "Never were such miseries to be removed — never was such a mighty good put within the power of one nation — the raising of a population of One Hundred Millions to a rational and happy existence, and through them, the illumination and civilization of all Asia!" (*Hindoos,* 1822, vol. 1, liv).

Ward's rhetoric here is markedly different from the preface of 1811. His earlier reluctance to offer an analysis of society is replaced here by a confident assertion that contemporary "Hindoo" society was suffused with a religiosity pervading all thought and action, one that produced dire social consequences for everyone, but especially women. There is no doubt here about what Ward would like readers to think: no question, as in 1811, of leaving them to form their own conclusions.

The objective of the work is also formulated differently. If in 1811 Ward's hope in publishing the book was to provide a fuller account of "Hindoo" society than was hitherto available, the work in 1822 is seen to have an explicitly instrumental dimension. The preface develops a lengthy argument for "improving" the natives, an argument which the volumes (unmentioned in the preface) are presumably intended to illustrate and confirm. The differences in tone and claims evident in the prefaces are also to be found in the bodies of the two editions. I now turn to the question of how the effect of authoritativeness is textually produced. Most of my examples are drawn from the treatment of specifically "non-controversial" items where one might least expect to find such contrasts.

One of the first things that strikes us about the two editions is the different order in which the material is presented. The 1811 edition consists of four volumes. It moves from a brief "history" of India to discussions of various "Hindoo" philosophical systems including textual extracts (volumes 1 and 2), "ceremonies of the Hindoos which are commanded in their Shastras" (volume 2), and gods, goddesses, temples, priests, and holy places (volume 3). The fourth and concluding volume deals with caste, marriage, and phenomena Ward characterizes as popular "Hindoo" philosophy and practice. The discussion moves, broadly speaking, from philosophical and religious texts to religious and social practices.

The 1822 edition, on the other hand, has quite a different arrangement. It also begins with a brief historical overview but proceeds swiftly to a discussion of caste and geography, and of family life under the rubric of birth and marriage. The first volume ends with Ward's reflections on the "moral conditions of the Hindoos" that includes an extract from Charles Grant's tract on the state of "Hindoo" society.[29] Volume 2 describes the founders and texts of different philosophical systems and concludes with a discussion of the prevailing state of education. Gods, goddesses, temples, religious rites, and religious sects are the burden of the third and concluding volume. Unlike the 1811 edition, which moves, generally speaking, from the abstract to the concrete, this collection begins with a firm focus on social conditions: thus the discussion of caste and family is set in the context of a brief "history" and a broader discussion of geography—climate, soil, and so on. Caste and marriage, which were deemed fit for the concluding volume in 1811, are now relo-

cated in the first volume. The rest of the material then proceeds in approximately the same sequence as before. I will return to the significance
of this change below.

The 1811 edition reads rather as a "miscellany." Loosely related items
are grouped together without a primary or dominant logic interweav-
ing them. By contrast, presentation of material in the 1822 edition is less
haphazard and seemingly more authoritative. The difference is well illustrated by contrasting how information on the "Dhunoorvadu Shastrus," or "Military Art," is presented in the two editions. In the 1811,
this section begins with the etymology of the term "dhunoorvadu,"
then proceeds to a detailed description of the bow, the training, de-
portment, and clothing of the archer, and the making of arrows. There
then follow paragraphs on bludgeons, wrestling, the flag on the chariot,
the engagement of troops, more details on chariots, different forms of
combat, and finally rules of combat. The information is laid out like a
random collection of curiosities: random not in their selection, for they
all relate to the craft of war, but in the order of their presentation, which
intermixes details of particular items, such as weapons, with more general discussions, such as how troops constitute themselves or are led into
combat.

The 1822 edition enacts a different logic. It begins with the training
and leadership of kings and then goes on to describe the arrangement
of troops, modes of warfare, laws of warfare, use and decoration of chariots, famed exploits of soldiers, and bad omens on going to war. This
discussion then sets the stage for detailed descriptions of weapons like
the bow, arrow, quiver, the training of archers, the use of clubs in war,
and wrestling as a preparation for combat. While the earlier edition
intermixed the particular and the general relatively haphazardly, in the
later edition the general description of warfare forms the framework for
the discussion of details of weaponry.

The move from a tentative to authoritative presentation is to be found
throughout the text. Furthermore, in the later edition, Ward is frequently apt to suggest, even assert, the relation between a given item and
his analysis of "Hindoo" society as a whole. Take for instance the contrast between the following fragments from the discussion of the bow.
In 1811, Ward writes:

Of the bow. There are different kinds of bows: From the bamboo Bruhma
made three bows. From the end nearest the roots he formed that called
Pinaku, which he gave to Shivu. From the second part of the bamboo he

made that called Kodundu, which was given to Vishnoo. (*Hindoos,* 1811, vol. 2, 381)

In 1822, Ward frames the same information about the bow as follows:

In the early ages, the bow was the principal instrument of war: and hence much is said of it in the history of the Hindoo wars: and, as everything described by the poets must have a divine origin, therefore from one bamboo the god Bruhma made three different bows: from the end nearest the roots he formed that called Pinaku, which he gave to Shivu. (*Hindoos,* 1822, vol. 2, 465)

Ward here re-presents the same information within a "historical" discourse (note the shift in tense, and the "thesis" statement about the importance of bows in earlier times). He also interprets the reference to Bruhma as evidence of the divine as source of poetic inspiration.

This shift in Ward's prose from the descriptive to the interpretive and evaluative is even clearer in those parts of the work concerned with religious practice. Take the example of *jupu*. Ward, in 1811, writes:

Jupu: Jupu is the repeating [of] the name of a god, in which a person, taking a bead-roll, repeats the name of his chosen god, counting by his beads, ten, twenty-eight, one hundred and eight, not less than one hundred more. (*Hindoos,* 1811, vol. 2, 466)

In 1822, however, Ward has this to say:

Repeating the Names of the Gods (Jupu)
The Hindoos believe that the repetition of the name of God is an act of adoration; some add that the name of God is like fire, by which all their sins are consumed: hence speaking the names of the idols is a popular ceremony among the Hindoos.
In this act the worshipper, taking a string of beads repeats the name of guardian deity, or that of any other God; counting by his beads 10, 28, 108, 208, and so on, adding to every 108 not less than one hundred more. (*Hindoos,* 1822, vol. 2, 282–283)

If in the 1811 edition Ward is prone to speak in terms of "they do *x*" or "they do *y*," in the later volumes, he is more likely to draw out the implications of his observations, claiming "they do *x* and *y*, and it means *z.*"

Such shifts are moves in a specifically ethnographic direction.[30] In tracing the emergence of the modern interpretative monograph, James Clifford notes the increasing predominance of argument over description. Evidence, he argues, is more and more related to a focused interpretation, unlike the older compendiums, which were "open text[s] subject to multiple interpretations." Clifford's description of one such text, as "content with low-level generalizations and the amassing of an eclectic range of material," can usefully be extended to the 1811 edition of Ward's *Hindoos*.[31] The greater emphasis on argument and interpretation in post-1920s ethnographic writing serves equally well as a description of the tendencies evident in the 1822 *Hindoos*.

In examining the two editions of *Hindoos*, it is important not to paint a picture of simple contrasts: analysis and critique are to be found in both. What distinguishes them, however, is that such elements are more likely to remain scattered or diffuse in the 1811 edition, while in 1822 they are mainly gathered into the full force of an argument. This effect is achieved in various ways: first, as in the examples of the bow or "jupu" above, through introductory sentences or paragraphs that delineate a specific context or meaning for the information that is about to follow; second, through concluding paragraphs that attempt to crystallize an argument by pulling together its various threads. Thus, for instance, a new conclusion to the discussion of caste is to be found in the 1822 edition, which represents contemporary brahmins as essentially corrupt. This portrayal clinches the argument of the chapter regarding the morally debilitating consequence of a system believed to have been the invention of such "corrupt" and "self serving" brahmins (*Hindoos*, 1822, vol. 1, 153–154). (The crafty brahmin was, as we saw in chapter 1, also a recurring trope in official discourse.)

Ward interweaves comments that further provide the connection between the particular and general. To draw again from the section on caste, discussion in both editions begins with a list of the four *varnas*. In the 1822 edition, however, this list is followed by the observation that, "like all other attempts to cramp the human intellect, and forcibly to restrain men within the bonds which nature scorns to keep, this system, however specious in theory, has operated like the Chinese national shoe, it has rendered the whole nation cripples" (*Hindoos*, 1822, vol. 1, 64). Here, as in other examples, Ward's later edition can be seen to move quickly from the textual to the social, from presenting a fragment to outlining and evaluating, often critically, its significance for society as a whole.

Robert Thornton's analysis of ethnographic holism is helpful here. Thornton argues that by imagining classificatory wholes a specifically ethnographic coherence is achieved. Where narratives produce closure through plot resolution, ethnographies attain it through successful descriptions of social structure, classificatory wholes within which specific items or domains are rendered intelligible.[32] Although Ward's term "Hindoo society" lacks the conceptual clarity we have come to associate with the concept of social structure, his move to relate items to a larger social entity implies the holism that Thornton identifies as a distinctly ethnographic trope, one which was reinforced by the new importance given to caste in the 1822 edition.

Further effects of an ethnographic shift are achieved in the 1822 edition in the following ways: through reorganizing the material to follow such principles as the notion of life-stages (so that, unlike the first edition, the section on marriage follows rather than precedes the one on birth); by a more systematic use of conventional paragraphing, if only through rewriting lists of related items as sentences and paragraphs; through the greater frequency with which Ward situates his data in the context of other European scholarship (the 1811 list of poetic texts is, in 1822, interwoven with an interpretive essay by H. T. Colebrooke); and by developing explicit principles of relatedness in grouping items (for instance, through reclassification and the introduction of new sections).

Given the transformed emphasis of the preface of 1822, it is perhaps not surprising that the sections on caste and marriage move from volume 4 in 1811 to volume 1 in 1822. This rearrangement, the most dramatic one undertaken by the later edition, reinforces the presentation of caste as the central structuring principle of society and the greatest barrier to evangelization.[33] It then proceeds to a discussion of marriage and family, institutions said to be fundamentally shaped by "Hindooism" and producing negative consequences for women and society. These chapters then frame ensuing volumes, providing a backdrop against which the details of gods, sects, and particular practices gather meaning and resonance.

## The Shifting Context of Evangelism

While analysis of the rhetorical strategies employed by the two editions enables us to grasp how these different effects of miscellany and ethnography are produced, for clues as to why such a shift might have occurred we must turn our attention to the political and discursive moments in which the volumes were published. The 1811 edition of

Ward's *Hindoos* was written and produced at a time when the position of missionaries in India was insecure. As noted in the previous chapter, there was considerable fear and suspicion among East India Company officials of the consequences of evangelical attempts to convert indigenous people from a religion to which they were believed to be jealously attached. (This view was also shared by Ward although it conflicted with his own record of the society around him.) Officials were especially concerned with the potential for social disturbance in missionary criticism of Hinduism and Islam.

Missionary presence was thus contingent upon the support in Bengal of sympathetic governors-general, and in Britain of Clapham Sect evangelists like Charles Grant and William Wilberforce who since the early 1790s had campaigned on behalf of missionization. When the East India Company charter came up for renewal in 1793, Wilberforce introduced clauses to urge the appointment of chaplains in India and the dispatch of "fit and proper persons" to act as "school masters, missionaries or otherwise" in order to "promote the religious and moral improvement" of its inhabitants.[34] The clauses would have legalized missionary activity. However, they were roundly defeated by legislators persuaded by East India Company fears about their potential for social and political chaos and consequent disruption of trade and commerce. The millions of India were accordingly left, as Wilberforce put it, "to the providential protection of Brama."[35]

In the meantime, the Baptists had worked cautiously and relatively unhindered except for periodic controversies with the East India Company, such as that over the implications of the 1806 Vellore Mutiny. The mutiny, in which Indian sepoys killed over one hundred British soldiers, was widely believed to have been sparked off by regulations requiring Indian sepoys to cut their beards, remove caste marks, and wear uniform head gear. This "culturalist" explanation of the event obviously raised anew official fear of religious interference and, by extension, concern over evangelical activity.[36] The following year another controversy erupted over a pamphlet printed at the Serampore press that contained comments denouncing Islam.[37] This episode had resulted in the East India Company requiring the Baptists to submit all their publications for its prior approval, and it is thus that we found Ward in 1810 awaiting government permission for publication of *Hindoos*. Given all this, it is hardly surprising that Ward's critique of Indian society in 1811 is relatively muted, and the general tone of his writing tentative. While he does lament many practices, and even claims that the prevalence of certain customs are anathema in a "British" India, his prose is more suggestive than declarative and his exhortations more akin to pleas than to rallying cries.

The legal situation of missionaries, however, dramatically altered in 1813; the evangelists in Britain succeeded in introducing a clause in the East India Company's charter legalizing missionary work and founding an ecclesiastical establishment in Calcutta to be funded by the company. Henceforth, missionaries were entitled to reside and work under government protection so long as their conduct remained lawful and did not violate the right of indigenous people to the free exercise of their own religion. (As argued in previous chapters, the question of what constituted "their own religion" was itself a complex issue and very much at stake in such discussions.)

The success of Grant, Wilberforce, and other evangelists had been predicated on a broad-based and carefully orchestrated campaign in Britain, both inside and outside Parliament. In all, more than 837 petitions containing approximately half a million signatures were submitted to Parliament during the debate on the charter in 1813.[38] Although by no means spontaneous, this mobilization attested to the importance of evangelical protestantism as an influential and vital current in the sociopolitical life of early-nineteenth-century Britain. Evangelism drew its strength from its heterogeneous and multi-denominational character. It included Methodists, orthodox dissenters such as the Baptists, and Church of England evangelists like Grant and Wilberforce.

The features that were shared to a greater or lesser extent by post-1730 evangelism were as follows: conversionism (the belief that lives needed to be changed and that preaching the gospel was the chief method of winning converts); activism (the imperative to be "up and doing" as a result of the increasing conviction that human beings could become agents in bringing the gospel to unevangelized nations); biblicism (a particular regard for the text of the Bible); and crucicentricism (emphasis on the sacrifice of Christ on the cross).[39] Although various denominations in the evangelical movement emphasized different elements at different times, there was sufficient agreement on basic tenets for groups to work closely with each other, a cooperation that was critical to the number of petitions and signatures garnered in 1813.

If evangelism drew its force in part from its undogmatic character, its success is also perhaps attributable to the intersection of its reformist zeal with utilitarianism.[40] Despite their differences both were concerned with the idea of a "just" rule, a concern with specific valence in a post–French Revolution Europe. Francis Hutchins sums up their difference:

"Utilitarianism hoped to improve morals by reforming society; Evangelicals hoped to improve society by reforming morals."[41] Both drew on India to make their case. The evangelical position was articulated by Wilberforce in the House of Commons and beyond that in the pages of journals like the *Missionary Register*, while the classic utilitarian text in this regard is James Mill's *The History of British India*, a text published in 1817 but under preparation since 1806.[42] The themes of duty, obligation and improvement had been key to colonial ideology of rule from the start.[43] What the charter debate inaugurated in Britain was a public discourse on India in which these terms were explicitly brought to bear on matters social and cultural. Needless to say, the various participants inflected these terms in their own way.

Wilberforce was the chief spokesman for the evangelists within Parliament. Declaring at the outset his opposition to forcible conversion, he outlined the ethical imperatives of evangelism. Wilberforce emphasized the prudence with which missionaries, in particular the Baptists, had hitherto conducted themselves, the successes of their endeavors, and the moral obligation of Britain to engage in the task of improving the natives. He also challenged his opponents' defense of the Hindus and their religion, arguing that far from being friends, such men were enemies of the natives and did not wish to see them liberated from the yoke of oppression. The necessity and urgency of moral improvement constituted the burden of his interventions. Here, as we might expect, his argument turned on his analysis of indigenous society as "degraded." He drew extensively on Grant's analysis of India.[44] Everything from indigenous "character," to caste, polygamy, infanticide, idolatry, and *sati* was produced as incontrovertible evidence of the necessity for moral improvement. By extension, Wilberforce asserted the fundamental opposition between England and India:

Both their civil and religious systems are radically and essentially the opposites of our own. Our religion is sublime, pure and beneficent. Theirs is mean, licentious, and cruel. Of our civil principles, and condition, the common right of all ranks and classes to be governed, protected, and punished by equal laws, is the fundamental principle. Equality, in short, is the vital essence and the very glory of our English laws. Of theirs, the essential and universal pervading character is inequality; despotism in the higher classes, degradation and oppression in the lower.[45]

What is interesting about Wilberforce's arguments is that they are not framed in relation to a discussion of brahmanic scriptures, but in terms of a common orientalist trope: the degradation of contemporary indigenous society.[46] Even though "religion" was clearly at stake, and he does employ the description "Hindoo society," Wilberforce does not explicitly stress the relationship of such "degraded" practices to "Hindoo religion." His discussion of *sati*, for example, turns on the extent of its practice, the indifference of spectators, and its coercive character. By contrast with the official debate on the abolition of *sati* discussed in chapter 1, the question of its "scriptural" basis is conspicuous by its absence. It is not that Wilberforce did not have the information with which to make a scriptural argument. The "authorities" cited in his speech on *sati* were Alexander Dow, François Bernier, Claudius Buchanan, William Ward, and Joshua Marshman.[47] Wilberforce had been in active contact with Buchanan (former vice-provost of the College of Fort William in Calcutta) since the latter's return from India in 1808.[48] Both Buchanan's *Memoir of the Expediency of an Ecclesiastical Establishment for British India,* and Ward's first edition of the *Hindoos,* to which he also refers in the course of his speech, had explicitly discussed the scriptural status of *sati*.[49] Perhaps Wilberforce hoped that by focusing on contemporary social conditions he could make a case for the evangelical project without seeming to challenge Hindu religion per se. His opponents, though, were not convinced, especially since the campaign in evangelical papers like the *Missionary Register* clearly outlined "Hindooism" as the main enemy. Those against the clause thus saw it as representing potential religious intervention and it was this danger that they emphasized. (It is important to bear in mind that even in the same year that the question of religious intervention was thus being debated in the British Parliament, the East India Company in India, under the guise of "tolerance," was busily intervening by codifying a particular version of *sati* as scripturally authentic; see chapter 1.)

Sir Stephen Lushington may be taken to represent the lobby opposing the clause.[50] Lushington addressed the three issues that he saw as inevitable consequences of the passage of a clause permitting missionary activity: its political danger, its impracticality, and its undesirability. The specter of the Vellore Mutiny was raised to signal the political dangers of interference. Lushington also believed that hopes for religious conversions were impractical. According to him, caste provided an insurmountable obstacle amongst Hindus, while Muslims, in his view, would never be open to conversion. He described missionaries already in India not as harbingers of social revolution as Wilberforce had suggested, but as mere "tub preachers" (a reference to the social basis of evangelism among the artisanal and laboring classes) incapable of debating the "intelligent Hindoo."

Finally, Lushington insisted that conversion was undesirable. He defended the Hindus as a moral and virtuous people, praised their literature, architecture and arts, and criticized his opponents' analysis for relying on a literal reading of the scriptures. As he put it, "If Menu said that the women of India were prone to anger, does it prove that every woman in India is a scold?" One may readily concede Lushington's point. However, it is interesting to note that, having warned his opponents against such extrapolations from the scriptures, he draws upon these texts in very similar ways: to illustrate the greatness of India and to argue that *sati,* one of "the principal charges in . . . [Wilberforce's] bill of indictment against the Hindoos," is not sanctioned by the scriptures but is "a species of overstrained interpretation of its duties." Lushington concludes that, given the moral state of Indian society and the obligation of Christianity not to produce civil strife, "commonsense, reason, and even religion itself, cry out against our interference." [51] He suggests, as an alternative, that the reformist energies of evangelists might best be employed in ameliorating English society.

In the event, it was Wilberforce, not Lushington, whose arguments were to prevail. The 1813 charter legalized the entry of missionaries into India and in doing so freed evangelists both in India and Britain. Henceforth, the activities of the Serampore Baptists, for instance, were not shaped by fear of deportation but by the local social and political context, and by material considerations such as their financial situation and collective capabilities. The clause also gave greater impetus to evangelists in Britain. Since their cause was no longer illegal, public support could be enlisted more vigorously. The measure of the evangelical triumph, however, did not lie in an immediate departure of missionaries for the colonies. Lushington's fears about India being overrun by zealous missionaries turned out to be groundless for, much to the embarrassment of evangelists, not a single person was found who was willing to go to India! [52]

What did prevail post-1813, however, was the kind of discourse on India that had been mobilized by Wilberforce. Sentiments expressed by him in the parliamentary debate became the staple of evangelical literature published in Britain. And the writings of the Baptists, including Ward, provided important material evidence for such analysis. Increasingly, that which was crafted by Ward and others in one context — from the margins of Bengal society and through their dependence on indigenous informants — was appropriated in quite another, as expert evidence in a self-confident and intensely moralistic evangelical discourse. The negative representation of India it popularized was to intersect with the more secularized and rationalized version to be found in Mill's *The History of British India,* marking the transition that historiography has conventionally described as the shift in British colonial attitude from a "sympathetic orientalism" to a "harsh anglicism."

## British Evangelism, Widow Burning, and the Writings of William Ward

European writing on the colonies addressed two distinct metropolitan audiences. Robert Thornton identifies these as the well-to-do who stored their literature in "cabinets of natural history" and the poorer folk and journeymen, whose staple was church bulletins, missionary tracts, and lectures delivered by returning or visiting evangelists in church halls and Sunday schools. Thornton notes that although missionaries wrote for both audiences, their participation in these latter "networks of information" has been inadequately explored.[53]

In this section I examine how the nature of material excerpted by populist evangelical publications from a work like *Hindoos* contributed to the consolidation of a particular discourse on India. I take as my focus the *Missionary Register,* a publication that explicitly sought to build popular support for evangelical work. *Sati* will provide the example. I compare the status of *sati* in Ward's *Hindoos* and journal writings with its subsequent representation in the *Missionary Register* and the *Periodical Accounts,* a publication primarily intended for internal circulation among members of the BMS. What shifts or transformations are discernible in the selection and framing of fragments from Ward's writings? What does the *Missionary Register* foreground and what are the effects of its procedures?

The first issue of the *Missionary Register* appeared in London in January 1813, its timing related to the impending renewal of the East India Company's charter. The journal was a publication of the Church Missionary Society, with which Wilberforce and company were associated. However, in the heterodox spirit of evangelism in this period, in addition to proceedings of the CMS, the journal also contained abstracts of the reported activities of the principal missionary and Bible societies operating throughout the world. The *Missionary Register* also published articles on the society and culture of the colonies, India among them. Perhaps not surprisingly, the themes that predominated in the journal's discussion of India were "Hindoo Superstitions," "Hindoo Mythology and Deities," and "Human Sacrifices."

One "Hindoo superstition" in which the journal took particular interest was widow burning. In June 1813, at the height of the parliamentary charter debate in which *sati* served to illustrate indigenous degradation and, by implication, the importance of evangelical work, the *Missionary Register* published an extract on widow burning from Ward's 1811 *Hindoos*.[54] In the fragment in question, Ward does not describe any particular incident of widow burning so much as construct a picture of widow burning in general. Ward begins,

I do not find it common for women to reveal their intention of being burnt with their husbands while both parties are in health. A few, however, do reveal this intention to their husbands alone, and there may be circumstances in the family which may lead [one] to expect such a circumstance. When the husband is ordered by the doctor to be carried to the river side, there being no hopes of his recovery, sometimes the wife then declares her resolve to be burnt with him. In this case she is treated with great respect by her neighbours, who bring her delicate things to eat, &c. When the husband is dead, she again declares her resolution to be burnt with his body. Having broken a small branch from the mango tree, she takes it with her, and proceeds to the body, where she sits down. The barber then comes and paints the sides of her feet red; then she bathes, and puts on new clothes. During these preparations, the drum beats a certain sound, by which it is known that a widow is about to burn with the corpse of her husband. On hearing this all the village assembles.

Ward proceeds in this vein to describe the preparation of the pile and the other practices that precede the burning of the corpse and the widow. The latter is described as follows:

The widow, having gone round seven times, ascends the pile, or rather throws herself down upon it by the side of the dead body. A few trifles belonging to women, as a box containing red paint, &c. are laid by her. The ropes are then drawn over the bodies, and they are tied together, and faggots put upon them. When this is done, the son, turning his head, puts fire to the head of his father, and at the same moment several persons light the pile at different sides. After lighting the pile, the women, relations, &c. set up a cry. Then with haste more thorns are thrown on the pile, and two bamboo levers are brought over the whole to hold down the persons and the piles. Several men, generally brahmuns, are employed in holding down these levers. . . . While the fire is burning, more clarified butter and pitch is thrown into it; then more thorns, &c. till the whole be consumed. It may take about two hours before the whole is burnt, but I conceive the woman must be dead in two minutes after the fire has been kindled.

Ward similarly details the disposal of the bones, the cleaning of the spot on which the immolation has taken place, and the practices that accompany the return of relatives to their homes. (Descriptions of *sati* are analyzed in detail in chapter 5.)

Ward's description of this "typical" *sati* expresses neither horror nor critique, although both were present in other accounts penned by him. Rather, his tone is matter-of-fact and similar to that adopted in describing mundane, noncontroversial events. The *Missionary Register,* however, frames the extract in such a way as to make crystal clear its purpose in reproducing the passages: "Let every Christian Woman who reads the following Statement, pity the wretched thousands of her sex who are sacrificed every year in India to a cruel superstition, and thank God for her own light and privileges, and pray and labour earnestly for the salvation of these miserable fellow subjects."[55] Ward's appropriation into a discourse of horror is here undertaken by means of a simple reframing of his text. The following month, the *Missionary Register* published another fragment from Ward's discussion of *sati* in the 1811 *Hindoos* under the title "Instance of the Cruelty of Hindoo Superstition." The incident, which Ward himself had described as a "most shocking and atrocious murder," is one in which the widow is said to have escaped from the pyre only to be dragged back by her family, bound to it, and burnt.[56]

Ward's own presentation of *sati* in the 1811 *Hindoos* had proceeded from a discussion of the scriptural basis of *sati,* to a generalized description of the practice referring to no particular incident, to descriptions of actual immolations.[57] The structure of Ward's discussion is consonant with the Baptist approach to preaching in the initial phase, which, as we saw, was concerned to establish the scriptural basis for contemporary social practices.

By contrast, the *Missionary Register* seems unconcerned with questions of scripture. Like Wilberforce in the parliamentary debate, the *Missionary Register* did not address *sati*'s relation to brahmanic scripture, but focused almost entirely on the domain of practice. In choosing to publish Ward's descriptions of a "typical" *sati* and a reported incident, the periodical was interested in "revealing" the "real," that is to say, immoral state of indigenous society. Here we see not just the introduction of a discourse of horror, but also a shift in discursive emphasis:

from a focus on *sati* in relation to scripture, to one on *sati* as evidence of social degradation.

This emphasis is perfectly intelligible given the ideological and practical objectives of periodicals like the *Missionary Register*. In addition to disseminating information on missionary activity, the purpose of such journals was to raise funds for mission work through repeated "exposés" of indigenous "superstition." The horrors they catalogued were designed to convince British readers of the enormity of the evangelical task and of the paramount importance of supporting such endeavors. They may thus be regarded as a genre of conversion literature for the metropole. They sought to enlist and constitute domestic support for evangelism and, by extension, colonialism.

Women represented a special constituency within the more general appeals to duty and philanthropy made by such literature. The address of the Ladies Association of the Southwark Church Missionary Society, published in the *Missionary Register* in April 1814, illustrates clearly the relationship asserted within these materials between womanly compassion, Christian "horror," and evangelical motivation. The Southwark Ladies Association was formed for the "purpose of collecting Weekly and Monthly Contributions, in aid of the funds of the Southwark Church Missionary Association."[58] The impulse for such an organization was formulated as follows:

The Ladies, who circulate this Address, do not feel it necessary to enter into a detail of the various and urgent wants of the millions who are involved in the darkness of heathen ignorance and superstition; for such information they refer to the Reports of the Church Missionary Society, and to the Missionary Register. One picture of misery, however, which appeals to their own sex, they venture to exhibit.[59]

The address then appeals to women's capacity to "commiserate with suffering humanity," asking them to imagine "the poignant anguish which must rend the breast of that mother, who, in the decease of her children's best support, hears the summons for her to forsake them, at a time, too, when they most need her fostering care; and to immolate herself on her husband's funeral pile!— The affecting representation excites our sympathy: let it stimulate our exertions."[60]

The Southwark Ladies Association was only one among many women's auxiliaries established in Britain in this period. (The first such organization was reputedly the Northampton Female Missionary Society of the BMS founded in 1805.)[61] Their rise signaled the critical involvement of women in evangelism, a participation facilitated by the movement's privileging of activism and service over doctrine. Moreover, nature appeared to converge with evangelical decree. Women's supposedly innate qualities of compassion, patience, and self-sacrifice were said to make them particularly suited to philanthropic work. Evangelical arguments also intersected with medical, scientific, and philosophic literature in this period, all of which gave new importance to the family as the fundamental social unit whose well-being determined that of society as a whole.[62] Within this scheme, women were defined as the natural guardians of households, and in the increasing demarcation of the private from the public worlds, middle-class women in particular became identified with the private.[63]

In this context, philanthropy became a legitimate sphere for women's agency, enabling them to extend the arena of their labor without disrupting the premises of turn-of-the-century gender ideology.[64] It is perhaps not surprising, then, to find that 15 percent of BMS subscribers in 1800 were women, the figure rising to 17 percent in 1825, while the proportion of women in the Church Missionary Society was 12 percent in 1801 and 29 percent in 1823.[65] Women's financial contributions were commensurate with their numbers even when, as in the case of the BMS, they had a large following among the laboring classes. Women also drew children into evangelical work. For women and children alike such activity had the promise of a double dividend: through it they could ensure their own salvation and prevent a backsliding into sinfulness, even while they labored to regenerate the heathen. Missionary literature and meetings sustained the energy for such work. In them, stories of horror and success were circulated, most often in print but occasionally in person, by visiting missionaries armed with fallen idols and other artifacts from the field. Given the specific function of cultural representations in enlisting the citizenry, it is not surprising that all of the extracts from Ward's *Hindoos* published by the *Missionary Register* between 1811 and 1822 served to illustrate, in one way or another, the supposed religious infatuation and degradation of indigenous people. In addition to the extracts from Ward on *sati* discussed above, the journal published excerpts from *Hindoos* on "human sacrifices"[66] and hook swinging.[67] Ward was also cited as a source in articles on idolatry[68] and on the "horrible festivities" at the Jagannath temple.[69] The new importance given to motherhood in early-nineteenth-century Britain also accounts in part for the special horror of *sati,* which, within this ideology, represented not just an individual but a social calamity.

Whatever the reasons for the nature of materials excerpted from Ward's four-volume *Hindoos,* the view of Indian society afforded by them is breathtakingly reductive. India emerges in these pages as a society stalked by "superstition," with the majority of people deluded and engaged for most of their waking hours in various forms of self-abuse, sacrifice, or murder. This picture of society, legitimized by missionary and other European writers, stands in striking contrast to that which is portrayed in the journals and letters of Carey, Marshman, and Ward.

In the critical reading of the journals of the Serampore trio undertaken in the previous chapter, "religion" emerges as a complex social domain. Despite missionary insistence to the contrary, both in their journals and elsewhere, the relation of "religion" to brahmanic scripture does not appear to be self-evident. More importantly, people's relationship to religion emerges as dynamic — contested, not all-consuming — and tempered by various "secular" considerations. It is not that the practices highlighted by the *Missionary Register* are undocumented in these other sources. Neither is it that missionaries were uncritical of them. Rather, it is that such practices are foregrounded less, and do not seem to inspire in missionaries the kind of special concern and horror that evangelical discourse in Britain would evince.

Take, for instance, the treatment of *sati* in Ward's journal. Given the emblematic status that *sati* was to assume in the discourse of popular evangelism in Britain, it is interesting that there are only nine entries on *sati* in the twelve-year period — October 1799 to October 1811 — during which Ward kept a regular diary. The entries mainly record individual instances of widow burning. They appear in the context of other entries and Ward's reports of them are fairly matter-of-fact. The incident is treated like other encounters with indigenous people recorded in his journal. When critique is expressed, it is limited to such brief expressions as "I was struck with horror to behold these infernal rites."[70]

Three of the entries on *sati* in Ward's journal refer to efforts made to ascertain the incidence of widow burning, first by the East India Company in 1802, and then by Claudius Buchanan in 1803.[71] Ward's journal records two figures for widow immolation. The first, noted in 1802, is said to be a guess and appears to be exaggerated: twenty-five to thirty thousand immolations a year.[72] Two years later Ward writes, "From actual enquiry at all the villages & towns for 30 miles around Calcutta it appears that no less than 438 widows have been burnt with their husbands in this circuit during the last year."[73] The region to which this figure refers is the area in which the Baptist missionaries lived and preached.

Yet, given the importance which Ward himself was to give to *sati* and to the social position of women in later years, there is surprisingly little mention in his journal of either subject.

Only once is *sati* reported as an item in Ward's conversation with indigenous people. On December 19, 1802, Ward writes that he was summoned to the house of a rich native: "As proof that Hindooism was true, this man among many other things mentioned that last week a woman had burnt with her husband near that place. I told him that women of bad character were known to burn with their husbands, & therefore it was no proof that this holiness was any thing."[74] This interaction is interesting for at least two reasons. First, the way in which *sati* is proposed by the rich man as "proof" of "Hindooism" appears to prefigure the manner in which it was to come to represent some essential feature about the religion (its truth, falsehood, or contemporary disgrace) for all participants in the debate on its abolition. On the other hand, this statement could conceivably have been a response to Ward's practice of exhorting indigenous people to demonstrate the relation between social practice and brahmanic scripture (see chapter 3). This reading is plausible given missionary preaching strategy and Ward's retort to the man. Ward claims that such immolations did not prove anything, since the women who committed them were known to be "of bad character," implying thereby that since such *satis* were not undertaken by women of virtue, they were scripturally inauthentic and as such not holy. There is in this fragment neither critique nor horror, but an ambivalence toward the ideal of *sati* reminiscent of the 1813 official regulation which institutionalized as law that dubious concept, the "voluntary" *sati*.

I point to the meager references to *sati* in Ward's journal neither to dispute the prevalence of the practice nor to imply that Ward was in favor of *sati*. This was far from being the case. We have already noted his comment in relation to the incident reprinted in the *Missionary Register* that it was "a most shocking and atrocious murder." Similar sentiments are expressed by him in his journal entry for April 18, 1803: "Last Monday was a horrible day. . . . three women burnt with their husband on one pile near our house."[75] Later in the same year, when the widow of one of the pundits employed at the mission press burnt with her husband, Ward writes that the missionaries chased the pundit's brother away "as a murderer."[76] Ward was no supporter of *sati*. But neither did he represent the practice, as he did in later writings, as a symbol of all that was degraded about "Hindoo" society.

Comparing the status of *sati* in Ward's journals and in the missionary press clarifies that *sati* did not always occupy a privileged place in the missionary imagination. Furthermore, the *Missionary Register*'s representation of the Indian landscape as drenched with the blood of human sacrifice and religious superstition is in sharp contrast with the social descriptions available in Ward's journal. Nor is a conclusion about the rampant superstitiousness of Indian society easily generalizable from Ward's 1811 *Hindoos*. Examined in its entirety, this work is, as I have suggested, a loosely structured compilation that intermixes textual extracts and social observation, but not within a totalizing narrative. What enables the reductive representations of Indian society popularized by journals like the *Missionary Register* is the selection and foregrounding of particular items, and their framing within a tightly sutured evangelical discourse. Evangelical fundraising texts drew on journal writings and compendiums like *Hindoos,* but did so selectively, privileging certain features and practices in a way that altered the materiality that had been accorded them in these sources.

The shift in such a reductive direction was, however, neither uniform nor complete. For instance, in the *Missionary Register,* Ward's non-horrified description of an ideal typical *sati* could be contrasted with its reductive framing. Furthermore, the *Missionary Register* can also be read against another contemporaneous publication, the *Periodical Accounts* of the BMS. Published in London for circulation in Britain, *Periodical Accounts* was a series of edited compilations of letters and journals received from Baptist missionaries in India. Letters were arranged either chronologically or by mission, although selected items were sometimes highlighted in the section on "Miscellaneous Intelligence." For instance, in the volume of the journal covering 1812–14, three instances of *sati* are reprinted from the letters of Moore of the BMS. Moore reports each incident and concludes his description with a brief critical comment such as, "The scene was calculated to strike the mind with inconceivable horror."[77] *Periodical Accounts* reproduces his report, but does not stage it as the *Missionary Register* might have done. Neither does it pause to assert the wider implications of such practices as *sati,* whether for Indian society, women, or the evangelical project.

Sources like *Periodical Accounts* in Britain (and *Circular Letters,* its counterpart in India) lie midpoint on the continuum between the relatively complex journals and letters, and the comparatively reductive conversion literature of fundraising. If we trace the status of widow burning across these sources we find that in the letters or journals, widow immolation was only one item among many, one event in a life filled with myriad activities and concerns. It may have been merely noted, or described in some detail, and may, or may not, have been accompanied by missionary critique of the practice. In the *Periodical Accounts* attention might be drawn to a particular account of *sati* by its insertion in a section on "miscellaneous intelligence," but the item is not likely to be accompanied by general observations on society. In the *Missionary Register*, on the other hand, the practice would achieve a different materiality. Accounts of *sati* were always framed within a critique of society, a critique which drew its force precisely from such practices, seen to be emblematic of society itself.

So far we have examined the ways in which Ward's journal writings, located at one point in the continuum identified above, could become raw material in another. But Ward was not merely a passive source in this process. As we have seen in comparing the tentative 1811 edition of the *Hindoos* with the authoritative 1822 edition, he himself produced both kinds of material. Indeed, Ward's rhetoric in the preface to the 1822 edition is reminiscent of the *Missionary Register*. This shift in Ward's prose was already beginning to take place in the speeches he delivered to missionary and Bible societies during his visit to Britain in 1819–20, versions of which were published in epistolary form as *Farewell Letters* in 1821.[78] In his innumerable addresses to British congregations, Ward had passionately defended evangelical work, detailed the obstacles in its path, elaborated, even exaggerated its "successes" (he claimed seven hundred converts!) and made rousing appeals for financial support of missionary work, particularly in the realm of female education, a project in which the Serampore missionaries had recently become involved.[79]

One theme that dominated Ward's sermons and lectures was the so-called state of female society in India. This issue was developed in the *Farewell Letters*, in his letter to Miss Maria Hope of Liverpool, a long-time activist in the British and Foreign Bible Society. In it Ward drew a harsh and misleading portrait of the life of Hindu women. Ward based his sketch on the position of upper-caste women, whose lives were far more circumscribed than those of most women. Ward argued that women were neglected or rejected at birth and prohibited from education by both scriptural injunction and popular opinion. Denied the opportunity to cultivate the mind, such women were not to be found engaged in tasks Ward viewed as befitting womanhood, such as knitting, sewing, or drawing. Rather, having spent the first ten years of her life "in sheer idleness immured in the house of her father, a woman was usually "betrothed without her consent."[80] The succeeding phase of her life is conceived by Ward in equally bleak terms. If her husband died before the consummation of the marriage, she was seen to have an option between death on the funeral pyre of her "nominal husband" or (since widowhood was prohibited "by law") a life of concubinage or as sexual prey. If her husband did not die, she was said to become his prisoner and slave. (It is important to bear in mind here that widow remarriage was in fact common among all but upper-caste women.)

According to Ward, lack of education made Indian women unsuitable companions to their husbands, even less suitable mothers, and, above all, "slave[s] of superstition." Ward elaborates a number of superstitious practices undertaken by women. Perhaps not surprisingly (given the importance accorded it by a section of the evangelical press) *sati* occupies a central place in his discussion. Contrary to the arguments being made at same time by his colleagues in India, Carey and Marshman, Ward claims that the "Hindoo legislators have sanctioned this immolation, showing herein a studied determination to insult and degrade woman," and argues that the circumstances which usually attend the practice confirm the base feelings of the people.[81] Ward challenges the claims of many that such immolations are voluntary, asking: "But has not all knowledge been denied to the Hindoo female; and have not their minds been shockingly perverted by superstition? Can a child, in the same sense as an adult be called a free agent?"[82]

Ward concludes by exhorting women in Britain to unite to "deliver these females doomed to a horrible death," and "become the guardians of the . . . Ten Thousand orphans" abandoned by both parents.[83] In another letter in the same collection Ward cites the same highly inflated figure and wishes he could "collect all the shrieks of these affrighted victims, all the innocent blood thus drunk up by the devouring element, and all the wailings of these ten thousand orphans, losing father and mother on the same day, and present them at our missionary anniversaries, and carry them through every town of the United Kingdom."[84] This Ward, the champion of "Hindoo" woman, traveling across Britain carrying with him the shrieks of widows burning, represents a far cry from the journal writer and author of the 1811 *Hindoos*. From a journal in which *sati* did not figure in any prominent way, from a discourse in which criticism of *sati* was at best muted, from an unwillingness to generalize about society in the first edition of his *Hindoos* he has moved to a rhetoric wherein the will to totalize is expressed without apology and where *sati* circulates as emblematic of indigenous degradation and of the oppression of Hindu women. This shift is most evident in Ward's speeches and writings during and following his visit to Britain in 1819. The new rhetoric did not require him to abandon his earlier discourse, merely to transform it, as the evangelical press had, by reordering its elements.

The shift in Ward's discourse is intelligible given that in his speeches to British congregations, he tried to do in person what periodicals like *Missionary Register* were attempting to achieve through print—raise funds for missionary work. Convincing people to keep donating money involved a careful balancing of two related arguments: the absolute difficulty of evangelizing the "heathen" and the dire necessity of continuing in the face of such odds. The former was amply confirmed by the poor record of conversions, something which evangelists were always having to defend to their detractors. Evangelists argued that caste represented the greatest barrier to the progress of Christianity. As Ward asserted in another epistle in *Farewell Letters,* from the very moment a Hindu accepted Christianity, he was required to be a "living martyr."[85] Converts were frequently disowned by friends and family and deprived of employment. Missionaries lamented this situation and hoped that education would in time weaken the hold of caste.[86]

If caste thus provided a perfect alibi for missionaries' lack of success, it could also have functioned to call into question the evangelical project. For if caste was so insurmountable, why persist in supporting missionary activities? It is here that the discourse on women's oppression (a rhetoric that resonated powerfully with the ideology of motherhood as social mission and family as a primary cell of the social organism) served a function in enlisting support for evangelism, far superior to any concrete "successes" evangelists might claim in conversion, language acquisition, translations, or education. By continually invoking horror and pity for women's condition as their raison d'être, the evangelists made an argument for supporting missionary activity that was entirely independent of such questions as practicality or success.

*Sati* lent itself to such deployments since it evoked both horror and pity simultaneously and in several ways. One could be horrified at the society and culture that sanctioned such a practice while pitying the women who were especially its victims. One could also be horrified at women for deserting their offspring, while pitying the children so abandoned. Finally, one could be horrified at those "unfeeling officiators" of such incidents, brahmin pundits, while pitying society for being, as it were, under their spell.

Locating evangelical horror of *sati* in the logic of fundraising is not in any way to condone the cruel and indefensible practice of widow burning. The purpose of this discussion is to explicate the recourse to horror and to *sati* in populist evangelical fundraising literature. The high profile assumed by *sati* in such materials suggests that these texts deployed the specter of *sati* to convert British Christians to evangelism.

We can see how the centrality accorded to caste and to women's oppression powerfully sustained evangelical fundraising efforts. Obviously, Ward's 1822 edition of *Hindoos* was not a fundraising document. But it, too, bears the traces of the discursive and political moment of its production. Nowhere is this more evident than in the way the discussion of caste, and of women under the rubric of marriage and family life, is to be found in the first volume of this edition, unlike in the 1811 *Hindoos*, where Ward had seen fit to consign these topics to the concluding volume of his work. Ward's reorganization of *Hindoos* bears the signature of this history.

## Baptists and the Representation of *Sati* in Bengal

If fundraising formed metropolitan evangelical discourse in particular ways, other factors shaped the direction of Baptist writing on *sati* published in Bengal. Between 1818 and 1826, in the monthly and quarterly *Friend of India*,[87] the Baptists published a series of six articles on widow burning in India. The first three of these were subsequently reprinted in England in 1823, in a collection entitled *Essays Relative to the Habits, Character, and Moral Improvement of the Hindoos.*[88]

In these essays, *sati* did not illustrate the degraded state of India (as in fundraising texts) or the manners and customs of the people (as in a work like *Hindoos*). Neither was it noted, as in missionary journals, as one event in the day's occurrences. Rather, these articles in the *Friend of India* were primarily arguments in favor of the abolition of *sati*.[89] As such they addressed prevailing official and indigenous arguments on widow burning. The scriptural basis of *sati* and the political expediency of intervention accordingly became recurring themes. Where populist evangelical literature in Britain emphasized the horror of widow burning and asserted its religious foundation, these articles sought to undermine *sati*'s claim to being religious, elaborated its material basis, and argued for the safety of abolition. This strategy was, as we have seen, also that of officials and indigenous elite men in favor of legislative prohibition of the practice.

A progressive alteration in emphasis is discernible in these articles. The first three, published between 1818 and 1819, focused primarily on the scriptural status of *sati*, with analysis of the social consequences of widow burning being a subordinate theme.[90] The emphasis, however, was reversed in subsequent articles published between 1821 and 1826. Here, the abolition of *sati* was represented primarily as a civil question, making discussion of its religious basis a secondary issue.[91] This shift is comprehensible in that, by 1821, the publication of Rammohun Roy's pamphlets on the dubious place of *sati* in Hindu scriptures had provided sufficient textual support for prohibition of the practice. Indeed, all the major scripture-based arguments for and against *sati* had been developed by 1821, and discussions thereafter largely repeated points that had already been made.

Missionary discussion of *sati*'s scriptural foundation drew entirely on indigenous sources. The first article published in December 1818 summarized, without crediting by name, Rammohun's first pamphlet on *sati*.[92] The following year the journal reproduced the conservative pro-*sati* riposte to Rammohun's first pamphlet, as well as the main outlines of the *vyawastha* of Mrityunjay Vidyalankar on the scriptural position on *sati*.[93] Yet although missionaries reprinted, paraphrased, and excerpted the arguments of others in the debate on *sati*, they brought a distinctive set of considerations to bear on the issue, namely, the consequences of *sati* for family and society. This was a theme which was simultaneously finding elaborate, if more dramatic, expression in Ward's sermons to congregations in Britain discussed above. The prose in the *Friend of India* was, however, less theatrical and more measured.

The main thesis of these articles is that *sati* is "destructive both to public happiness and domestic enjoyment."[94] Missionaries argue that the widow is "torn from her family at the very climax of her grief," and in dying, forsakes her children.[95] "The family compact is destroyed with the suddenness of an earthquake."[96] The prospect of such an event, it is argued, implies constant anxiety about the future. Family life, under these circumstances, is not "a source of joy," but an "aggravation of expected wretchedness."[97] The accumulated miseries of each family are said to seriously affect society at large, doubling the loss of life in epidemics and leading, in general, to untold misery.

One article specifically drew out the investments family members and pundits might have in *sati*.[98] The argument here echoes that advanced by some East India Company officials and *bhadralok*. Among the chief considerations listed are the desire to preserve family honor by enforcing the chastity of the widow through death, and the elimination of the widow as financial burden and potential controller of her husband's property. For her part, the widow is said to be tempted by delusory ideas about future reward, and fear of living among those who desire her destruction. (The role of fear as a factor motivating the widow is discussed in chapter 5.) Brahmin pundits are said to have a financial stake in supporting the desires of surviving relatives who would likely be sources of future employment for them.

These articles represented *sati* as a social practice in which diverse interests converged. This picture is considerably more sophisticated than that suggested in fundraising texts which deployed *sati* simply as an indicator of the evils of an idolatrous religion. In fact, the burden of the articles published in the *Friend of India* was precisely to undermine the so-called religious basis of *sati*. Arguing the opposite of what was being simultaneously asserted in metropolitan evangelical texts, missionaries stressed the material forces at work in widow burning, citing as evidence the testimonials of women who had been prevented from burning. The statements of widows, they claimed (and this is borne out by my analysis in chapter 5), clarified that feelings other "than those of unconquerable affection" had brought them to the pyre.[99] As further proof of *sati*'s civil status, it was noted that *sati* was not widespread outside of Bengal, that it prevailed only among a section of the population, and that no goddess was propitiated through the practice. Thus they concluded, "It has scarcely enough of religious ceremony connected with it to varnish it over with the name of religion."[100] Even as Ward's British sermons proposed *sati* as emblematic of Hindu religion, his colleagues in India were dismantling, brick by brick, the edifice on which his argument stood. But this mattered little, for Ward could confidently depend on the ignorance of his audience. His discourse, to borrow a phrase from Malek Alloula, was meant for a "public incapable of questioning its truthfulness."[101]

Missionary efforts to draw out the implications of *sati* for family life, and by extension for society, reflect concerns similar to that evident in British evangelical literature of this period. Baptists strove to promote the ideal of a heterosexual family in which parents were joined by conjugal love and were dedicated to parenting as a social mission. They lamented that women in India were peculiarly ill-prepared, given lack of education and early marriage, for the tasks of wife and mother. As the article "On the State of Female Society in India" put it, the Indian mother "knows nothing of books and as little of mankind; how then can she impart to her son that instruction which may form his mind, or those lessons of conduct which shall shield him from the danger amidst the busy scenes of a treacherous world."[102]

Given the importance accorded to parenting, it is not surprising that missionaries were critical of *sati,* at least in part because they believed it to be a desertion of motherhood. This concern for children orphaned by *sati* was reflected in the informal record of widow immolations undertaken by the Baptists in 1812, which included information on the number of children left behind by the widow.[103] (This figure was not collected by the East India Company when it began to record the incidence of widow burning.) Elsewhere, in their fundraising material, for instance, the missionaries made much of the fact that Hindu women were not mothers but unfeeling monsters.[104] (We will see in chapter 5 how, far from being absent, maternal anxieties were at times part of the calculus compelling women to the pyre.)

Missionary writing in India was not entirely discontinuous with that produced primarily for a British audience. A number of themes cut across these materials, including the repercussions of social practices for family and society. A common analysis of women's position in Indian society also united these texts. In India, however, such concerns were tempered by consideration of the issues privileged by official discourse: the scriptural basis of *sati,* and anxiety over the political consequences of its prohibition. While it did not develop, as did official discourse, entirely within the domains of scripture, tradition, law, and state control, the tone and direction of the missionary crusade against *sati* in India strove to address and accommodate the dominant anxieties of the East India Company.

The measure of the Baptists as good propagandists, able to weave their own concerns with those of the East India Company, is evident in the way they argued for the safety of abolition.[105] In addition to drawing, as officials had, on previous instances in which interference in "religious tradition" had failed to produce social unrest, missionaries argued for the government's right to intervene as a matter of principle. Citing John Locke, they argued that toleration ceases where crime begins, and asked who, if not the ruling power, had the right to determine what was permissible in society? If the government cannot take life without a trial, on what grounds, they queried, could citizens be entitled to decide the fate of others? *Sati* was either suicide or murder, and in either case a cognizable offense. This argument for the right of the state to control all means of legitimate violence was interwoven with evidence of the civil nature of *sati,* a fact that, in their view, enabled the East India Company to combine justice with good government, achieving thereby a "virtuous employment of power": "Will it be too much while we dispense blessings with one hand, with the other to snatch the helpless victims from the flames?"[106]

Arguments for the safety of this civilizing mission were always carefully qualified. In the Indian context, missionaries did not elaborate, as they had in Britain, an entirely moral and melodramatic discourse. The tension between the desirability and feasibility of abolition, which had structured official debate from the start, also exerted its pressure on the evangelists. In fact, missionaries went so far as to say that "if the continuance of the British empire in India . . . absolutely depended on the burning of a thousand widows annually on the funeral pile, to permit these sacrifices, might be to act on a principle of . . . benevolence . . . [a]s the only prospect of ever seeing this unnatural practice abandoned, is dependent on the perpetuity of the British power in the East."[107] The interests of missionaries and those of the East India Company were thus consistently represented as, in all respects, complementary.

Simultaneously with taking account of the concerns of the East India Company, missionaries urged the British in India to bring greater pressure to bear on Parliament in Britain. The *Friend of India* urged its readers to address the issue regularly in their correspondence with friends and family in Britain. Pointing to the examples of the abolition of the slave trade and the 1813 East India Company charter renewal, it suggested that letters would generate public pressure on members of Parliament, push periodicals to devote more space to the subject, and eventually force widespread debate on the issue.[108] In many ways, their prognosis was borne out by events.

## Afterword

Taking printed missionary materials as its focus, this chapter has examined how missionary discourse was consolidated in the aftermath of the legalization of evangelical activity in 1813. In "tracking" and "excavating" these materials, I have attended to twin processes evident in evangelical discourse. On the one hand, one notes an increasing directionality, certainty, and authoritativeness; on the other hand, there remains an abiding flexibility, contradictoriness, and pragmatism in the mobilization of specific components. I have analyzed the impact of the socio-historical context and location on what is foregrounded out of the complexity of items in a given text or field of texts. Analysis of material extracted from Ward's 1811 *Hindoos* for publication in the *Missionary Register* has provided one instance of the highly selective appropriation of an otherwise complex work. The other example developed here has been the "career" of *sati* in these materials. The differential status of *sati* in various sources suggests that its constitution in evangelical discourse as emblematic of "Hindoo" women's status was a post-1813 phenomenon.

This material also suggests traffic between Britain and India; although in the initial phase, Ward's finished work functioned as raw material for British evangelical discourse, he himself came to produce this reductive rhetoric after his visit to Britain in 1819, as can be seen from his *Farewell Letters* and 1822 *Hindoos*. The consolidation of missionary discourse was, however, not uniform. Even as the *Missionary Register* produced textualized descriptions of India, the *Periodical Accounts* reprinted letters from Baptists which, like those analyzed in the previous chapter, contained social descriptions that disputed dominant missionary claims regarding the religious infatuation of indigenous people. But there was little for missionaries to gain in drawing out the implications of such reports. Horror stories of indigenous superstition were good fundraising material. As a result, these more complex, or at least less stereotypical, descriptions failed to challenge or unsettle the conceptions of India that were at this time gathering force. It would be inappropriate, however, to suggest that missionaries somehow deliberately simplified matters, for similar processes are also evident in official discourse.

Even though there are important distinctions, even disjunctions, between the richer accounts of the journals and letters and the textualized representations of the *Missionary Register*, both shared key assumptions about Indian society. These included the centrality of religion, the passive relation to it of indigenous people, the importance of brahmanic scripture, and the domination of brahmins. Different elements were emphasized by different literatures at different times. Thus the fundraising literature stressed social conditions and ignored, by and large, questions of brahmanic scripture, while missionary preaching accounts and the 1811 *Hindoos* addressed the former in terms of the latter. While evangelists in Britain could choose to dispense with questions of scripture, missionaries in India were compelled to engage them. Even as Ward was ignoring the issue in Britain, Marshman and Carey were publishing in *Friend of India* arguments for the abolition of *sati* which turned crucially on questions of scriptural interpretation.

Context and constituency are important in accounting for the differences of emphasis and inflection in missionary discourse. The "authoritativeness" of post-1813 evangelical discourse is, at least in part, a function of the legalization of missionary activity. The ideological tone and cast of the *Missionary Register,* for example, was largely shaped by its metropolitan constituency and financial goals. Fundraising discourse was sustained by specters and passions independent of "practical" questions. But such issues were central to Baptist concerns in India, where missionaries, although legal, had another master to serve, or at the very least, to take into account and placate, namely, the East India Company. Thus we find in their Indian publications attention to questions of scripture, and insistence on the safety of *sati*'s prohibition. Baptist strategy was well considered. Practical concerns remained paramount for East India Company officials and administrators, the only ones in the final analysis with the power to legislate against widow burning.

## CHAPTER 5

# The Female Subject, the Colonial Gaze

## *Eyewitness Accounts of* Sati

---

*To track . . . through the colonial representations of Algerian women — the figures of a phantasm — is to attempt a double operation: first to uncover the nature and meaning of the colonialist gaze; then, to subvert the stereotype that is so tenaciously attached to the bodies of women.*

Malek Alloula, *The Colonial Harem*[1]

*One never encounters the testimony of the women's voice-consciousness. Such a testimony would not be ideology-transparent or "fully" subjective, of course, but it would have constituted the ingredients for producing a countersentence. As one goes down the grotesquely mistranscribed names of these women, the sacrificed widows, in the police reports included in the records of the East India Company, one cannot put together a "voice." The most one can sense is the immense heterogeneity breaking through even such a skeletal and ignorant account.*

Gayatri Chakravorty Spivak, "Can the Subaltern Speak?"[2]

We turn in this chapter to eyewitness accounts of widow burning. Our analysis will attend to the narrative structure and focus of such accounts as well as to their descriptions of women's testimonials and actions at the pyre. Themes that have cut across earlier chapters resurface here with particular poignancy. It may have been theoretically possible thus far to bracket the materiality of widow burning for the purposes of discursive analysis; after all, widow burning was less often the

158

object of consideration than the ground for a range of deliberations and contestations. Such bracketing is, however, difficult to sustain in reading reports of burning. Even though the discursive and the material were densely interwoven in them, it becomes impossible to disarticulate the violence of the rhetoric from that of the practice.

In simultaneously engaging the material and discursive registers of these accounts, I depart from Malek Alloula's strategy in analyzing French colonial postcards of Algerian women. In *The Colonial Harem* Alloula demonstrates how these semi-pornographic postcards staged the wished-for encounters with Algerian women not available to European men, and convincingly argues that they represent the art of simulacrum in both the theatrical and compensatory senses of the term. According to Alloula, such postcards say more about the vivisecting gaze and libidinal investments of colonialism than about the women hired by the studio photographer. Analyzing them is for him a form of exorcism. He attempts, as he puts it, "to return this immense postcard to its sender."[3]

As a woman, as a feminist, it is impossible for me to read descriptions of *sati* in this way, simply turning the glare of analytic scrutiny back on the colonizer. The violence of widow burning is in constant tension with the "epistemic violence" of colonialism,[4] even if European descriptions are themselves exemplary instances of colonial discourse. My analysis is structured by this tension, which is not merely an intellectual one, but is also emotional and visceral. Engaging it has been my strategy for developing a critique of the discourse on *sati* that is simultaneously anti-imperialist and feminist.

If *The Colonial Harem* compromises its critique by neglecting the question of women's position in Algerian society, Gayatri Spivak's "Can the Subaltern Speak?" disappoints by foreclosing too quickly a set of complex issues about voice and agency. Spivak's insistence that the "female subaltern cannot speak" is to be read in the context of her examination and interrogation of the multiple determinations of archival sources, and her well-founded rejection of any simplistic desire to counter discourses of domination by "letting the native speak." As a general conclusion about colonial discourse, however, this position raises as many questions as it answers.[5] In claiming "the subaltern cannot speak," does Spivak mean "cannot" as in "does not know how to" or "cannot" in the sense of "is unable to under the circumstances"? Further, is there not a slippage between noting, as she does, that the female subaltern *does* not speak in police records of the East India Company, and in concluding from this that "the subaltern cannot speak" at all, in any voice, however refracted? Spivak's conclusion is called into question by the testimonials of women available in the accounts that are the focus of this chapter. Be that as it may, as will become evident, we would do well to heed her methodological concerns if we are to avoid some of the dangers she elaborates.

Eyewitness accounts of widow immolation bring to crisis the complexities of reading against the grain. Accounts were almost exclusively the product of European male observers. Most were initially published in the English-language press in India, frequently as letters to the editor. Many were reprinted in the British evangelical press and in secular journals concerned with East India affairs. The Bengali press mainly carried obituaries giving particulars of the (male) deceased and (his) widow, and the date, place, and time of burning (see chapter 2). These obituaries were at times republished in English papers in Bengal.

By contrast with the Bengali press wherein *sati* was almost always reported in the context of men's obituaries, in the English-language press, incidents of burning were assumed to be newsworthy in their own right. Here, the male corpse is simply the sine qua non, and the focus is on the burning alive of the widow. Reports were most often published without comment, although on occasion the editor or narrator prefaced the description with such remarks as the following:

In the hope of seeing more effectual regulations adopted, to do away, or render difficult the barbarous and inhuman practice of immolating a widow on the funeral pyre of her departed husband, I am induced to offer you a short account of a suttee, to which I was an unwilling witness.[6]

We call the attention of our readers to another of those distressing, and really heart rending recitals, which we are certain Governments of this country would rejoice in being able to render a tale of other times.[7]

Such contextualization was, however, exceptional. *Sati* was considered "news," and publication of its details required no explanation. It was only from mid-1827 onward that reports were increasingly accompanied by discussions of East India Company policy. The lay press in Britain treated widow burning incidents in a similar fashion. The *Asiatic Journal,* for example, mostly published accounts in its section on "Asiatic Intelligence." As for the evangelical press, *sati* was, as we have seen, newsworthy in a different sense (see chapter 4). Here we will turn to a close reading of the structure and focus of descriptions of widow burning.

Accounts of incidents in the English-language press vary in detail and scope. Some are akin to obituaries and furnish only basic information about the event. More frequently, however, they are detailed accounts, organized around four cardinal moments: that of the narrator receiving information that a burning was about to occur and hastening to the spot; the narrator's monitoring of the widow and relatives, as well as his (or other Europeans') attempts at dissuasion; the narrator's observation of the practices that preceded the burning; the setting alight of the pyre and destruction of the widow. The degree of emphasis placed on each of these moments varies, although, in general, the bulk of the narrative is given over to a scrutiny of the widow, her demeanor, and her actions. Narratives frequently include conversations between the observer and the widow. Reports of these minimal and overdetermined exchanges give us some sense of the subjectivity of the widow and of the logic of her actions. Some observers also describe the practices that precede the burning. The structure and emphasis of European eyewitness accounts are a product of the fundamental colonial ambivalence toward so-called "voluntary" *sati*. This ambivalence was enshrined in a law which tolerated *sati* so long as it was found to be based on the widow's "consent." (If the terms "voluntary" and "consent" are set off by the use of quotation marks, it is because, as will become painfully clear, these are exceedingly dubious concepts.)

Human activity at the pyre is almost always represented as ritualistic. This was so, not only for the "ceremonies" (as they were called) that preceded the burning, but for the entire set of practices that constituted widow immolation. The language and tenor of such descriptions are tied to colonial insistence on *sati* as fundamentally "religious." It will be remembered that the colonial conception of religion implied three interlocking notions: the presumed hegemony of brahmanic scripture, with religion as scriptural rather than customary; religious motivations as separate from and incompatible with worldly concerns; and an extraordinarily reductive conception of indigenous agency. All three assumptions are to be found in eyewitness accounts of *sati*.

The form and focus of European accounts of *sati* incidents had particular discursive and ideological consequences, but the partiality of these descriptions in one respect must be addressed at the very start. While we may read these narratives for a more nuanced (although by no means exhaustive) understanding of the widow and the European observer, their representation of the widow's relatives and of pundits are, in general, without complexity. Both groups emerge in these descriptions as almost entirely devoted to the widow's destruction. No doubt pundits and relatives stood to gain materially from burning the widow, and by the same token, there is insurmountable evidence that women were coerced, drugged, and tied to the pyre. But most accounts suggest a uniformity of purpose shared by those around the widow. With some exceptions, there is little hint of disagreement or of competing interests over her fate. Such is the limit of these texts. Even while we may, for example, press them for a richer conception of the widow's agency, we must be mindful of the accounts' homogenization of the collective agency of those around her. The gains, however, are neither minimal nor insignificant.

We have already noted how within the discourse on *sati,* women are represented in two mutually exclusive ways: as heroines able to withstand the raging blaze of the funeral pyre or else as pathetic victims coerced against their will into the flames (see chapter 2). These poles preclude the possibility of a female subjectivity that is shifting, contradictory, inconsistent. This reductive and binary view of agency is unable to capture the dynamic and complex relation of women to social and familial expectations. In particular, the constrained notion of agency that underwrites the representation of women as victims discursively positions women as objects to be saved — never as subjects who act, even if within overdetermined and restricted conditions. Such a representation of Indian women has been fertile ground for the elaboration of discourses of salvation, in the context of colonialism and nationalism. In large part both have constructed the Indian woman not as someone who acts, but as someone to be acted upon.

This view of women is contestable through eyewitness accounts of incidents in which the widow escapes or is successfully dissuaded from burning. Even when such descriptions are squarely within a colonialist framework, they provide a sense of the forces that converge in bringing the widow to the pyre, and of the widow's shifting relation to them. The following account appeared in the *India Gazette.*[8] Receiving information that an incident is about to occur, the narrator, who identifies himself as "an eyewitness," states that he

with several Gentlemen proceeded to the Ghaut, in order to expostulate with the infatuated creature, where the Police Darogah was in attendance. . . . Every argument that could be thought of was now urged by him to dissuade her from her purpose . . . and the remonstrances of her own relations, also, not proving successful after many persevering efforts, the Magistrate reluctantly retired and the other Gentlemen also withdrew to a distance.

They wait there until the immolation is about to begin at which point they "placed themselves nearer the scene of action." The widow's movements are then described in detail.

With most inimitable composure the *Suttee* went through the performance of various preparatory rites. Having conversed with the *Goroo,* washed her hands in the *Gunga* water, and been decked out according to established forms by kinswomen, she slowly and calmly raised herself from the ground, poured some rice into her lap, and scattering the grain as she marched in a direction contrary to the sun's course, encircled the pile three times, and [at] last unassisted, with unblenched lip, mounted the structure, and threw herself on the remains of her husband.

Her son then sets the pile alight and the cry "Hari bol" is raised by those present. The narrator continues to watch the widow who, he says, acknowledged the spectators: "by waving her hand until the flames began to envelop her, when her courage, which had been wrought to the highest pitch, failed, and she sprung from amid the devouring fire in a state of extreme agitation from pain and terror."

The relatives are described as disappointed by this turn of events: "her son seemed plunged in the depths of despair: some unfeelingly bid her throw herself into the flames." The widow herself is said to have been "scarce[ly] sensible of what was taking place. After remaining in a sort of stupor, at length she seized her son's hand, and led by him moved away from the spot without venturing to cast one look behind." The widow is then conveyed to the house of the British Resident, given medication and questioned "into the motives that had led her to ascend the funeral pyre." Her responses are reported in indirect speech.

Her determination to become a *Suttee* had been the result *not of choice, or of any notion that by so doing she would escape some undefined misery in some future state;* but fear of personal obloquy and neglect from her friends, and of bringing disgrace on them and her son; indeed her apprehensions that her want of firmness would prejudice the boy's interests and success in life were with great difficulty quieted by repeated assurances of *protection.*

The narrator speculates that "she had sprung from the pile from an instinctive impulse," continuing that the attempted dissuasions and the presence of persons "who would shield her from immediate injury or insult" should she change her mind, no doubt influenced the widow's actions. The account ends with the return home of a now "tranquil" widow with her relatives "who also appeared quite reconciled to the course that the affair had taken."

This incident is interesting for the light it throws on the question of the widow's subjectivity. An apparently "voluntary" act (note her reported resistance to dissuasion, her ostensible composure, her being unassisted at every stage) turns out to have been the effect of fear of disgracing family and friends and of jeopardizing her son's future prospects. By her own account, it is such material pressures that have brought the widow to the pyre of her deceased husband. The family is noted as discouraging her from burning, then being disappointed by her escape and eventually as reconciled to it, an account which undercuts the claim for any unilateral familial stance. The ideology of *sati*, as an act undertaken by a devoted wife with a view to future spiritual reward, is nowhere alluded to by the widow. The narrator highlights this, possibly because Europeans remained drawn, however ambivalently, to the possibility and legitimacy of "voluntary" *sati*, and persisted in evaluating incidents they observed against this idealized notion. This move was, of course, entirely consonant with the colonial assumption that all social practices derived from scriptural texts and were therefore to be measured against them.

The narrator describes the widow first as an "infatuated creature," then in terms of her composure, and finally, in the aftermath of her escape, as "scarce[ly] sensible of what was taking place." While the shock and trauma of her narrow escape might indeed have made her appear barely conscious of her surroundings, the logic of her decision-making process, as she is reported as having described it, hardly warrants the adjective "infatuated." In this, the narrator is firmly within a colonial discourse which conceives women as dreamily enacting "tradition" (*sati*, for example), being woken from their misguided reverie primarily by European dissuasion and the shock of physical pain, whereupon they are saved by their (usually Western) protectors. This version of events may well contain an element of truth; the presence of the police and European spectators could have ensured, for instance, that the widow was not thrown back on the pyre. However, this narrative occludes the agency of the widow, both in her "decision" to submit to destruction, and in her leaping off the pyre. It fails, in other words, to acknowledge her as capable of evaluating the conditions of her life and overlooks her part in her own rescue, not to mention the rationality of her response to fear and pain. Part of what sustains this discourse is the representation as "ritual" of the practices that precede the burning. I will return to this later.

Other accounts of successful prevention further underscore the complexity of the widow's motivations and the importance of conceiving of her consciousness as a dynamic process. The following account from the journal of William Bowley of the Church Missionary Society was published in the *Missionary Register*.[9] On being informed that a burning is about to take place, Bowley writes that he hurried to the spot accompanied by two Bengali converts to Christianity, identified as Charles Doss and Christian Tryloke. The widow is described as "seated by the corpse of her husband, with a string of beads in her hand, and her face toward the sacred stream" (323). Having pointed out to the police officer irregularities in the construction of the pyre which would have effectively prevented her escape once upon it, he approaches the widow: " 'Why do you destroy yourself?' [asks the narrator] 'My Thakoor,' was her reply. [The narrator responds] 'This perishing corpse is not your Thakoor . . . nor have you any relation to him now that he is dead. He came into the world alone, and is gone alone. Wait till you are also called away' " (323). Bowley pleads with her not to "fly in the face of your Creator," and writes "she seemed to listen with attention" (323). It being late, it was decided to burn the corpse alone and get permission to burn her the following day with a relic belonging to her husband. The narrator, afraid that she might be administered intoxicating drugs in the night, and distrusting Hindu police officers, arranges for Muslim functionaries to guard her and departs from the scene. He returns later in the evening "thinking that a favourable opportunity served to speak to her during the night."

I was somewhat pleased to find her preparing to bathe: yet she still moved about like one deprived of her senses. I then addressed her as before— when, all on a sudden as if the spell was broken by which she was held, and she had returned to her right mind, she gave vent to her feelings: with tears and lamentations bewailing her lord, she said, that she should now be in Paradise—that all were her enemies—who would protect her?—how should she drag out a whole life from her sixteenth year?—she had no children to beguile her days &c. I told her that if none of her Relations would protect her, she might send to me, and I would see that justice was done her. I also got the Police Officers to offer their services in the event of her being oppressed; and she seemed somewhat eased. (324)

Bowley returns home convinced that "the danger was passed." Word had it, he observes, "that the Padre's persuasion and the bewitching powers of the Bengalee whom he brought with him, deprived the Woman of her Sutya" (324). The account ends with the observation that Christianity was a beautiful palace compared to the "slaughter-house" of Hinduism.

The change of the widow's heart is described as the breaking of a spell enabled, it would seem, by the interventions of the narrator and his indigenous Christian friends, who deprived her of her "sutya" (resolution). Given *sati*'s presumed status as a Hindu religious practice, and the assumption that Hindus could not accordingly be trusted to prevent it, Bowley arranges for a Muslim guard for the widow. Interestingly, however, the widow's reasons for contemplating *sati* are "secular." The ideology of *sati* as the act of the devoted wife is merely hinted at in her statement that "she should now be in Paradise," but the rest of her speech is about fear—"all were her enemies." If she bewails "her lord," it is with regard to her fear for the future in the absence of the assured protection of a living husband. Yet, notwithstanding the worldly basis of her motivations, *sati* remains in this as in many other missionary accounts emblematic of the "slaughter-house" of Hindu religion. Equally interesting, credit for the widow's change of mind is taken entirely by the narrator, none of it being shared with his companions upon whom he may very well have depended for translation. It is nowhere suggested that the widow, compelled to *sati* by fear of the future, takes advantage of the presence of the narrator to save *herself* from immolation by fire.

Fear of future financial insecurity seems to have been a predominant consideration for widows. In an account published in the *Asiatic Journal* in 1823[10] the European narrator describes his interaction with "the intended victim of a superstitious and barbarous religion" (344) in the following way:

I asked her, if she intended to ascend the flaming pile of her deceased partner in life? she unhesitatingly replied that she did; and that the time for the ceremony had arrived. I then explained to her that self-destruction was the worst of acts, and a heinous crime in the sight of the Supreme Ruler of the universe; that if she did not at once retract her vow, she would in a very short time rashly force herself into the presence of her Maker. To all of which she answered with composure, that it was her own free will; having no family or near relations, she could not survive her husband, and would follow him; and having bathed the corpse according to custom, she could not now return to her dwelling, but must destroy herself as other females of her family had done before her, or be considered in the light of an outcaste the remainder of her life. She then inquired, over and over again, if she did not burn herself, how she could, deprived as she was of her husband, alone manage to earn a subsistence for her future support? To this I immediately replied that I would willingly provide her during life with every necessary she might stand in need of. (344)

The narrator addresses himself to the "other actors in the ceremony," as he calls them, but finds them unwilling to interfere in the matter. He approaches her again:

I perceived from her manners and actions some symptoms of wavering, arising, as I supposed, from what she often repeated, about a provision for her future life, in the event of retracting the rash step she was on the point of committing. . . . After a considerable time had been spent in this manner, I plainly saw she began to listen more attentively to what I urged in dissuading her from her dreadful crime of self-immolation. (344)

The author writes with surprise that he was aided in his efforts by several Hindus who had accompanied him and who "reasoned with the woman to comply with my wishes. Upon which soon after she gave a tacit assent" (344). The corpse is then taken to be burnt. The narrator stays behind to watch the burning lest "the widow who had taken her seat near me, should again consent and follow the procession." Regarding the widow, he continues, "At the period of my arrival, the woman was decked out in her best attire . . . dancing and singing a doleful and melancholy song. . . . She appeared perfectly sensible and composed. She is between forty and fifty years of age, and now appears happy and contented at having been timely rescued from the worst of deaths, through the humble exertions and persuasive means adopted by a single European" (344).

The narrator employs a specifically Christian argument against widow burning conceived as sinful in contrast with the ideology of *sati* as future reward as articulated in some Hindu texts. The widow's explanation of her action begins by clarifying that she is acting of her own accord. She then proceeds to concerns about her future subsistence and the negative social consequences of retracting her resolution, and returns to the question of financial support. It is this concern, repeatedly expressed, that gives the author room for optimism in his efforts at dissuasion. Nothing in what the widow is reported as having said points to a "religious" basis for *sati* or suggests it is the result of wifely devotion. Even so, the widow is described as the "victim of a superstitious and barbarous religion." What is more, in concluding his account, the narrator expresses surprise that the burning was to take place two days after the husband's death, dubbing it a "gross violation of Hindooism, for on the demise of any of them, whether of a high or a low caste, no food should be eaten, or water drunk by any of the family or relations of the deceased person, till his body has either been consumed by the flames, buried, or thrown into a river" (345). Here we have that move so characteristic of colonial discourse: the reinscription of *sati* as religious tradition, and critique of practices that were seen to deviate from their "scriptural" versions. This view was shared by colonial officials and missionaries alike. Insistence on *sati* as religious had led, as we know, to its legalization in 1813 and had made its abolition a complicated and drawn out affair.

In the meanwhile, women's efforts at negotiating their way out of the pyre, with the help of those like our narrator above, were marginalized. When the widow decides against immolation, having repeatedly sought promises from the narrator, she is said to have "compl[ied] with my wishes," and to have given "a *tacit* assent" (emphasis mine, 344). Credit for her decision, the narrator believes, rests entirely with himself, being the result of "the humble exertions and persuasive means adopted by a single European." As with Bowley, even the indigenous persons assisting him remain unacknowledged.

Bowley's account and the one just analyzed illustrate the specifically Christian elements present in attempts at dissuasion that are to be found in missionary narratives, although not restricted to them. Where others sought to prevent burnings through assurances of protection and efforts to ensure the absence of coercion, missionaries additionally argued that *sati* was suicide and, as such, was an unpardonable sin against God. John Peter of the BMS attempted unsuccessfully to make this point by reading from the Bible. "I am sorry I was not able to do her any good. I followed, warning her and the crowd against the horrible crime, with the New Testament in my hand."[11] It is unclear whether such arguments made any impression on widows, whose testimonies suggest that they were operating within a different universe of discourse from that of the missionaries, and to whom the idea of *sati* as sinful must surely have been alien.

Accounts of *sati* illustrate the adage that actions can speak louder than words. Indeed women's actions sometimes contradicted the expectations generated by their speech. In an account published in the *Bengal Hurkaru* the narrator writes of the efforts to dissuade the widow as follows: "every endeavour was made to induce the misguided and infatuated woman to abandon her resolution of destroying herself. Protection and support were promised to her and her family provided she would relinquish her horrid purpose. She rejected every proposal, however, with disdain, but with mildness, obstinately bent on self-destruction."[12] She persists in her decision even after the arrival of

the magistrate's written permission: "with a firm step and a mind un-
daunted, [she] repaired to the banks of the Ganges, where the pile was
raised." The proceedings are delayed by an insufficiency of wood but
once reinforcements are brought, she is said to have mounted the pile.

The brushwood was soon set fire to in several places, and soon rose into an
awful and majestic blaze, aided by a strong westerly wind. I shall never for-
get this appalling moment. As the flames reached her I observed her move,
as if about to lay down, that the conflict might the sooner be over, but what
was my astonishment and delight to see her make a jump from the pile,
throwing the body of her husband from her lap with a strong convulsive
start. (2)

The narrator observes that she sank to "the ground in a state of exhaustion. . . . we had the proud satisfaction of conducting this infatuated devotee to Brahminical influence, from the ground to her village,
where she now is, and I believe thankful for her rescue" (2). He goes on
to note that, given the exhaustion and hunger caused by three days of
awaiting permission to burn, and the badly burnt state of her back and
arms, her survival had been miraculous.

   Having said that, however, the narrator cannot refrain from claiming
that the act had been, until her escape, a "voluntary" affair: "No intoxicating drugs were administered to stupefy her, so far as I could ascertain, and the determined heroic fortitude she displayed throughout the
whole of the ceremony, till the moment of pain and trial, was worthy
[of] a better cause, and would have done honor to a Christian Martyr"
(2). What kind of "voluntary" act is this that is undertaken in a state of
exhaustion and hunger? And on the part of the narrator, what else is this
if not the fascination for *sati* that is the underside of horror? The narrator remains transfixed by her so-called fortitude, even as he laments
what he believes accounts for it. Indeed, it is her apparent willingness to
attempt immolation, not her courage in rescuing herself, that is seen as
heroic. Drawn as he is to the idea of "voluntary" *sati*, the widow's escape is intelligible to him primarily as a failure of nerve. Meanwhile her
escape is rewritten as "rescue." The language used to describe her jump
from the pyre is instructive. The widow is said to have made the jump
"with a strong convulsive start." This phrase recalls that used by the narrator in the account analyzed earlier, that she had "sprung from the pile
from an instinctive impulse." Both descriptions imply a primarily
physical process, not one that involves both mind and body. They represent the widow's escape not as a decisive act but as a bodily reflex. As

a consequence, even after such a dramatic act of self-affirmation as escape from the burning funeral pyre, she remains the "deluded young widow" and "infatuated devotee to Brahminical influence."

Not all widows were as fortunate in surviving the burns they sustained before jumping off the pyre. In another deeply disturbing description, the widow, having declared "it was her own pleasure to burn," is said to have escaped soon after the pyre was set alight.[13] The author writes that there ensued a struggle between the European observers seeking to protect her and the brahmins who were said to be intent on throwing her back onto the pyre. One of the observers is sent to inform the magistrate of what had happened, "but before the messenger could return with an answer from the civil authority, the Bramins had persuaded the unfortunate woman once more to approach the pile. And as she declared, on being questioned by those present, that it was her own wish to ascend the pile, they stood aloof, fearful of giving offence to the prejudices of the native population on the one hand, or to the civil authorities on the other" (570). Thus was the official sanction of "voluntary" *sati* upheld. Alas, the saga was far from over. The widow declines to ascend the pile for some time, is lifted onto it by force, escapes and is once again followed by pundits said to have been determined that she should burn. At this time, the European spectators take her to their side and guard her until the arrival of the magistrate. But the injuries she had suffered were too serious. She died the following day in the hospital "forsaken by her own relations."

The accounts of *sati* incidents available to us suggest many of the external pressures on the widow. These included fear of future economic hardship and the absence of protection by family. These reports confirm the argument made by Rammohun Roy, the missionaries, and some anti-*sati* East India Company officials that access to the property due to the widow on her husband's death was a key motivating factor in *sati*. In an account published in the missionary journal *Friend of India,* the narrator suggests that the dissuasions of the widows' in-laws were insincere and half-hearted, since they stood to gain property and money from her death.[14] By contrast, the parents of one of the widows were said to have been "exceedingly affected with the fate of their daughter, and besought her earnestly not thus to throw away her life, particularly as her husband had left behind him an abundance of support."[15]

In another incident in which the "concubine" of a wealthy and landed person perished, it was said "that his relatives apprehending the woman would inherit all his estates, promoted her death."[16] The widow's life was sometimes determined by a power struggle between contending parties. The following report is unusual for not representing those around the widow as united in their purpose. A widow, said to be under the age permissible for *sati,* was prevented from burning. Her prevention was, however, not the consequence of concern for her. Rather, it was said to have been the outcome of a contest between her in-laws, anxious to promote her destruction in order to control the property that would fall to her, and her deceased husband's spiritual mentor, equally anxious to prevent it since she was a minor and "in all probability, the expenditure of her property will principally pass through his [the mentor's] hands."[17] Another woman who had been successfully dissuaded confessed that her elder brothers had pressured her to commit *sati* to get hold of the money due to her.[18]

Women were not merely persuaded to commit *sati.* They were also physically coerced into immolating themselves. There are numerous examples of women being tied to the pyre,[19] held down with bamboo poles,[20] or else weighted down with wood.[21] Sometimes a combination of such coercive techniques were applied. The *Asiatic Journal* published an account of a widow weighted down with wood and additionally held down by bamboo poles.[22] In another incident reported in the *Baptist Magazine,* the widow was said to have been tied, following which, wood was piled upon her.[23] The *Bengal Hurkaru* printed details of an incident in which all three means were employed to prevent the widow's escape from the pyre.[24]

The technology of widow immolation was geared to ensure incineration, not escape. Pyres were constructed such that logs of wood were interwoven with faggots, reeds, and dry leaves, and bamboo poles were used to hold down the bodies. The following graphic description, which is instructive on this score, was published alongside plate 4 in the *Baptist Magazine* in February 1922:

I saw a cord fastened tightly round the two bodies, and thick pieces of wood heaping on by which they were pressed as closely together as possible. Together with the wood there was a great deal of straw, and long dry rushes. . . . At first the blaze was very great, but the materials being light it was obliged to be kept up by adding more, which the brahmans were officious in supplying both above and below the pile of wood, while a number of persons were fetching jars of water to pour over them lest the fire should hurt them. The two bamboos were constantly applied to jam the wood together. . . . the brahmans bus[ied] themselves in keeping up the fire, running in every direction about the pile, some calling for more light stuff to be supplied, and pouring out abuse upon some who had put it above instead of below.[25]

Fires were also fed by ghee, resin, and other inflammable substances, the purpose of which was to facilitate speedy combustion.

When women were not so entrapped under logs of wood or held down by bamboo poles, their opportunities for escape were greater. Mr. Smith, a Baptist missionary, reports the following case from the city of Benares (the only incident discussed here which is from outside Bengal, the focus of this study):

After they had performed their superstitious ceremonies, they placed the woman on the pile with the corpse, and set fire to the wood. As soon as the flames touched her, she jumped off the pile. Immediately the brahmuns seized her, in order to put her again into the flames: she exclaimed —"Do not murder me! I don't wish to be burnt!" The Company's officers being present, she was brought home safely.[26]

Safety, however, turns out not to be life in her marital family, who proceed "to transport her to Juggernauth, there to end her days."[27] The widow, in refusing forcible burning, is left with enforced asceticism in the grounds of the Jagannath temple as the only alternative.

In addition to being subject to physical coercion, women were frequently drugged. One widow, who managed to escape from the pyre, testified to having been given large quantities of opium and *bang*.[28] Other women were observed to be barely sensible: "her eyes were open, but apparently beyond the power of recognition of surrounding objects."[29] Such women were usually said to have been physically assisted through the practices that preceded the burning and to have been barely conscious by the time the pyre was set alight.

Such practices as drugging the widow or binding her to the pyre were illegal under East India Company law. Yet, for the most part, local newspapers routinely published details of coercion without comment. Only occasionally did a newspaper editor request others to come forward and confirm a given account.[30] There was, then, sufficient evidence to severely undermine the idea of "voluntary" *sati*. Yet this conception endured even in accounts of women whose deaths were secured by coercion. Thus a newspaper item which goes on to detail an incident in which the widow was weighted down with wood begins, "The Cholera Morbus has put the *fidelity* of many a Hindoo Widow to the test" (emphasis mine).[31]

Fascination for *sati* was most clearly expressed in accounts of apparently voluntary burnings. This is a problematic and pernicious concept given the testimonials of widows at the pyre; descriptions of women bound, drugged and otherwise coerced; and stories told by women who successfully escaped their immolation. One wonders how many other tales of coercion overt and subtle perished untold in the pyres of those so-called voluntary burnings.

This fundamental ambivalence toward *sati,* and especially the valorization of the apparently voluntary burning, shaped eyewitness accounts of widow immolation in important ways. First, there is the hastening to the pyre on news of *sati.* Something in excess of the hope of dissuading the widow is often expressed in the desire to witness widow burning: "I beheld a sight I long felt to see, but a more horrible one I never witnessed. It was an immolation of a human creature in the prime of life, with health and youth blooming in the countenance."[32] Or, having reached the spot, there is the urge to stay: "I had almost determined to leave the spot, when observing that the magistrate went and stood close to the pile, I felt a wild and impatient desire to remain."[33]

Then there is the admiration of women who burnt in incidents deemed to be "voluntary," but whose real nature we can guess at, given what we know of *sati.* Such admiration is frequently expressed in relation to women described as unusually beautiful.

the great personal beauty of the victim gave unusual interest and importance to this Suttee, and rendered the tragic spectacle very imposing.[34]

I stood close to her, she observed me attentively. . . . She might be about twenty-four or five years of age, a time of life when the bloom of beauty had fled the cheek in India; but she still preserved a sufficient share to prove that she must have been handsome. Her figure was small, but elegantly turned; and the form of her hands and arms was peculiarly beautiful.[35]

though too short for a fine form, [she] had a fair and interesting countenance. Her natural beauty heightened by her resolution, would have affected . . . [the] heart of [the] adamant.[36]

Such "tender" descriptions of the personal appearance and beauty of widows suggests the voyeuristic pleasure of a specifically male gaze, contemplating what it constructs as the wife devoted to her husband in death as in life. Malek Alloula is helpful here: "It is the nature of pleasure to scrutinize its object detail by detail, to take possession of it in both a total and fragmented fashion. It is an intoxication, a loss of oneself in the other through sight."[37] This phallocentric reverie, by mystifying coercion as the devotion and free will of the widow, enacts a discursive violence that is every bit as cruel and indefensible as the practice that is its referent.

One effect of such a valorizing of the beautiful widow engaged in apparently voluntary *sati* was that "sympathy" was reserved for such women. Their deaths are rendered empathetically. However, the pathos expressed here is not for the widow's predicament but for the imminent loss of one so attractive. In an account from the *Calcutta Journal* reprinted in the *Asiatic Journal,* the narrator writes of a widow who he says was so drugged that she had to be lifted onto the pyre.

She was twenty-one years of age, beautiful to my conception, by far the most so of any native female I have ever seen; combined with the beauty of face, the figure was perfect, which heightened the distress, if possible, in the minds of those who were witnesses of the sacrifice, and felt their inability to prevent it.[38]

The qualifier, "if possible," is unconvincing. It is her beauty, not her coercion, that provokes his sympathy. Could it be that, in a repetition of the masculinist gaze noted earlier, this observer is distressed for himself, not for the widow?

Eyewitness accounts have relatively few kind words for women who struggled, escaped, were badly burnt, or were, in the eyes of the observer, not beautiful to behold. Such women are invariably described as "miserable wretches," "suffering wretches," "unfortunate women," or "unfortunate victims." The descriptive repertoire in these cases is neither rich nor elaborate. For instance, a letter to the editor in arguing that widows were invariably coerced describes them as "wretched and deluded . . . harrassed and goaded into assent[ing] to . . . they know not what."[39] The struggles of women against their coercion are seen as neither imposing nor admirable — they merely inspire horror and distaste.

There is strikingly little description of suffering in most eyewitness accounts of *sati*.[40] As already noted, much of the narrative is taken up with the efforts at dissuasion and in describing the practices leading up to the burning. The widow's death itself occupies very little of the account. The following are typical descriptions:

she fell on the fire and was soon burnt to ashes.[41]

a load of hemp (*pout*) . . . was thrown on her, and a blaze kindled, which in a few minutes consumed the living and the dead.[42]

they laid themselves, the one on one side and the other on the other of their departed husband, and were quickly enveloped in flames.[43]

some logs of wood having been placed upon her, the son fired the pile, and things of a combustible nature being thrown in, she was soon consumed.[44]

This abrupt conclusion to narratives that otherwise closely detail every aspect of the proceedings at the pyre, is surprising indeed. It forecloses discussion of the widow's suffering. Some accounts suggest that the flames and the fact that the widow was tied down made it difficult to see whether she struggled, while the cries of "Hari bol" drowned the screams of widows, if such were issued.

It was impossible to have heard the woman, had she groaned, or even cried aloud, on account of the mad noise of the people; and it was impossible for her to struggle, on account of the bamboos which are held down upon them like the levers of the press.[45]

When the flames reached the unfortunate victim a scream was heard but the multitude having immediately shouted *hure bole,* it was impossible to hear if she again uttered the groans of torture.[46]

This difficulty of actually knowing how the widow experienced burning does not seem entirely satisfactory as an explanation of the absence, in general, of an explicit thematization of her suffering. After all, her motivations and subjective state in relation to *sati* were equally difficult to access. Yet observers frequently made the widow ground for their own speculations in the matter. Why, then, this reticence in the issue of her pain and distress? The contrast between a willingness to narrativize the widow's emotions at the pyre and hesitation to describe her suffering is well captured in the following poem:

> Her last fond wishes breathed — a farewell smile
> Is lingering on the calm unclouded brow
> Of yon deluded victim, — Firmly now
> She mounts, with dauntless mien, the funeral pile
> Where lies her earthly Lord — The Brahmin's guile
> Hath wrought its will — fraternal hands bestow
> The flaming brand — the crackling embers glow
> And flakes of hideous smoke the skies defile
> The ruthless throng their willing aid supply
> And pour the kindling oil — The stunning sound
> of dissonant drums — the Priests exulting cry —
> The failing Martyr's pleading voice have drowned
> While fiercely burning rafters fall around
> And shroud her from Horror's straining eye![47]

The adjectival flourish that characterizes the poem up to this point deserts the poet at the moment of burning. All that "Horror's straining eye" can imagine is the "pleading voice" of the "failing Martyr," not her torture under the "burning rafters." Paintings and engravings of *sati* also contribute to the marginalization of the agony of widow burning. In them, the widow frequently appears as though reposing on a bed of flames or under a blanket of fire, an arm thrust heavenward (plates 3, 5). Or else, as in the drawing by the Indian artist Bahadur Singh, c. 1780 (plate 2), she is shown sitting peacefully untouched amidst the surrounding flames.[48] The fire billows around her but does not consume her.

One exception to this general neglect of the widow's suffering was an account published in the *Calcutta Journal* on May 2, 1819. The narrator suggests that, although "the wailings of the poor wretch" could not be heard over the cries of spectators, the "high wind blowing the flames under the pile, I fear, must have greatly prolonged her torments."[49] Sometimes observers reported having seen a little of the widow's struggle.

The fire with the aid of a strong South-East wind quickly reached its victim, who by the contraction and spasmodic twitching of her limbs, seemed but too plainly to feel the excruciating torments she laboured under, but not long, for the raging element now fed by Bramins with fresh combustible matter soon put an end to her sufferings and closed the horrid scene.[50]

surely none that saw the convulsed twitching of the hand and sinews could hesitate for an instant in thinking, that if they had not been prevented by the weight of wood, they would have endeavoured to escape from the excruciating death.[51]

Even if her suffering can only be read through surface bodily signs of "spasmodic" or "convulsed" "twitching," signs that in stressing the physicality of suffering, tend, at another level of analysis to efface the widow as *agent* of suffering, or "subject in /of pain,"[52] such fragments give us some indication, however minimal, of the torture of *sati*.

The few descriptions we have of women's agony are of those who escaped from the pyre.

I arrived at the ground as they were bringing her . . . from the river [to which the widow had escaped from the pyre]. . . . I cannot describe to you the horror I felt on seeing the mangled condition she was in, almost every inch of skin on her body had been burnt off, her legs and thighs, her arms and back were completely raw, her breasts were dreadfully torn and the skin hanging from them in shreds, the skins and nails of her fingers had peeled wholly off and were hanging.

The widow was taken to hospital where she lingered "in the most ex-cruciating pain for about 20 hours and then died."[53] In another equally explicit account, the narrator describes the state of the escaped "unfor-tunate woman" as follows:

I returned to the scene and beheld a sight that made me shudder and the recollection of which sends a thrill of horror yet thro' my body, the unfor-tunate woman had only succeeded in extricating herself from the wood and rolling down the pile; for the struggle and heat had nearly deprived her of life. She lay gasping for breathe [sic], her face and body exhibiting the most revolting spectacle imaginable.[54]

Such accounts are exceptional in their attention to the palpable, vis-ceral torture of *sati*. They are also unusual in representing the woman as agent in pain. She is portrayed as actively suffering, not merely as a body whose response to the flames is to be decoded from the jerks and movement of limbs, a type of description which effaces the agency in-volved in struggle, rewriting it as a purely physical, animal, reflex.

In most descriptions of *sati*, however, as the widow ascends the pyre details vanish as magically as the narrator would have us believe the widow herself evaporates.[55] Accounts conclude cryptically or, we might say, evasively: "the widow was soon consumed." Or worse, they posi-tively romanticize the widows' experience on the pyre: "in a moment the souls of the devoted girls fled in shrieks to the world of spirits."[56] Such metaphoric excesses achieved full expression in poems on widow burning. The following excerpt is from "Description of a Suttee," by James Lovewell. Only one stanza is devoted to the actual burning in the twenty-two verse poem which describes an incident supposedly wit-nessed by the author.

> The fire was quickly kindled, and soon spread,
> And as its fury caught her tender frame,
> Spite of her shrieks and struggles, Brahmans fed,
> With savage zeal, the fast devouring flame!
> Soon all was hushed! Koomaree's spirit fled,
> For death in mercy to the victim came,
> To waft her where the seraph band adore,
> Where grief shall cease, and pains assail no more![57]

Anguish or sorrow for the widow are uncommon in such descrip-tions. Grief, when expressed, is frequently articulated as horror. Horror distances the observer, objectifies the practice, and excludes, by defini-tion, empathy even for victims of horrible acts. Within such a framework, anguish for the victim can frequently be displaced by anguish for the observing self:

God forbid I should ever witness such another horrid scene.[58]

I can safely aver, that I suffered more on the occasion than her cruel connexions, who prepared her for burning with all the apathy and unfeeling barbarity that we may suppose apparent in the savages of America, when urged by a sentiment of revenge acting upon a savage mind, and in retaliation for injuries received. I would willingly endure a week's gout, rather than suffer again what I did on this day, in the vain hope of saving a life; for though frequent repetitions of these cruel scenes have not blunted my feelings on the subject, I could not divest myself of the hope of success without a trial, though the cholera might have been the result.[59]

The twin compulsions of horror and fascination whereby Europeans were drawn to the site of burnings even though they claimed to be unwilling witnesses is well captured in plate 5. Additionally, in plates 3 and 5, indigenous men are shown waving swords around the pyre, something that is not mentioned in eyewitness accounts. One might suggest that horror of the practice is signaled here by the wielding of swords and, in plate 5, by the averted gaze of the Europeans, while fascination is dramatized by the widow's representation. Or, to return to Lovewell's poem,

> Lovewell felt quite distracted at the scene,
> And many a silent tear bedewed his cheek;
> He would have given worlds he had not been
> A witness to the deed, and tried to seek
> In vain for solace round; for what between
> horror and grief, he scarce had pow'r to speak,
> Or give his servants orders to prepare
> To quit the scene, of terror and despair
>
> Oh! that't had been, said he, the evening hour
> When the moon's beams afford but glimmering light,
> Or when dense clouds upon th'horizon lour,
> And, spreading round, involve the world in night;
> That I'd not viewed the sweet and spotless flower
> In anguish perish, sickening at the sight;
> That I'd not seen, with sorrow and dismay,
> The harrowing proof of superstition's sway.[60]

It would seem that widows could become marginal even in reflections ostensibly prompted by their own suffering.

There were descriptions in which a more genuine concern was expressed for the widow. One such example was an item carried by the Baptist *Friend of India* in July 1820. To the account is appended a discussion of the absurdity of the concept of "voluntary" *sati* that conveys pathos without sensationalism. It would seem the reader is being directed to the facts themselves and not, as is more typical of evangelical fundraising materials, to what such facts may imply about Indian society.

[O]n whom had these two young persons to lean on for counsel at this awful moment which was to decide their fate? Their own father and mother? These were far away as is generally the case. Their husband's uncle, and his sons! It is probable that these felt quite as much for them as is felt for widows in general; but could they be ignorant that if they chose to live they must remain a perpetual burden on them, of which nothing could rid them but death itself? These two young widows, in their husband's death had indeed *lost their all*. . . . Can we contemplate all these circumstances without feeling that no one amidst them *could act freely*? (emphasis in original)[61]

In general, missionaries were least likely to produce fascinated accounts of *sati*, although they also continued, the above report notwithstanding, to lend credence to the notion of "voluntary" *sati*. On a pragmatic level, the notion of "voluntary" *sati* was useful since it confirmed the all-powerful influence of Hinduism, or, as William Ward put it, "the amazing power which this superstition has over the mind of its votaries."[62] Compare also the preceding discussion of the material forces underpinning *sati* with Ward's fictional testimonial of what the widow might have been thinking at the pyre:

Such a widow reflects thus: "It is right that the wife leave the world with her husband; a son can never be to the mother what a husband is to a wife; the extinction of life is the work of a minute; by strangling, by drowning, how soon does the soul leave the body: there are no terrors then in the funeral pile, and I shall at once enter on happiness! What multitudes have died in this manner before me; and if I live, I have nothing but sorrow to expect."[63]

These are words of which the pro-*sati* lobby would have been proud, for they suggest that short-term suffering is rewarded by long-term happiness. They are, however, at variance with what most women were reported as actually having said at the pyre. For although women do emphasize that they have "nothing but sorrow to expect" (fear of economic uncertainty and the prospect of familial abandonment), nowhere do they suggest the torture of widow burning as a temporary suffering of no matter. Ward's fabricated testimonial suggests that even missionaries were not entirely immune to that troubling and tenacious concept, the apparently voluntary *sati*.

Related to the conception of *sati* as voluntary was its construction as a practice that exemplifed wifely devotion. As Lovewell puts it,

> She thought not of the pleasures which were past,
> Her heart with hope of brighter realms was cheer'd,
> And sighed for joys which would for ever last!
> The world to her no longer was endeared
> But seemed as if a wilderness't had grown,
> Since with her husband all its charms had flown![64]

This portrayal of the widow as driven to burning by inconsolable loss and a broken heart, of *sati* as expressing "the deep vow of undivided, yea, unshallow'd love,"[65] is in tension with women's testimonials and, indeed, even with the substance of men's obituaries, which were the primary context for reporting widow burning in the indigenous press. Where many Europeans persisted in understanding *sati* in terms of a notion of conjugal love, women's testimonials stressed not grief over the loss of a husband, but rather fear and uncertainty of what lay ahead of them. They focus, in other words, not on the affective ties of marital union rent asunder by the death of their spouse, but on the vulnerable social and economic status of widows.

This is equally true of the obituaries published in the Bengali press, which, even while normalizing the violence of *sati*, typically address the widow's motivations as follows:

His wife not willing to endure the distresses of a widow at that old age . . .[66]

His widow thinking herself altogether worthless in the world . . . and anticipating the many distresses that she would have to suffer if she survived . . .[67]

Here the sense of worthlessness attributed to the widow and the explanation of her apparent unwillingness to continue living are related not to the loss of her husband, but to her devalued status in society. Questions of women's virtue and chastity which had formed a strand, albeit a minor one, in pamphlets and petitions, are largely absent in such reports. Not so in European accounts. These persisted in locating widow burning within a bourgeois notion of companionate marriage and conjugal love, constructs that in their turn continued to lend credence and energy to the idea of voluntary *sati*. Together they contributed to the refrain—"did she go willingly?"—a question that centrally structured debate on *sati,* mystifying the practice and delaying its prohibition.

Representation of the practices surrounding immolation illuminate European conceptions of indigenous culture and agency. The terms are, as we shall see, inextricably linked. An article on "Female Immolations in India," published in the *Calcutta Journal,* carried the following description:

[Her] nearest relations leave the house, and accompany her to the Ganges, where she bathes; and is assisted by a brahmun in repeating the formulas which are to prepare her as the victim for the fire. These being gone through, she comes up from the river (about 10 to 12 yards) to the funeral pile, which consists of a heap of faggots laid on the earth, and rising from the ground about three feet. On this the dead body of her husband has been laid. She walks round the pile four or five times, scattering parched corn as she goes; and then lays herself down by the dead body, laying her arm across the body. With two cords laid under the body, and across the pile, the dead and the living bodies are now tied fast together; and then a large quantity of faggots are thrown on the pile, which are held down, . . . [lest] . . . the widow . . . disentangle herself, and escape . . . by two bamboo levers. Her eldest son then, with his head averted, touches, with a lighted torch, the mouth of his deceased father; and then sets fire to the pile. The beating of the drums, and the shouts of the crowd, drown the cries of the dying victim.[68]

The account is rendered in the ethnographic present. As many critics of the rhetorical conventions of ethnography have argued, this strategy has the effect of reifying, naturalizing, and de-historicizing social practices, locating them "in a time order different from that of the speaking subject."[69] In the example above, events follow one another without interruption. Persons involved seem to be enacting a transhistorical tradition, in "synchronic suspension," rather than actively engaging in a social practice.[70] The activities seem "unmotivated" in that their logic is not apparent from the description. The seamless narrative even naturalizes violence, neither hesitating nor stuttering at the tying of the widow to the pyre. The use of the passive voice and the limiting of description to actions represented as if unfolding in a predetermined sequence contribute to this effect. *Sati* here is decontextualized, not just temporally, but also spatially: the account is of a "typical" instance occurring nowhere in particular.

Eyewitness accounts of *sati* only infrequently carried elaborate descriptions of the practices surrounding immolation, the narrative center being efforts made by the observer to dissuade the widow. However, when such descriptions were included, they shared many elements with the so-called representative account quoted above. As the narrator begins to describe these practices, he moves from "particularized narrative" to "generalized description."[71] Accounts often reverted to "particularized narrative" at the very end with the observer's comments on the incident. The effect is a textualized eyewitness account of the practices surrounding immolation. In the following example, the narrator, having stated the exact dimensions of the pyre as nine feet long, six feet broad and four feet high, continues:

loose cords (or rather unlaid jute) were thrown across on which the body was laid after having been washed in the river water by Bramins and widows. One of the sons then put a small piece of gold in its mouth, nostrils, eyes and ears. The Widows then washed themselves and prayed in the river, putting red powder or paint on the front of the head where the hair is parted. While they were praying, one of the sons walked three times around the pile with some lighted Straw in his hand and touched the mouth of the Corpse with it, some native music striking up at the same time. When the women came out of the river, they took off their earrings and the ornaments of their arms and legs and gave them to the priest for distribution to those they named, some were given to the musicians: the women were next led around the pile amidst the shouts of spectators: we were told that they should have gone 7 times round, but they appeared unable to walk more than once round, being very old, probably between 50 and 60 years of age (the husband was said to be 72). They were then assisted on to the pile from which they threw cowries to the surrounding people, who seemed anxious to obtain them, after which they laid down one on each side of the body—when instantly the cords above mentioned were drawn across them and the bodies tied together.[72]

The narrator claims "the women appeared passive and indifferent" and, in the same dispassionate tone, notes that wood was piled upon them and bamboo poles held across the pyre to prevent their escape. The son then lights the pile and shouts are heard from the crowd. Typically, the account's representation of the widows' suffering on the pyre is minimal: "so immediately does the whole ignite that suffocation must take place in a very short time."

Even in this account of a burning witnessed by the narrator, *sati* emerges as a timeless, unmotivated ritual. Things seem to succeed one another steadily and without interruption. No one appears to be in control, supervising the proceedings, getting things done. It would seem that the widow, relatives, and pundits are actualizing roles accorded them in a prior script. Such representations of *sati* seriously mystify the social and material roots of the practice, insistently rewriting it as an event intelligible primarily, if not solely, within a presumed religious master-narrative. It would appear that nobody stood to gain from *sati;* that it was merely a disinterested religious performance whose repetition is to be understood as unreflective obedience to scripture. "Religion" or "culture" is seen here to have the force of nature. Erasure of the agency of persons involved in *sati* is an inevitable consequence. This notion of culture further contributes to the marginalization of the widow as subject and to minimizing her coercion, resistance, struggle, and suffering. Equally significant, by representing the family as uniformly subjected to the eternal imperatives of "religion" or "culture," such accounts homogenize the agency of family members and obscure their competing and/or complementary material investments in the practice. In short, this conception of culture produces a discourse which severely attenuates the material forces underpinning *sati,* severs the material from the religious realms of social life, and eliminates the agencies, either in perpetuating the practice or in resisting it, of those involved.

Descriptions of *sati* as ritual also normalize its violence. The rhythmic cadence of the prose is not interrupted even by the coercion of women, their restraint under ropes, wood, bamboo poles. The violence of this rhetoric, in the face of the evidence in narrated accounts of the coercive and material basis of *sati,* leaves one breathless. One is tempted to ask, is it, as the Europeans insisted, "Hindus" who are hypnotized by brahmanic texts? Is it not, rather, the European observer who is paying obeisance to "their" scriptures?

Interestingly, the representation of *sati* as ritualized activity is to be found even in accounts which are explicitly critical of the practice, unlike those just discussed. Take, for instance, the following incident from the *Asiatic Journal:*

On arrival at the edge of the river, some pots of water were thrown over the head of the woman, and a bunch of leaves placed in her hand, which she appeared to be almost without strength to support; and after this operation, she was stripped of a few ornaments. A parcel of combs were stuck in her hair, and her apparel being changed, she was conveyed towards the pile, on which the body of her husband lay extended.

On reaching the pile, she was released from the arms of the woman who had hitherto supported her, and hustled round it three or four times midst the vociferations of the multitude; and then with the aid of the ruffians that surrounded her, she mounted the pile, apparently as inanimate as the deceased body of her husband. At this interval I observed one of the most active of the attendants, fasten her with a cord to the dead body of her husband and instantly a quantity of straw, dry bamboos, fire-wood were thrown over the victim . . . to prevent her . . . extricating herself . . . A long bamboo pole was then laid across the whole . . . In two minutes the whole was enveloped in smoke and flames, and the work of destruction was complete.[73]

The narrator concludes that this was "wilful and deliberate murder." The observer's critical perspective is evident. There is no sense that the widow's actions were in any way "voluntary." She is said to be assisted and hurried through the various stages. She is "stripped" of her jewels, combs are "stuck" in her hair, and she is bound to the pile.

Apart from these important differences, this account of *sati* as murder has more in common than we might expect with those descriptions in which it approximates a religious ritual. Except when the narrator interrupts to make a comment about one of the attendants, actions mechanically follow each other suggesting a deterministic unfolding of events. In addition, neither type of description advances an "explanation" for the burning other than relating it in a general way to religion or the will to murder. If the former codes *sati* as a "religious ritual," the latter represents it as a secular one. It is unclear, at least from these particular descriptions, precisely what is at stake in *sati*, why women were thus sacrificed to religion or willfully murdered.

Such considerations are, in a sense, foreclosed by the way in which both narratives abstract the events they describe from the landscapes in which they take place. In both incidents the narrator positions himself in that privileged location which Mary Louise Pratt terms "monarch of all I survey."[74] And, in this instance, what this unwavering gaze surveys is the widow's movements. This insistent visual tracking of the widow has been extremely valuable in reconstructing some sense of her subjectivity. However, this focus bleaches out the surrounding landscape, details of which are rare in such accounts. Many incidents are said to have taken place on riverbanks. Were there boats plying on the river, washermen and women laboring? What about the crowds said to have gathered around the pile? Most accounts say very little about them. They tend to erupt into the narrative only when the widow reaches the pyre or is set alight. Are we to assume they stood still and were silent until that moment? Did they never mill around or get in the way? The following account, exceptional in its detail, gives us a glimpse of particulars others might have left out. Perhaps not surprisingly, given that they were least likely to produce fascinated accounts of *sati,* it comes from the pen of a missionary.

The Darogah and his attendants were sitting under a tree writing out the necessary papers, the crowds were pouring in from every quarter, and at the scene of the river were an immense noise and bustle; some were pushing about the multitude to bring in materials for the pile; some were cutting up wood, some laying it in order, and others roaring out orders and directions,— to which was added the deep hum of spectators.[75]

Sound and smell are consistently subordinated to sight.[76] The sound most frequently registered is that of the crowd at the moment of the burning. Mention of smell, the odor of burning flesh, for instance, is also infrequent in these descriptions. Only a few accounts note the odor of putrefying carcasses, which surely must have been common and pungent, to say the least, given the climate and the delays often caused by waiting for the magistrate's permission to burn.[77] To cite a final example, none of the accounts mention birds of prey. Surely dead bodies would have attracted scavengers?

Ann Chaffin's and W. Bampton's descriptions of *sati* are significant in this context.[78] Their narratives diverge from most others in their structure and in the kind of details they furnish. Each tells not an unbroken tale but a story with many beginnings and interruptions. Both are exceptional in setting the event within a larger frame. Chaffin's is of additional interest as a detailed account by a woman.[79] Chaffin was a female missionary and was at the Serampore Baptist Mission at the time of the incident. When Chaffin first hastens to the spot, she discovers that permission has yet to be granted for the burning. She returns home having spoken to the brother of the deceased about the particulars of the death and having "contemplate[d] the surrounding objects."

It was near a ghaut adjoining the estate of Rev. Mr. Brown. Many natives were engaged in different occupations such as carrying bricks, mending boats; and quite unconcerned as tho' the burning of the Woman alive was a circumstance of no moment whatever. Just on the brink of the Ganges lay the corpse of the poor Woman's Husband covered with cloth.

The narrative begins a second time when she receives news that the burning was about to start. Chaffin locates her perspective as being from a boat.

The tide being high our boat came within 3 yards of the corpse lying on the bank. We beheld a large multitude hastening down towards us leading the poor woman to the place of her death. Her mother supported on one side and attended her. . . . I was much struck . . . by her appearance, she was young, not above 20 very agreeable, more so than any other I have seen amongst the Natives. She looked remarkably stout and healthy, well dressed and ornamented as usual with nose jewels, bracelets round the waist and large spot of red paint on the forehead. Her countenance betrayed no fear, tho there was something of a pensive cast on it, and at times I thought I could discover a look which indicated absence of mind.

Chaffin, like other, male observers, is concerned to monitor the widow's subjectivity and, like them, finds the widow apparently in her senses. Like many male observers she also finds the woman unusually attractive. But just as she appears to be reproducing the formulaic male description, she interrupts to note "a circumstance which greatly affected my mind. . . . while the poor woman was engaged in performing the last gloomy rites if anything was heard beyond the general clamour it was this noise occasioned by the men driving stakes into the ground which was to form the pile. To me this was a dismal noise." By drawing back from the widow, and enlarging the canvas thus, Chaffin undermines the tendency toward haunting description produced by many other accounts. The sound of stakes can hardly sustain an aestheticized narrative of "devotional sacrifice." Even when Chaffin follows the widow's actions, they are not represented as continuous. She is noted as pausing between things. For instance, Chaffin writes, "She then sat down by her husband and for the space of half-an-hour or more fanned his face. . . . Occasionally her Mother would speak to her. . . . Then she would resume the fan again and drive away the flies for they were swarming in abundance round the head of the corpse." Chaffin depicts the event as one in which the pace varies. Sometimes little seems to be happening. This contrasts with the bulk of descriptions, where the tempo is even until the widow's ascent onto the pyre and where the practices surrounding immolation are represented as though unfolding in one elongated moment. Furthermore, not everything that happens at the pyre is related by Chaffin to the "ritual" of *sati*. Thus, for example, she notes the widow as fanning flies away from the corpse. (One wonders why more accounts do not mention flies.) The account does not sustain a division between the "sacred" and "secular," but intermixes both. This, together with Chaffin's representation of *sati* as an unevenly paced process, situates it firmly in the domain of everyday practice, undermining the tendency toward idealization found in many other European accounts.

Chaffin's perspective in narrating the incident is not a unilinear one. She notes the simultaneity of actions, her account moving between the widow seated by the pyre and the brother-in-law at the river's edge. She also clarifies the differing distances between her and the events taking place. When she first arrives, she states her boat was "within 3 yards of the corpse." Later, when the widow is brought to the riverbank to be bathed, Chaffin claims, "she was so near, I could have touched her with a walking stick." Finally, as the body is in flames, she writes "we were obliged to go farther off. . . . the end of one of the bamboos which crossed the pile came upon our boat." Locating herself in relation to the events undercuts the singular view of things implied by the unspecified vantage points assumed by most narratives.

Chaffin's description of the widow lacks, by and large, the disdain that is often evident in male accounts. Even though she comes away more deeply impressed about the need for Christianity in India, Chaffin speaks of the widow as the "poor woman," or the "poor devoted widow," not the "miserable, deluded wretch." Since she in no way idealizes *sati,* her account of the tying of the woman serves to foreground its coercive nature. The rope is described as "the noose" and the person tying it is said to have put "both his knees upon her stomach and pull[ed] the noose just as we do in packing up parcels." The analogy to the tying of parcels once again inscribes *sati* as a material event. Interestingly, Chaffin makes no comment on the pain the widow might have felt at the pressure of the knees or ropes. Indeed, Chaffin does not speculate on the suffering of the widow on the pyre. In this she is like other observers. However, her account does not end with the bursting of the pyre into flames. After the boat moves off, she turns and takes "a last view of the hated spectacle and the flames having subsided a little . . . [I] could plainly discover the mutilated head of the man and the arm of the woman already shrivelled and blackened." Chaffin does not conclude her account by taking shelter in the presumption of the widow's instantaneous death. With the attention to particularity that is characteristic of her narrative, she simply notes that the widow's arm is "shrivelled and blackened" and that the burning is still in progress.

Bampton's narrative also shares many of the features to be found in Chaffin's account. Among these we might note the type of detail and contextualization, and the representation of the event as a process with multiple elements which are neither synchronized nor enacted as ritual. Bampton begins with information about the deceased, the widow and family members, and then elaborately details the construction of the pit and pyre (in the burning he recounts the bodies are first burnt in a pit and then removed to be fully incinerated on a pyre). At this point in the narrative he receives a message from home recalling him. He returns as soon as he is able and proceeds to describe the arrival of the widow at the funeral pyre and in brief his unsuccessful attempts at dissuasion. Although disappointed that he had pleaded in vain, Bampton does not pause to speculate on the widow's subjective state. Instead, he turns to the mechanics of burning which are laid out in exacting detail.

What distinguishes Bampton's account from others, including Chaffin's, is its attention to the technology and labor of immolation: the digging of the pit, the construction of the pyre, the transportation and preparation of raw materials, and so on. In his description, widow burning emerges as an intricate and precise mechanism for cremation involving the labor and expertise of many.

Soon after my arrival, about twelve coolies came, each of them bringing a load of wood on his or *her* head, for several of them were women, and they came twice. I charged all the labourers with being accessory to the crime about to be committed, and the general reply was, in substance, that they worked for money, and did this work as they did any other because they were paid for it. (229)

He then describes the splintering of wood kindling and the preparation of the pit for the initial burning.

The pit being finished, a quantity of water was mixed with cow dung, and sprinkled on the margin, and about one third of the way down, in sufficient quantity to turn the sand its own colour; two ropes were also well wetted with the same mixture, the use of which will appear hereafter. On inquiring [about] the use of the two bamboos which lay near, I was told that they were to stir the fire, and turn about the bodies. The bits of wood prepared for the occasion, were between twelve and eighteen inches long, and I suppose on an average, five or six in circumference: a quantity of them were now thrown into the pit, and a man at the bottom proceeded to set them up on their ends, two or three thick round the sides. (229)

This meticulous attention to process is also to be found in Bampton's representation of the preliminary burning and the subsequent removal of the deceased man and widow from the pit and onto the pyre.

Now the ropes came into use, which, as I have said, were wetted with cow dung and water: one of them was doubled, and the middle thrown down to catch the man's chin. I think it was guided to his chin by a bamboo: one or two bamboo levers were then put under his head to raise it, and get the rope around his neck. The rope was then twisted, that is, the two ends of it were twisted together, in order to fasten it, and they began to draw; but they failed, for the rope slipped off. Another man then attempted to fasten the rope; he succeeded, and they drew up the body, with the exception, I think, of the legs; but it was quite dark, and nothing could be seen but by the light of the fire. (231)

Similar problems were encountered in dragging the widow's body from the pit:

they put . . . [the rope] on her arm, which projected in such a way as to favour their doing so, and after twisting it well, they drew her nearly to the top of the pit, but they seemed afraid that they should lose her again, if they trusted entirely to her arm, so she was held just below the edge of the pit, till another man put the other rope under her chin, and she was then drawn quite up. Some of the people then employed themselves in arranging the wood for the fires that were to consume the bodies, and I stood perhaps ten minutes longer, finally leaving both bodies on the brink of the pit, that of the woman still blazing. The joints of her knees were exposed, and most of the flesh burnt off one leg. (231)

These extracts illustrate that which is especially noteworthy about Bampton's narrative, namely, its attention to the labor of widow immolation. The involved processes he relates foreground the irreducible materiality of widow burning: *sati* is systematically produced, not simply enacted.

There are multiple ways in which, taken together, the accounts of Chaffin and Bampton help to contest representation of *sati* as spectacle or ritualized activity, whether it be coded as religious or secular. The portrayal of *sati* as oneiric sacrifice or ritual murder depends on the singular focus of the observer on a widow who is represented as if moving through proceedings that unfold as a coordinated sequence of events. Chaffin and Bampton undermine such a rendering of *sati* in a number of ways: enlarging the frame of description, telling an explicitly situated story, attending to practical details as well as technical hitches, remarking on the bodily consequences of burning, and narrating widow burning not as a single extended episode but as a phenomenon with several components. These aspects of the event and of the practice were omitted or glossed over in most other representations. Chaffin's and Bampton's narratives suggest how outside of the singular line of vision of the apparently all-seeing narrator lay the details large and small of the rootedness of widow burning in material and social contexts, the different motivations and interests that converged in it, and the individuals whose agency sustained, resisted, and enforced the practice.

In this chapter, eyewitness accounts of widow burning have been read with the double purpose of mapping "the obsessive scheme that regulates the totality of the output . . . and endows it with meaning,"[80] and of foregrounding the particular exclusions, inflections, and inscriptions that sustain enduring fictions about *sati* and its victims. If in the official debate or pamphlet literature women were the ground of the discourse on *sati,* in these descriptions, they move between being object and ground. For example, women are, at times, the object of description; at other times, women are ground for the elaboration of distinctively male constructions of *sati,* and specifically colonial notions of culture. Reading against the grain, contrary to "the obsessive scheme," I have attempted to reconstruct woman as subject, to restore to the center the traces of active suffering, resistance, and coercion elided or marginalized in these narratives. While these descriptions do not yield elaborate representations of women's subjectivity, there is sufficient evidence here to unsettle the image of her as passive, willing, or silent.

Women's testimonials similarly call into question colonial insistence on the religious basis of *sati.* The concerns of widows were explicitly material and social. If we were to abandon a dualistic colonial conception of religion in which the sacred and the secular were posited as autonomous domains, we might concede that a practice with a primarily material basis was given form in terms that were "religious"; notice the officiating of pundits, the recitation of mantras, the cries of "Hari bol." For their part, widows nowhere drew on a scripturally derived rationale for *sati,* such as the presumed spiritual rewards insisted upon by the pro-*sati* indigenous lobby. Rather, the testimonials of widows repeatedly addressed the material hardship and social dimensions of widowhood. However, the colonial conception of religion as the structuring principle of indigenous society meant that, though acknowledged early in the debate on widow burning, evidence for the material basis of *sati* was unable to displace insistence on its fundamentally "religious" character. This insistence intersected with the ambivalence toward *sati* (discernible even in those opposed to the practice) and delayed its prohibition. The issue, returning to Spivak's question, may not be whether the subaltern can speak so much as whether she can be *heard* to be speaking in a given set of materials and what, indeed, has been made of her voice by colonial and postcolonial historiography. Rephrasing Spivak thus enables us to remain vigilant about the positioning of woman in colonial discourse without conceding to colonial discourse what it did not, in fact, achieve — the erasure of women.

# Afterword

In this brief afterword, I delineate some of the themes of my analysis of the multiple stakes and determinations of the discourses that constituted the debate on widow burning between 1780 and 1833. In undertaking a work of this kind one is in critical dialogue not merely with the ideologues of the time but also with what has been claimed about them by subsequent historiography. Such claims, as we have seen in the case at hand, are often very misleading. Colonialist historiography, for example, has represented the prohibition of widow burning as an instance of the civilizing mission, an assertion hardly sustainable in a close reading of the terms upon which the discussions proceeded. Similarly, the argument that the Bengal Renaissance initiated a radical break turns out, upon inspection, to require a reconceptualization.

Perhaps the most striking feature is the astonishing marginality of the widow to this debate over whether she should survive her husband or be burned on his funeral pyre. She is buried under a welter of official deliberations on "Hindu law," and becomes hostage to colonial superstition about the political and economic chaos that it was presumed would ensue from intervention in a practice insistently coded as religious, despite evidence to the contrary. In *bhadralok* discourse she disappears behind an abstract scripturalism. Although the *bhadralok* were cognizant that the justification for widow burning rested on particular conceptions of women's nature, they were ultimately more interested in debating the proper place of ritual within Hinduism. Missionaries appear to show concern for the widow's plight. However, their frequent recourse to a discourse of horror, especially in the metropolitan context, caricatured her suffering and dehumanized her existence. Furthermore, in their case, the social ill-treatment of indigenous women largely served as evidence for the paramount necessity for evangelism.

All parties normalized the violence of *sati,* and ambivalence toward the practice is evident in the writings of both those for and those against it. Thus Rammohun could approvingly cite *sati* as exemplifying women's fortitude even as he articulated his opposition to the practice and argued that it was in most cases involuntary. Meanwhile, European officials and missionaries could read into widow burning their own narrative about conjugal love — a claim for *sati* nowhere made by the indigenous literati. A conception of wifely duty given credence by some brahmanic scriptures was thus translated into a bourgeois notion of a woman's love and sacrifice for her husband, adding another layer of obfuscation to the violence of *sati.*

A key argument of this book is that a specifically colonial discourse on Indian society informed the debate on widow immolation and initiated shifts in indigenous perception. British colonial officials conceived of brahmanic texts as authentic, legitimate, and exhaustive guides to indigenous society. Religion was presumed to structure social life, and all practices were seen to derive from the scriptural texts. Religion was equated with scripture, and any evidence of a divergence of social practice from scriptural texts was seen to confirm the practice's inauthenticity. Thus it was that a particular version of *sati* was codified as legal in 1813 and policed by East India Company officials. Likewise we find the Baptist missionaries challenging the natives they met to defend their practices in terms of brahmanic scriptures, seeking to shame them for their "ignorance" of these texts, which was widespread. This discourse on India was not invented from whole cloth. It drew on contemporaneous European intellectual and philosophical currents, among them orientalism, protestantism, evangelism, and utilitarianism. These structured a colonial view of Indian society which was shared by missionaries and colonial officials alike, among whom numbered many preeminent orientalists.

Colonial perception was incommensurable with the heterogeneous actuality of the society officials and missionaries encountered. It is clear from the early interactions of colonial officials with court pundits, that the discourse of the former was alien and puzzling to the latter. A similar process was observable in the interactions between the Baptist missionaries and their subaltern audiences. Both court pundits and street audiences articulated their own understanding of the circumscribed place of text in religion and daily life, the importance of custom, and a view of the relationship of religion to material practice which was not one of correspondence. Such evidence did not, however, challenge colonial knowledge. Officials and missionaries secured an insistence on their own view by ignoring, marginalizing, domesticating, and exceptionalizing whatever did not accord with their presumptions. These tactics were not always instrumental in the narrow sense. They illustrate how ideology literally constructs "reality." The extraordinary way in which colonial discourse continued to constitute the object of its perception in its own terms is clearly illustrated in European eyewitness accounts of widow burning, which represent *sati* as a religious act of wifely devotion in the face of the coercion of women, and of widows' testimonials regarding the material basis of the practice. In addition, there was the a priori arrogation of the supremacy of colonial over indigenous knowledge. Thus although indigenous persons were integrally involved in the production of colonial knowledge, their writings were recast in specific ways, making their discourse a structurally subordinate one, especially when they were employees of the East India Company. Accordingly, in chapter I we traced the contest between colonial officials and pundits over the form, status, and interpretation of scriptural texts. Colonial officials, however, through their disciplinary procedures and evidentiary protocols laid down the principles by which these texts were to be read, guidelines that over time shaped the *vyawasthas* of pundits.

The shifts initiated by colonial discourse were far from total. The discursive traces of colonialism are most discernible when *bhadralok* sought to communicate with the East India Company, as in *vyawasthas*, or in petitions for or against widow burning. Elsewhere the terms of *bhadralok* discussion were quite distinct, and relatively autonomous from official concerns. Indigenous pamphlets on *sati* are a good example here. For although these, too, engaged scripture, they did so in ways that differed from official deliberations. In general the *bhadralok* were less concerned about the form of these texts and more interested in contesting their content. Thus, we find them challenging each other on particular interpretations of textual fragments, and their philosophical implications as well as social consequences. They are engaged in a frankly evaluative process, and in no way seek to erase the impress of their own readings, even while claiming transparency and authenticity for their positions. The disagreements of texts on virtually all the issues raised by widow burning (its necessity and purpose, the right of individuals to take their own life, the goal of human existence, the place of ritual in religious worship, etc.) were seen not as contradictions but as differences of opinion. The texts are not conceived, as in the official view, as static mirrors of an ideal society. Nor is there an obsessive concern with ordering texts according to their antiquity. Rather, there is a tendency to simultaneously cite a great variety of sources, and to mix genres of texts, features that are absent from petitions that tend to focus on the Vedas and *Manusmriti* to the exclusion of other texts, in recognition of the interpretive priorities of officials.

*Bhadralok* discourse was thus not derivative of colonial rhetoric. As argued in chapter 2, this relationship is better characterized as one of intersection and disjunction. Even when both framed their arguments within scripture, for example, each brought a distinctive set of concerns to their articulation of it. Notwithstanding this fact, however, one may note that over time there is in *bhadralok* discourse a drift in a specifically colonial direction. Among the elements that one may point to here are the increasing equation of scripture and law, the conflation of tradition with brahmanism, and the conviction of the existence of a prior Hindu golden age and its fall as precipitated by an Islamic tyranny. Thus we see that even when issues that had been engaged in precolonial India are taken up, such as monotheism or the place of ritual in religious life, there is a discernible transformation in the mode and goal of the argument. This shift is clearly traceable in the writings of Rammohun Roy, which move from a forceful critique of religion in terms drawn from Islamic rationalism and devotional vaishnavism, to the reform of Hinduism conceived as a return to vedantism.

The increasing entanglement of *bhadralok* with official discourse is comprehensible not merely because of the growing consolidation of colonial power, but also in part because contests over tradition became integral to colonial ideology of rule, and this class could take upon itself the custodianship of tradition proper. No wonder, then, that the making of this class proceeded in part through the supposed remaking of tradition in relation to a range of social issues, the most célèbrated of which involved the status of women. The increasing focus on women has been mistakenly conceived as signifying a new and thoroughly modern concern for their rights as individuals. What is, however, abundantly clear in examining the debate on *sati,* the first of these causes célèbres, is that, far from signaling any such concern, these debates became the context in which the *bhadralok* remade itself in relation to the so-called lower orders and to colonial power. In that sense, it may be no exaggeration to say that these debates reconstituted patriarchy and caste much more than liberating women into modernity. This is not to say that women experienced no social gains. Such gains were mostly limited to upper-caste and upper-class women, however, and were made in return for a greater scrutiny of their behavior, which was now seen increasingly to reflect upon the honor of the men of their families and, by extension, their communities. As for non-brahmin women, the generation of colonial law from brahmanic texts deprived them of their customary rights and freedoms by placing them within the enclosure of its restrictive purview.

While elements of colonial rhetoric might be found to inflect and at times reshape *bhadralok* consciousness, the uneven reach of the colonial state implied a differential relation between colonial and subaltern discourses. One must proceed carefully here for our access to subaltern discourses in the present study is minimal, certainly compared to that of the *bhadralok,* among whom widow burning predominated. Furthermore such material as we do have is from the early years of the period under consideration. These qualifications notwithstanding, it seems clear that these groups were largely impervious to the cultural logic of colonialism. One may note here that the street audiences of missionaries neither comprehended nor cared to engage missionary critique of their faith, life, and religious practice. To the despair of missionaries, they either walked away or else simply stated their view of things: that their practice was customary, that those who had leisure might pay attention to the *shastras,* that the nature of their employment reflected material necessity, and so on. The poor record of conversions suggests a general, continued indifference to the evangelists' message. If the missionaries had little power to enforce their worldview on these groups, the colonial state had little interest in doing so. The latter established a relation of force with the laboring classes, not one in which they were either invited or enlisted into its cultural logic and remade through disciplinary, reformist projects.

As should by now be clear, official, missionary, and *bhadralok* discourses were not homogeneous but internally differentiated. Although official and missionary perceptions densely overlapped and reiterated one another, each brought its own concerns to bear. Ultimately, for the East India Company in Bengal the prohibition of widow burning was a law-and-order problem, given their analysis of Indian society. The Court of Directors in London also took this view, although the pressure of public opinion and their distance from the colony made them more apt to note, without in any way belaboring, the ethical issues involved in tolerance of *sati*. Missionaries, especially in Britain, expressed vociferously their opposition to the practice in moral terms. Baptists in India, however, explicitly engaged the terms by which the discussion proceeded in Bengal, their ethical concerns being incorporated into such arguments as a minor and infrequent theme. However, both in Britain and India, evangelists brought a specific concern for the consequence of widow burning for family and society which was absent from official discussions. *Bhadralok* writings on *sati* were similarly varied. There was a specificity to the discourse of Bengali newspapers, pamphlets, and petitions to the East India Company. Petitions most directly engaged colonial rhetoric; newspapers were a primarily autonomous realm, except in the period immediately before and after legislative prohibition; and pamphlets occupied an intermediate third space. These discourses existed in determinate, evolving, and specifiable relations of complementarity, contestation, and disjunction with each other.

As a final word, I would like to clarify the burden of the project undertaken here. In the years that I have presented this material I have on occasion been criticized for bringing to it a late-twentieth-century feminist perspective which, it is claimed, makes me unsympathetic to the cultural milieux of the late eighteenth and early nineteenth century. The point, however, is not to blame colonialists for not properly enacting the civilizing mission; nor to berate the *bhadralok* for not being authentically modern. Rather, it is to sort through the grand claims of the historiography of both groups, so that the submerged truths, ironies, contradictions, and paradoxes can be brought to the surface. Without such a move, the real legacies of colonialism and of nineteenth-century social reform cannot be narrativized. While both have arrogated to themselves the agency of history, the widows' valiant and persistent efforts at self-preservation and self-affirmation have been fatally occluded. Even though widows who were questioned at the pyre consistently spoke the naked truths of terror, of their coercion by family members, and of the material distresses of widowhood, their voices have not been attended to. It is hoped that the testimonials here analyzed will serve to bury once and for all that violent fiction of *sati* as a dutiful act of religious volition.

# Notes

## Introduction

1. Romila Thapar, *The Past and Prejudice* (Delhi: National Book Trust, 1975), 3.

2. For the non-Indianist, it might be helpful to note that "communalism" is the term used to designate interreligious tensions, in particular social, cultural, and political antagonisms between Hindus and Muslims. For analysis of the emergence of communalism in the nineteenth century, see Gyanendra Pandey, *The Construction of Communalism in Colonial North India* (Delhi: Oxford University Press, 1992).

3. Edward Said, *Orientalism* (New York: Vintage, 1979).

4. See, for example, Bernard S. Cohn, "The Command of Language and the Language of Command," in *Subaltern Studies IV,* ed. Ranajit Guha (Delhi: Oxford University Press, 1985), 276–329; Cohn, *An Anthropologist among the Historians and Other Essays* (Delhi: Oxford University Press, 1990), chs. 7, 10, 20, 23; Ranajit Guha, *An Indian Historiography of India: A Nineteenth-Century Agenda and Its Implications* (Calcutta: Centre for Studies in Social Sciences, 1987); Sudipta Kaviraj, "On the Construction of Colonial Power: Structure, Discourse, Hegemony," paper presented at Berlin conference on "Imperial Hegemony," June 1–3, 1989; Timothy Mitchell, *Colonising Egypt* (Cambridge: Cambridge University Press, 1988); David Arnold, *Colonizing the Body: State Medicine and Epidemic Disease in Nineteenth-Century India* (Berkeley: University of California Press, 1993).

5. See, among others, Sudipta Kaviraj, "Imaginary History," Occasional Papers on History and Society, 2d ser., no. 7 (New Delhi: Nehru Memorial Museum and Library, September 1988); Pandey, *The Construction of Communalism in Colonial North India;* Gyan Prakash, *Bonded Histories: Genealogies of Labour Servitude in Colonial India* (Cambridge: Cambridge University Press, 1990);

Kumkum Sangari and Sudesh Vaid, eds., *Recasting Women: Essays in Colonial History* (New Delhi: Kali, 1989); Mrinalini Sinha, *Colonial Masculinity: The "Manly Englishman" and the "Effeminate Bengali"* (Manchester: Manchester University Press, 1995).

6. See, for example, Partha Chatterjee, *Nationalist Thought and the Colonial World: A Derivative Discourse?* (London: Zed Press, 1986); Sudhir Chandra, *The Oppressive Present: Literature and Social Consciousness in Colonial India* (Delhi: Oxford University Press, 1992). Dipesh Chakrabarty, "Postcoloniality and the Artifice of History: Who Speaks for 'Indian' Pasts?" *Representations* 37 (Winter 1992): 1–26, is an excellent discussion of the problematic category of "history" and of the complexities of writing "counter-histories."

7. Work in this area includes Gauri Viswanathan, *Masks of Conquest: Literary Study and British Rule in India* (New York: Columbia University Press, 1989); Lisa Lowe, *Critical Terrains: French and British Orientalism* (Berkeley: University of California Press, 1991); Tejaswini Niranjana, *Siting Translation: History, Post-Structuralism and the Colonial Context* (Berkeley: University of California Press, 1992); Robert Young, *White Mythologies: Writing History and the West* (London and New York: Routledge, 1990); Javed Majeed, *Ungoverned Imaginings: James Mill's* The History of British India *and Orientalism* (Oxford: Clarendon Press, 1992). See also Jenny Sharpe, *Allegories of Empire: The Figure of Woman in the Colonial Text* (Minneapolis: University of Minnesota Press, 1993).

8. See, among others, Benita Parry, "Problems in Current Theories of Colonial Discourse," *Oxford Literary Review* 9, 1–2 (1987): 27–58; Aijaz Ahmad, *In Theory: Classes, Nations, Literatures* (London: Verso, 1992); Rosalind O'Hanlon and David Washbrook, "After Orientalism: Culture, Criticism, and Politics in the Third World," *Comparative Studies in Society and History* 34, 1 (January 1992): 141–167; Gyan Prakash, "Can the 'Subaltern' Ride? A Reply to O'Hanlon and Washbrook," *Comparative Studies in Society and History* 34, 1 (January 1992): 168–184; Svati Joshi, "Rethinking English: An Introduction," in *Rethinking English: Essays in Literature, Language, History,* ed. Svati Joshi (New Delhi: Trianka, 1991), 1–31, especially 9–11; Sara Suleri, *The Rhetoric of English India* (Chicago: University of Chicago Press, 1992).

9. See Sangari and Vaid, "Recasting Women: An Introduction," in *Recasting Women,* 1–26; Sumanta Banerjee, *The Parlour and the Streets: Elite and Popular Culture in Nineteenth-Century Calcutta* (Calcutta: Seagull Books, 1989).

10. Ranajit Guha, "Dominance without Hegemony and Its Historiography," in *Subaltern Studies VI,* ed. Guha (Delhi: Oxford University Press, 1989), 210–309.

11. No one seriously proposes the conclusion that colonialism ushered in a total transformation; the second position is principally characteristic of the Cambridge School of Indian historiography.

12. See, for example, Sangari and Vaid, *Recasting Women;* Susie Tharu and K. Lalita, "Literature of the Reform and Nationalist Movements," in *Women Writing in India, 600 B.C. to the Present,* ed. Susie Tharu and K. Lalita (New York: Feminist Press, 1991), 145–186; Banerjee, *The Parlour and the Streets;* the several volumes of essays published by the Subaltern Studies Collective have analyzed the reconstellation of class relations under colonialism; see Ranajit Guha, ed., *Subaltern Studies I–VI* (Delhi: Oxford University Press, 1982–89).

13. Chatterjee, *Nationalist Thought and the Colonial World;* Chakrabarty, "Postcoloniality and the Artifice of History."

14. Lata Mani, "Multiple Mediations: Feminist Scholarship in the Age of Multinational Reception," *Feminist Review* 35 (Summer 1990): 24–41; Ruth Frankenberg and Lata Mani, "Crosscurrents, Crosstalk: Race, 'Postcoloniality' and the Politics of Location," *Cultural Studies* 7, 2 (May 1993): 292–310.

## Chapter 1: Equivocations in the Name of Tradition

1. G. Dowdeswell to the Register of the Nizamat Adalat, December 5, 1812, Parliamentary Papers on Hindoo Widows (hereafter PP on Hindoo Widows), 1821, 18: 31.

2. Bernard S. Cohn, "Law and the Colonial State in India," in *History and Power in the Study of Law,* ed. Jane Collier and June Starr (Ithaca, N.Y.: Cornell University Press, 1989), 131–152.

3. Ranajit Guha, *An Indian Historiography of India: A Nineteenth-Century Agenda and Its Implications* (Calcutta: Centre for Studies in Social Sciences, 1987), 27.

4. See, for example, Michel Foucault, *Discipline and Punish* (New York: Vintage, 1979).

5. Guha, *An Indian Historiography of India,* 10.

6. Sudipta Kaviraj, "On the Construction of Colonial Power: Structure, Discourse, Hegemony," paper presented at conference on "Imperial Hegemony," Berlin, June 1–3, 1989, 3.

7. See, for example, C. A. Bayly, *Indian Society and the Making of the British Empire,* vol. 2, pt. 1, *The New Cambridge History of India* (Cambridge: Cambridge University Press, 1988); Ranajit Guha, ed., *Subaltern Studies I–VI* (Delhi: Oxford University Press, 1982–89); Sumit Sarkar, *A Critique of Colonial India* (Calcutta: Papyrus, 1985); Kaviraj, "On the Construction of Colonial Power."

8. Kaviraj, "On the Construction of Colonial Power," 11–15.

9. Bernard S. Cohn, "The Census, Social Structure and Objectification in South Asia," in his *An Anthropologist among the Historians and Other Essays* (Delhi: Oxford University Press, 1990), 224–254; Cohn, "The Anthropology of a Colonial State and Its Forms of Knowledge," background paper for conference on "Culture Consciousness and the Colonial State," Isle of Thorns, July 23–27, 1989; Thomas R. Metcalf, "The Indian Empire: Its Structures and Processes under the British," *Indo-British Review* 6, 2 (1973): 31–38; David Arnold, "Some Observations on the Theory and Practice of the Colonial State," paper presented at conference on "Culture Consciousness and the Colonial State," Isle of Thorns, July 23–27, 1989.

10. Kaviraj, "On the Construction of Colonial Power," 10–12.

11. Ranajit Guha, "Dominance without Hegemony and Its Historiography," *Subaltern Studies VI,* ed. Guha (Delhi: Oxford University Press, 1989), 210–309.

12. In earlier versions of my analysis of the official debate on *sati,* page numbers of Parliamentary Papers cited referred to the handwritten, not the printed

pagination. In this text, all references to the Parliamentary Papers are to the printed pagination. See Lata Mani, "The Production of an Official Discourse on *Sati* in Early-Nineteenth-Century Bengal," in *Europe and Its Others*, ed. F. Barker et al. (Colchester: University of Essex, 1985), vol. 1, 107–127; also in *Economic and Political Weekly; Review of Women's Studies*, April 26, 1986, 32–40; "Contentious Traditions: The Debate on *Sati* in Colonial India," *Cultural Critique* 7 (Fall 1987): 119–156; also in *Recasting Women: Essays in Colonial History*, ed. Kumkum Sangari and Sudesh Vaid (New Delhi: Kali, 1989), 88–126.

13. See, for instance, B. Hjejle, "The Social Policy of the East India Company with Regard to Sati, Slavery, Thagi and Infanticide, 1722–1855" (D. Phil., Oxford University, 1958); Dorothy K. Stein, "Women to Burn: Suttee as a Normative Institution," *Signs* 4, 2 (1978): 253–268; C. A. Bayly, "From Ritual to Ceremony: Death Ritual and Society in Hindu North India since 1600," in *Mirrors of Mortality*, ed. J. Whaley (London: Europa, 1981), 154–186, especially 171–175.

14. Hastings is said to have convened a synod of ten pundits from all over India to compile a digest of Hindu law. Their text, *Vivadharnava-Setu*, was later translated by N. B. Halhed as *A Code of Gentoo Laws, or Ordinations of the Pundits* (London, 1776); Bernard S. Cohn, "The Command of Language and the Language of Command," in *Subaltern Studies IV*, ed. Ranajit Guha (Delhi: Oxford University Press, 1985), 288–295. There is a substantial literature on law in the colonial period. See especially J. D. M. Derrett, *Religion, Law and the State* (New York: The Free Press, 1968), chs. 8, 9; Lloyd I. Rudolph and Suzanne H. Rudolph, *The Modernity of Tradition*, pt. 3 (Chicago: University of Chicago Press, 1967); Bernard S. Cohn, "Anthropological Notes on Disputes and Law in India," in *An Anthropologist among the Historians and Other Essays*, 575–631; D. A. Washbrook, "Law, State and Agrarian Society in Colonial India," *Modern Asian Studies* 15, 3 (1981): 649–721; Richard Saumerez Smith, "Rule-by-Records and Rule-by-Reports: Complementary Aspects of British Imperial Rule of Law," *Contributions to Indian Sociology*, n.s., 19, no. 1 (1985): 153–176.

15. For other accounts of colonial state policy on *sati*, see A. Mukhopadhyay, "Sati as a Social Institution in Bengal," *Bengal Past and Present* 75 (1957): 99–115; K. Mittra, "Suppression of Suttee in the Province of Cuttack," *Bengal Past and Present* 46 (1933): 125–131; G. Seed, "The Abolition of Suttee in Bengal," *History* (October 1955): 286–299; B. Hjejle, "The Social Policy of the East India Company"; A. F. Salahuddin Ahmed, *Social Ideas and Social Change in Bengal, 1818–1835* (Leiden: Brill, 1965), 108–128; V. N. Datta, *Sati: Widow Burning in India* (Riverdale, Md.: Riverdale, 1988), 19–70.

16. PP on Hindoo Widows, 1821, 18: 22.

17. Ibid., 23.

18. Ahmed, *Social Ideas and Social Change in Bengal*, 109.

19. The government's position was elaborated in December 1812, but instructions to district courts and magistrates were not dispatched until April 1813. PP on Hindoo Widows, 1821, 18: 37.

20. Datta, *Sati: Widow Burning in India*, 24.

21. PP on Hindoo Widows, 1821, 18: 30.

22. Ibid., 31.

23. Ibid., 242.

24. Ibid., 38–39.

25. Ibid., 42.

26. Ibid., 41, 44.

27. PP on Hindoo Widows, 1824, 23: 43.

28. S. N. Mukherjee, *Sir William Jones: A Study in Eighteenth-Century British Attitudes to India* (Cambridge: Cambridge University Press, 1968); David Kopf, *British Orientalism and the Bengal Renaissance: The Dynamics of Indian Modernization, 1773–1835* (Berkeley: University of California Press, 1969); Javed Majeed, *Ungoverned Imaginings: James Mill's* The History of British India *and Orientalism* (Oxford: Clarendon Press, 1992), ch. 2, "Sir William Jones," 11–46.

29. PP on Hindoo Widows, 1821, 18: 229.

30. PP on Hindoo Widows, 1825, 24: 148.

31. PP on Hindoo Widows, 1821, 18: 218.

32. Ibid., 219.

33. PP on Hindoo Widows, 1830, 28: 226–228.

34. PP on Hindoo Widows, 1825, 24: 10.

35. Gayatri Chakravorty Spivak, "Can the Subaltern Speak?" in *Marxism and the Interpretation of Culture,* ed. Cary Nelson and Lawrence Grossberg (Urbana: University of Illinois Press, 1988), 298–299 and passim.

36. PP on Hindoo Widows, 1825, 24: 153.

37. This figure is computed from data in Benoy Bhusan Roy, *Socioeconomic Impact of Sati in Bengal and the Role of Raja Rammohun Roy* (Calcutta: Naya Prokash, 1987), 43–48.

38. PP on Hindoo Widows, 1825, 24: 84–85.

39. PP on Hindoo Widows, 1826–27, 20: 1–34, especially 29–31.

40. Articles on *sati* in the *Oriental Herald* included "Burning of Hindoo Widows," April 1824, 551–560; and "On the Burning of Hindoo Widows," January 1826, 1–20.

41. "Bedfordshire Petition against the Burning of Hindoo Widows," *Missionary Register,* June 1823, 250–251; "An Account of the Proceedings at a Public Meeting, Held at the City of York, on the Nineteenth January 1827, to take into Consideration the Expediency of Petitioning Parliament on the Subject of the Immolation of Widows in British India," York, 1827; "Meeting for the Abolition of the Burning of Widows in India," *Oriental Herald,* March 1829, 539–545; "Appeal to Britain on the Burning of Widows," *Oriental Herald,* May 1829, 306.

42. See, for example, "Burning of Hindoo Widows," debate at the East India House, June 18, 1828, *Asiatic Journal* 26 (1828): 115–121.

43. Letter from the Governor-General in Council to the Court of Directors, December 4, 1829, appended to PP on Hindoo Widows, 1830, 28: 3–4.

44. Iqbal Singh, *Rammohun Roy: A Biographical Inquiry into the Making of Modern India* (Bombay: Asia Publishing House, 1958), vol. 1, 214; Datta, *Sati: Widow Burning in India,* 64. Singh and Datta are rightly critical of the East India Company's slowness to implement prohibition of *sati,* but they tend to take at face value the Company's claims to noninterference. However, even as the East India Company refused legislative intervention, it was intervening discursively, making its conception of tradition, for instance, the basis of law.

45. "Lord William Bentinck's Minute on Suttee," in *Raja Rammohun Roy and Progressive Movements in India: A Selection from Records, 1775–1845,* ed. J. K.

Majumdar (Calcutta: Art Press, 1941), 141. For an assessment of Bentinck's attitude toward and role in the prohibition of *sati,* see Datta, *Sati: Widow Burning in India,* 82–118.

46. Regulation 17 (1829) of the Bengal Code, appended to PP on Hindoo Widows, 1830, 28: 4–5.

47. For discussion of the events that followed on the abolition of *sati,* including the appeal of the pro-*sati* lobby to the Privy Council, see Roy, *Socioeconomic Impact of Sati in Bengal and the Role of Raja Rammohun Roy,* 101–119; Datta, *Sati: Widow Burning in India,* 136–150; and Singh, *Rammohun Roy,* vol. 2, 209–249, vol. 3, 461–471.

48. Vasudha Dhagamwar, "Saint, Victim or Criminal," *Seminar,* no. 342 (special issue on *sati*), February 1988, 36; clause 298 of draft of the Indian Penal Code prepared principally by T. B. Macaulay, cited in Dhagamwar, 36.

49. Ibid., 36.

50. Spivak, "Can the Subaltern Speak?" 298–299 and passim.

51. PP on Hindoo Widows, 1821, 18: 27.

52. Ibid., 227–229. Further references to Ewer's letter will be included in the text.

53. This conception of crowds as enacting primordial instincts and loyalties was to become, as Gyanendra Pandey has argued, central to colonial representations of collective action. See Pandey, *The Construction of Communalism in Colonial North India* (Delhi: Oxford University Press, 1992).

54. PP on Hindoo Widows, 1821, 18: 235.

55. Arvind Sharma, "Suttee: A Study in Western Reactions," in Sharma, *Thresholds in Hindu-Buddhist Studies* (Calcutta: Minerva, 1979), 83–111.

56. Detailed Statement of Suttees or Hindoo Widows Who Were Burnt or Buried With Their Deceased Husbands, In the several Zillahs and Cities during the Year 1815, PP on Hindoo Widows, 1821, 18: 70.

57. Ibid., 74.

58. Detailed Statement of Suttees or Hindoo Widows Who Were Burnt or Buried With Their Deceased Husbands, In the several Zillahs and Cities during the Year 1816, PP on Hindoo Widows, 1821, 18: 90.

59. PP on Hindoo Widows, 1830, 28: 136.

60. PP on Hindoo Widows, 1828, 23: 21.

61. PP on Hindoo Widows, 1830, 28: 136.

62. Cohn, "The Command of Language and the Language of Command."

63. PP on Hindoo Widows, 1821, 18: 238.

64. Ibid., 116, 117.

65. Ibid., 116–117.

66. Ibid., 118.

67. Ibid., 130.

68. Ibid., 27.

69. PP on Hindoo Widows, 1830, 28: 124.

70. The representation of Indian women as caught in the grip of culture has a long and enduring history and persists today even in the liberatory rhetoric of much international feminism. See, for example, Chandra Talpade Mohanty, "Under Western Eyes: Feminist Scholarship and Colonial Discourses," *Feminist Review* (Autumn 1988): 60–88.

71. Roy, *Socioeconomic Impact of Sati in Bengal and the Role of Raja Rammohun Roy,* 48–49, 167.

72. PP on Hindoo Widows, 1821, 18: 110.

73. Ronald Inden, *Imagining India* (Oxford: Basil Blackwell, 1990), especially ch. 1.

74. PP on Hindoo Widows, 1821, 18: 112.

75. Ibid., 28.

76. Ibid.

77. Ibid., 29.

78. Ibid., 31.

79. This is an illustrative instance of how my own analysis diverges from Datta's in *Sati: Widow Burning in India.* While both of us have consulted the same official sources, Datta tends, in my view, to naturalize what I have described above as the social relations of knowledge production in the colonial context. Thus Datta concludes after describing this very encounter that East India Company "policy on suttee was formed in accordance with the advice tendered to the Court of Nizamat Adalat by Pundits, the guides and philosophers of the Hindus whose interpretations of Hindu religious texts convinced the government that the practice of suttee was 'founded on the religious notions of the Hindus and was expressly stated with approbation in their laws'" (25). This analysis does not consider the specific context and relations of power between East India Company officials and court pundits and as such is unable to document the emergence and institutionalization of a historically specific interpretive apparatus.

80. PP on Hindoo Widows, 1821, 18: 37–38.

81. Ibid., 114.

82. Ibid., 39–40.

83. Ibid., 40. The undermining of custom and customary law was not particular to *sati* but was a general feature of colonial rule and has been noted, among others, by Derrett, *Religion, Law and the State;* Rudolph and Rudolph, *The Modernity of Tradition;* Marc Galanter, "The Displacement of Traditional Law in Modern India," *Journal of Social Issues* 24 (1968): 65–91.

84. PP on Hindoo Widows, 1821, 18: 114.

85. Ibid., 111.

86. Ibid., 113.

87. Ibid.

88. Arvind Sharma, "Hinduism," in *Our Religions,* ed. Sharma (San Francisco: HarperCollins, 1993), 28.

89. Ibid., 26.

90. Sudipta Kaviraj, "The Myth of Praxis: The Construction of the Figure of Krishna in *Krishnacaritra,*" Occasional Papers on History and Society, 1st ser., no. 50 (New Delhi: Nehru Memorial Museum and Library, 1987).

91. Guha, "An Indian Historiography of India," 11.

92. Ricoeur's discussion of textualization is rooted in his analysis of what happens to discourse — speech — when it becomes textualized in language, action, or ritual. See Paul Ricoeur, "The Model of the Text: Meaningful Action Considered as a Text," *Social Research* 38, 3 (Fall 1971): 529–562.

93. The regressive consequences for women of the extension of high-caste

law have been analyzed, among others, by Lucy Carroll, "Law, Custom and Statutory Social Reform: The Hindu Widow's Remarriage Act of 1856," *Indian Economic and Social History Review* 20, 4 (1983): 363–89; Jana Everett, *Women and Social Change in India* (New Delhi: Heritage, 1981); Madhu Kishwar, "Toiling without Rights: Ho Women of Singhbum," 3 parts, *Economic and Political Weekly*, January 17, 1987, 95–101; January 24, 1987, 149–155; January 31, 1987, 194–200; Maria Mies, *Indian Women and Patriarchy: Conflicts and Dilemmas of Students and Working Women* (Delhi: Concept, 1980); Rosalind O'Hanlon, "Issues of Widowhood: Gender and Resistance in Colonial Western India," in *Contesting Power: Resistance and Everyday Social Relations in South Asia,* ed. Douglas Haynes and Gyan Prakash (Delhi: Oxford University Press, 1981), 62–108.

94. PP on Hindoo Widows, 1821, 18: 33.

95. PP on Hindoo Widows, 1823, 17: 29.

96. Foucault, *Discipline and Punish,* 78.

97. See, for example, the remarks of Nizamat Adalat judges on the returns for Jangal Mahals and Midnapur, in PP on Hindoo Widows, 1824, 23: 34.

98. Ibid., 44.

99. John Wolfe, *The Protestant Crusade in Great Britain, 1829–1860* (Oxford: Clarendon Press, 1991), 109–127.

100. See, for instance, Hjejle, "The Social Policy of the East India Company"; Stein, "Women to Burn"; Bayly, "From Ritual to Ceremony," 171–175; Giles H. R. Tillotson, "Sacrifice of an Hindoo Widow upon the Funeral Pile of Her Husband," in *An Illustrated History of Modern India, 1600–1947,* ed. C. A. Bayly (Delhi: Oxford University Press, 1990), 220.

101. Quoted in Javed Majeed, *Ungoverned Imaginings,* 134. See also Eric Stokes, *The English Utilitarians and India* (Oxford: Oxford University Press, 1959).

102. Singh, *Rammohun Roy,* vol. 3, 302.

## Chapter 2: Abstract Disquisitions

1. A. F. Salahuddin Ahmed, "The Bengal Renaissance and the Muslim Community," in *Reflections on the Bengal Renaissance,* ed. David Kopf and Safiuddin Joarder, (Rajshahi: Institute of Bangladesh Studies, 1977), 34.

2. Ramananda Chatterjee, *Rammohun Roy and Modern India* (Calcutta: Sadharan Brahmo Samaj, 1918), 6.

3. This is the case even with A. F. Salahuddin Ahmed who has otherwise argued the importance of attending to the shared class basis and social formation of *bhadralok.* See his *Social Ideas and Social Change in Bengal, 1818–1835* (Leiden: Brill, 1965), ch. 2.

4. S. N. Mukherjee, "Class, Caste and Politics in Calcutta, 1815–1838," in *Elites in South Asia,* ed. Edmund Leach and S. N. Mukherjee (Cambridge: Cambridge University Press, 1970), 33–78; Pradip Sinha, *Calcutta in Urban History* (Calcutta: Firma KLM, 1978), 62–85.

5. Ranajit Guha, *A Rule of Property for Bengal: An Essay on the Idea of Permanent Settlement* (Paris: Mouton, 1963).

6. There is a vast literature on the impact of colonial rule on tenurial structures and agrarian relations. Some idea of key issues may be gained from the following: N. K. Sinha, *The Economic History of Bengal*, vols. 2 and 3 (Calcutta: Firma K. L. Mukhopadhyay, 1962); Ratnalekha Ray, *Change in Bengal Agrarian Society, c. 1760–1850* (Delhi: Manohar, 1979); Dharma Kumar, ed., *The Cambridge Economic History of India*, vol. 2 (Cambridge: Cambridge University Press, 1983); David Washbrook, "Progress and Problems: South Asian Economic and Social History, c. 1720–1860," *Modern Asian Studies* 22, 1 (1988): 57–96; for Bihar, see Gyan Prakash, *Bonded Histories: Genealogies of Labor Servitude in Colonial India* (Cambridge: Cambridge University Press, 1990), especially ch. 3.

7. See the essays in V. C. Joshi, ed., *Rammohun Roy and the Process of Modernization in India* (New Delhi: Vikas, 1975), especially those by Rajat K. Ray, Sumit Sarkar, Asok Sen, and Barun De.

8. S. N. Mukherjee argues that there is no evidence prior to 1799 of *bhadralok* as a term designating a social group and that its use in this manner became common only after 1815. For a history of the word, see his "Bhadralok in Bengali Language and Literature," *Bengal Past and Present* 95 (July–December 1976): 181, 225–237.

9. This thesis was first proposed by A. K. Bagchi, "De-Industrialization in India in the Nineteenth Century: Some Theoretical Implications," *Journal of Development Studies* 12 (1975–76): 135–164.

10. Ranajit Guha, *An Indian Historiography of India: A Nineteenth-Century Agenda and Its Implications* (Calcutta: Centre for Studies in Social Sciences, 1987); Sudipta Kaviraj, "Imaginary History," Occasional Papers on History and Society, 2d ser., no. 7 (New Delhi: Nehru Memorial Museum and Library, September 1988).

11. Rajat K. Ray, "Introduction," in *Rammohun Roy and the Process of Modernization in India*, 19.

12. Sumit Sarkar, "The Radicalism of Intellectuals," in his *A Critique of Colonial India* (Calcutta: Papyrus, 1985), 65.

13. Hiren Mukherjee, *Indian Renaissance and Raja Rammohun Roy* (Poona: University of Poona, 1975), 39.

14. Ahmed, *Social Ideas and Social Change in Bengal*, 26–51; Ray, "Introduction," 16–17; Sumit Sarkar, "The Complexities of Young Bengal," in *A Critique of Colonial India*, 18–36; Krishna Kriplani, *Dwarkanath Tagore, A Forgotten Pioneer: A Life* (Delhi: National Book Trust, 1980), ch. 4; Mukherjee, "Class, Caste and Politics in Calcutta," 67–69.

15. Rammohun's interest in *sati* is said to have been kindled by the death through immolation of his sister-in-law in 1812. See editors' notes, Sophia Dobson Collet, *The Life and Letters of Raja Rammohun Roy*, ed. D. K. Biswas and P. C. Ganguli (Calcutta: Sadharan Brahmo Samaj, 1962), 106. According to Collet, Rammohun also formed a vigilance committee to intercede in cases of widow burning. Ibid., 89.

16. S. N. Mukherjee has argued that divisions between Calcutta *bhadralok* are also attributable to their affiliation to different dals, multicaste factions that arbitrated caste disputes, brokered marriages, and so on. Mukherjee, "Class, Caste and Politics in Calcutta," 33–78; "Bhadralok and Their Dals—Policies of Social Factions, 1820–1856," in *The Urban Experience: Calcutta*, ed. Pradip Sinha

(Calcutta: Riddhi-India, 1987), 39–58. See also Pradip Sinha, *Calcutta in Urban History,* 86–108, for continuities and discontinuities in the forms of social organization in early-nineteenth-century Calcutta.

17. Bengali-language papers *Samachar Darpan* and *Bengal Gazette* both began publication in 1818. The former was published by the Serampore Baptists and the latter by Harachandra Roy. See Ahmed, *Social Ideas and Social Change in Bengal,* chs. 2 and 3, for the history of the press in this period.

18. Rammohun Roy, "Translation of a Conference between an Advocate for and an Opponent of the Practice of Burning Widows Alive" (1818), in *The English Works of Rammohun Roy,* ed. J. C. Ghose (New Delhi: Cosmo Publications, 1982), vol. 2, 321–332. For Hariharananda's letter and the anti-*sati* petition to counter that of the pro-*sati* petitioners to the marquis of Hastings, governor-general in council of the East India Company, see *Raja Rammohun Roy and Progressive Movements in India: A Selection from Records, 1775–1845,* ed. J. K. Majumdar (Calcutta: Art Press, 1941), 112–117. It has been suggested that Hariharananda did not know English and that the letter was probably penned by Rammohun. See editors' notes, Collet, *The Life and Letters of Raja Rammohun Roy,* 102. For other accounts of Rammohun Roy's campaign against *sati,* see Collet, ibid., 76–95, 105–107; Iqbal Singh, *Rammohun Roy: A Biographical Inquiry into the Making of Modern India* (Bombay: Asia Publishing House, 1958), vol. 1, 187–215; Benoy Bhusan Roy, *Socioeconomic Impact of Sati in Bengal and the Role of Raja Rammohun Roy* (Calcutta: Naya Prokash, 1987), 81–125; V. N. Datta, *Sati : Widow Burning in India* (Riverdale, Md.: Riverdale, 1988), 119–135.

19. Rammohun Roy, "Abstract of the arguments regarding the burning of widows considered as a religious rite" (1830), in *English Works,* vol. 2, 365–372 (hereafter "Abstract"). Further references to this work will be included in the text; emphasis is in the original unless otherwise indicated.

20. "The Petition of the orthodox Hindu community of Calcutta against the Suttee Regulation, together with a Paper of Authorities, and the Reply of the Governor-General thereto" (January 14, 1830), in *Raja Rammohun Roy and Progressive Movements in India,* 156–163.

21. For further discussion of the politics of interpretation of *Rg Vedic* fragments in relation to *sati,* see Gayatri Chakravorty Spivak, "Can the Subaltern Speak?" in *Marxism and the Interpretation of Culture,* ed. Cary Nelson and Lawrence Grossberg (Urbana: University of Illinois Press, 1988), 303–304.

22. "The Petition of the orthodox Hindu community of Calcutta against the Suttee Regulation," 156–163. Further references to this petition will be included in the text; emphasis is in the original unless otherwise indicated.

23. Roy, "Abstract," 372.

24. Rammohun's first published response to criticism of his stand on idolatry was "A Defence of Hindoo Theism in Reply to an Attack of an Advocate for Idolatry at Madras" (1817), in *English Works,* vol. 1, 87–100. Vidyalankar's critique of Rammohun's anti-idolatry stance had been elaborated in his *Vedanta Chandrika, Mrityunjay Granthavali,* Calcutta, BS 1346, 193–213. Rammohun's critical riposte was published as "A Second Defence of the Monotheistical System of the Veds, in Reply to an Apology for the Present State of Hindoo

Worship" (1817), in *English Works*, vol. 1, 101–126. For discussions of this controversy, see Singh, *Rammohun Roy*, vol. 1, 136–146; A. K. Ray provides an overview of the controversies generated by Rammohun's publications in *The Religious Ideas of Rammohun Roy* (New Delhi: Kanak Publications, 1976), 31–42.

25. Singh, *Rammohun Roy*, vol. 1, 137–138.

26. Roy, "Translation of a Conference between an Advocate for and an Opponent of the Practice of Burning Widows Alive," 321–332. Rammohun's second tract was published in Bengali toward the end of 1819 and in English in early 1820. "A Second Conference between an Advocate for, and an Opponent of the Practice of Burning Widows Alive," in *English Works*, vol. 2, 333–363.

27. Tarkavagish's pamphlet was extensively excerpted along with a critical commentary in "Review of a pamphlet on the subject of burning Widows. Written in Bengalee by a learned Pundit; to which is added an English translation," *Friend of India*, monthly, October 1819, 453–484.

28. Ibid., 466.

29. Ibid., 465.

30. Roy, "A Second Conference between an Advocate for, and an Opponent of the Practice of Burning Widows Alive," 345.

31. Rammohun Roy, "Translation of an Abridgement of the Vedant" (1816), in *English Works*, vol. 1, 4.

32. Roy, "A Second Conference between an Advocate for, and an Opponent of the Practice of Burning Widows Alive," 360.

33. Singh, *Rammohun Roy*, vol. 1, 206.

34. "The counter-petition of some Hindoo inhabitants of Calcutta re: Suttee orders of Government," *Asiatic Journal*, July 1819, in *Raja Rammohun Roy and Progressive Movements in India*, 115. Further references to this document will be included in the text.

35. "Address to Lord William Bentinck" (January 16, 1830), in *English Works*, vol. 2, 475–477.

36. Ibid., 475.

37. Ibid., 475.

38. Ibid., 476.

39. Rammohun Roy, "Brief Remarks regarding Modern Encroachments on the Ancient Rights of Females according to the Hindu Law of Inheritance" (1822), in *The English Works of Raja Rammohun Roy*, ed. K. Nag and D. Burman (Calcutta: Sadharan Brahmo Samaj, 1945), pt. 1, 1–9.

40. Ibid., 4.

41. See "A pamphlet of Rammohun Roy containing some remarks in vindication of the Resolution passed by the Government of Bengal in 1829 abolishing the practice of female sacrifices in India" (1831), in *Raja Rammohun Roy and Progressive Movements in India*, 186–187.

42. See, for instance, Ashis Nandy, "Sati: A Nineteenth-Century Tale of Women, Violence and Protest," in *Rammohun Roy and the Process of Modernization in India*, 172–173; Roy, *Socioeconomic Impact of Sati in Bengal and the Role of Raja Rammohun Roy*, 39–40, 72–78; Datta, *Sati: Widow Burning in India*, 189–206.

43. PP on Hindoo Widows, 1821, 18: 243.

44. Brajendranath Bandhopadhyay, *Bangla Samayik Patra* (Calcutta: Bangiya Sahitya Parishad, BS 1384, 1948), vol. 1, 5–11.

45. Brajendranath Bandhopadhyay, *Sambadpatra Sekaler Katha*, 2 vols. (Calcutta: Bangiya Sahitya Parishad, 1949–50).

46. *Samachar Darpan,* July 7, 1821, in *Sambadpatra Sekaler Katha,* vol. 1, 250.

47. *Sambad Kaumudi,* May 22, 1824, in *Bengal Hurkaru,* May 29, 1824, 2.

48. *Samachar Chundrika,* July 30, 1825, in *Bengal Hurkaru,* August 10, 1825, 2.

49. *Samachar Darpan,* October 22, 1825, in *Bengal Hurkaru,* October 25, 1825, 2.

50. *Sambad Kaumudi,* October 8, 1825, in *Bengal Hurkaru,* October 10, 1825, 2.

51. *Samachar Chundrika,* June 12, 1826, in *Bengal Hurkaru,* June 15, 1826, 2.

52. *Samachar Chundrika,* August 22, 1825, in *Bengal Hurkaru,* August 29, 1825, 2.

53. *Sambad Kaumudi,* March 15, 1828, in *John Bull,* April 5, 1828, in *Raja Rammohun Roy and Progressive Movements in India,* 131.

54. *Samachar Darpan,* May 1, 1822, August 2, 1823, in *Sambadpatra Sekaler Katha,* vol. 1, 41–42, 253.

55. Letter to the editor, *Samachar Chundrika,* March 10, 1822, in *Calcutta Journal,* March 18, 1822, in *Raja Rammohun Roy and Progressive Movements in India,* 124.

56. Letter to the editor, *Samachar Chundrika,* March 18, 1822, in *Calcutta Journal,* June 25, 1822, in *Raja Rammohun Roy and Progressive Movements in India,* 125.

57. Letter to the editor, *Samachar Chundrika,* May 25, 1822, in *Calcutta Journal,* March 18, 1822, in *Raja Rammohun Roy and Progressive Movements in India,* 125.

58. *Samachar· Chundrika,* in *Samachar Darpan* August 8, 1829, in *Raja Rammohun Roy and Progressive Movements in India,* 256.

59. *Samachar Chundrika,* November 26, 1829, in *Bengal Hurkaru,* December 7, 1829, 2. See also *Bengal Hurkaru,* December 1, 1829, December 8, 1829, and January 5, 1830, for exchanges between *Chundrika* and *Darpan.*

60. *Samachar Chundrika,* November 19, 1829, in *Bengal Hurkaru,* December 1, 1829, 2.

61. Letter to the editor, *Bengal Hurkaru,* December 14, 1829, 2. See also *Bengal Herald,* December 27, 1829, for a report of prevented burning.

62. See, for instance, *Sambad Kaumudi,* August 2, 1830, in *Bengal Hurkaru,* August 17, 1830, 2; *Samachar Darpan,* in *Bengal Hurkaru,* August 30, 1830, 2–3; *Samachar Chundrika, Sambad Kaumudi,* and *Samachar Darpan,* in *Bengal Hurkaru,* September 6, 1830, 2; for *Samachar Chundrika*'s report of the miraculous death of a widow prevented from burning, see *Bengal Hurkaru,* December 27, 1830, 2.

63. *Sambad Kaumudi,* October 15, 1830, in *Bengal Hurkaru,* October 25, 1830, 2.

64. See, for instance, *Sambad Kaumudi,* in *Bengal Hurkaru,* November 1, 1830; *Sambad Kaumudi,* quoted in *Calcutta Monthly Journal,* January 1831, in

*Raja Rammohun Roy and Progressive Movements in India*, 181–182; letter to the editor, *Sambad Kaumudi*, in *Bengal Hurkaru*, April 25, 1831, 3.

65. Although the economic status of individual court pundits varied, none-theless their respectable social standing warrants their inclusion as a group in the category of *bhadralok*.

66. *Bengal Hurkaru*, December 24, 1822, 2; and *Bengal Hurkaru*, December 25, 1822, 2.

67. Sumit Sarkar, "Raja Rammohun Roy and the Break with the Past," in *Rammohun Roy and the Process of Modernization in India*, 46–68. See also Rammohun Roy, *Tuhfutul Muwahiddin*, trans. Obaidullah El Obaide (Dacca, 1883), in Kissory Chand Mitter and Rammohun Roy, *Rammohun Roy and Tuhfatul Muwahiddin* (Calcutta: K. P. Bagchi, 1975); Ray, *The Religious Ideas of Rammohun Roy*, 20–27.

68. Sarkar, "Rammohun Roy and the Break with the Past, 50.

69. Ibid., 50.

70. Ibid., 53–54.

71. See editors' notes in Collet, *The Life and Letters of Raja Rammohun Roy*, 37–41, 42.

72. Rajat K. Ray, "Introduction," 7.

73. "The Petition of the orthodox Hindu community of Calcutta against the Suttee Regulation," 162.

74. Ibid., 163.

75. "A pamphlet of Rammohun Roy containing some remarks in vindication of the Resolution passed by the Government of Bengal in 1829 abolishing the practice of female sacrifices in India," 188.

76. See, for instance, his "A Defence of Hindoo Theism in Reply to an Attack of an Advocate for Idolatry at Madras," 90–91.

77. Bentinck notes that Rammohun was apprehensive lest people view prohibition as the first of many religious infringements. "Lord William Bentinck's Minute on Suttee," in *Raja Rammohun Roy and Progressive Movements in India*, 142. On this point, see Datta, *Sati: Widow Burning in India*, 128–132, who argues that Rammohun was ultimately a moderate and became an accessory to abolition only after the fact.

78. "Address to Lord William Bentinck" (January 16, 1830), in *English Works*, vol. 2, 477.

79. "A pamphlet of Rammohun Roy containing some remarks in vindication of the Resolution passed by the Government of Bengal in 1829 abolishing the practice of female sacrifices in India," 189.

80. For a discussion of Rammohun's arguments against Trinitarianism, see Singh, *Rammohun Roy*, vol. 1, 216–274; Collet, *The Life and Letters of Raja Rammohun Roy*, 100–166; Ray, *The Religious Ideas of Rammohun Roy*, 46–51.

81. *Asiatic Journal*, June 1830, in *Raja Rammohun Roy and Progressive Movements in India*, 172.

82. In this respect it is interesting, as Sumit Sarkar notes, how Rammohun's painstaking detailing of the merits of ascetic widowhood was to complicate Vidyasagar's case for widow remarriage! Sarkar, "Raja Rammohun Roy and the Break with the Past," in *Rammohun Roy and the Process of Modernization in India*, 53.

83. Roy, "Translation of a Conference between an Advocate for and an Opponent of the Practice of Burning Widows Alive," 331.

84. Ibid., 331.

85. Ibid., 332.

86. Roy, "A Second Conference between an Advocate for, and an Opponent of the Practice of Burning Widows Alive," 359–363; Collet, *The Life and Letters of Raja Rammohun Roy,* 92; Singh, *Rammohun Roy,* vol. 1, 205–209.

87. "Review of a Pamphlet on the subject of burning Widows," *Friend of India,* monthly, October 1819, 465–466.

88. Roy, "A Second Conference between an Advocate for, and an Opponent of the Practice of Burning Widows Alive," 361.

89. Ibid., 361.

90. Ibid., 361.

91. Ibid., 360.

92. Ibid., 360.

93. "Lord William Bentinck's Minute on Suttee," in *Raja Rammohun Roy and Progressive Movements in India,* 139.

94. Ibid., 148.

95. See, for instance, "Bedfordshire Petition against the Burning of Hindoo Widows," presented to the House of Commons in 1823, reprinted in *Missionary Register,* June 1853, 250–251; for a similar petition drawn up in a public meeting in Coventry in February 1829, see "Meeting for the Abolition of the Burning of Women in India," *Oriental Herald,* March 1829, 543–545.

96. I use the term "classical" as formulated by Sudipta Kaviraj in "The Myth of Praxis: The Construction of the Figure of Krishna in *Krishnacaritra,*" Occasional Papers on History and Society, 1st ser., no. 50 (New Delhi: Nehru Memorial Museum and Library, 1987). According to Kaviraj, classicization moves an object toward its ideal form, making it conceptual and nonempirical and stressing its non-historically indexed features (80 and passim).

97. For an excellent analysis of the ambivalent attitudes toward women of social reformers active in the debate on widow remarriage, see Sudhir Chandra, "Conflicted Beliefs and Men's Consciousness about Women: Widow Remarriage in Later Nineteenth-Century Indian Literature," *Economic and Political Weekly, Review of Women's Studies,* October 31, 1987, 55–62.

98. The phrase "colonial rearticulations of gender" is Susie Tharu and K. Lalita's and is taken from their edited collection, *Women Writing in India: 600 B.C. to the Present,* vol. 1, *600 B.C. to the Early Twentieth Century* (New York: The Feminist Press, 1991), 154.

99. The following are some key texts in this burgeoning field: Kumkum Sangari and Sudesh Vaid, eds., *Recasting Women: Essays in Colonial History* (New Delhi: Kali, 1989); Susie Tharu and K. Lalita, eds., *Women Writing in India,* ibid.; Sujata Patel, "The Construction and Reconstruction of Women in Gandhi," *Economic and Political Weekly,* February 20, 1988, 377–387; Tanika Sarkar, "Bankimchandra and the Impossibility of a Political Agenda: A Predicament for Nineteenth-Century Bengal," Occasional Papers on History and Society, 2d ser., no. 40 (New Delhi: Nehru Memorial Museum and Library, July 1991); Gyanendra Pandey, *The Construction of Communalism in Colonial North India* (Delhi: Oxford University Press, 1992); Sudipta Kaviraj, "The Myth

of Praxis: The Construction of the Figure of Krishna in *Krishnacaritra*"; and "Humour and the Prison of Reality: Kamala Kanta as the Secret Autobiography of Bankimchandra Chattopadhyay," Occasional Papers on History and Society, 2d ser., no. 4, July 1988; *Subaltern Studies I–VI,* ed. Ranajit Guha, (Delhi: Oxford University Press, 1982–89).

100. Sangari and Vaid, *Recasting Women,* 1–26; Tharu and Lalita, *Women Writing in India;* Sumanta Banerjee, *The Parlour and the Streets: Elite and Popular Culture in Nineteenth-Century Calcutta* (Calcutta: Seagull, 1989); Prem Chowdhry, "Customs in a Peasant Economy: Women in Colonial Haryana," in *Recasting Women,* 302–336.

101. Rosalind O'Hanlon, "Issues of Widowhood: Gender and Resistance in Western India," in *Contesting Power: Resistance and Everyday Social Relations in South Asia,* ed. Douglas Haynes and Gyan Prakash (Delhi: Oxford University Press, 1991), 62–108.

102. Tharu and Lalita, *Women Writing in India;* Malavika Karlekar, *Voices from Within: Early Personal Narratives of Bengali Women* (Delhi: Oxford University Press, 1991).

103. See, for example, Mokshodayani Mukhopadhyay, "Bangalir Babu," in *Women Writing in India,* 219–221; Tarabai Shinde, "Stri Purush Tulana," in *Women Writing in India,* 223–235. For a critical analysis of Tarabai Shinde, see O'Hanlon, "Issues of Widowhood," 89–104.


## Chapter 3: Missionaries and Subalterns

1. John Thomas, "Narrative of Himself and his Labours," *Periodical Accounts Relative to the Baptist Missionary Society* 1, no. 1, 1800, 18–19.

2. William Ward, Journal, October 31, 1802, Baptist Missionary Society (BMS) Archives, London.

3. Other evangelists included Nathaniel Forsythe of the London Missionary Society and the Anglican Chaplains Claudius Buchanan and David Brown appointed by the East India Company to minister to the needs of its Christian employees. Relations between different protestant groups were cordial except for periodic tensions; see Potts, *British Baptist Missionaries in Bengal, 1793–1837* (Cambridge: Cambridge University Press, 1967), 54–57. The same is not true of the relationship between Baptists and Catholics, but the latter were not present in any sizable number in Bengal. S. Neill, *A History of Christianity in India, 1707–1858,* Cambridge: Cambridge University Press, 1985 and Kenneth Ingham, *Reformers in India, 1793–1833,* Cambridge: Cambridge University Press, 1956, provide general accounts of the situation in this period.

4. William Carey, *An Enquiry into the Obligation of Christians, to use means for the Conversion of Heathens in which the Religious State of Different Nations of the World, the Success of Former Undertakings, and the Practicability of Further Undertakings, are Considered,* Leicester, 1792. For a discussion of the establishment of the British Missionary Society and the problems encountered by its founders, J. C. Marshman, *The Life and Times of Carey, Marshman and Ward: Embracing the History of the Serampore Mission* (London: Longman, Brown,

Green, Longmans and Roberts, 1859), vol. 1, 9–19; Potts, *British Baptist Missionaries in Bengal*, is the most scholarly monograph on the Serampore Baptists. It attempts to evaluate their efforts, unlike Marshman or S. P. Carey, *William Carey*, Philadelphia, 1923, which take missionary claims at face value.

5. Marshman, *The Life and Times of Carey, Marshman and Ward*, 112–124.

6. For Carey's activities in India before the establishment of the Serampore mission, see Potts, *British Baptist Missionaries in Bengal*, 13–17.

7. Ranajit Guha defines as subaltern all those who do not constitute the elite (whether foreign or indigenous). This deliberately broad definition is appropriate to my purpose here, for although the exact social composition of street congregations is hard to specify, the listeners were rarely members of the elite. "On Some Aspects of the Historiography of Colonial India," *Subaltern Studies I* (Delhi: Oxford University Press, 1982), 8.

8. Potts, *British Baptist Missionaries in Bengal*, ch. 8.

9. David Kopf, *British Orientalism and the Bengal Renaissance: The Dynamics of Indian Modernization, 1773–1835* (Berkeley: University of California Press, 1969).

10. Ibid., 67–80.

11. The division of labor at the mission reflects their occupations prior to their departure for Bengal. Ward had been a printer in Coventry and Marshman a school master in Bristol.

12. Marshman to Dr. Ryland, n.d., BMS Archive. The letter was received in 1805 which suggests that it must have been written in 1804.

13. Marshman, Journal, March 28, 1805, BMS Archive.

14. Carey to Andrew Fuller, journal entry for October 21, 1800, in letter dated November 23, 1800, BMS Archive.

15. Ward, Journal, November 2, 1801, BMS Archive.

16. Ibid., May 11, 1800.

17. Carey to the Church at Leicester, December 16, 1793, *Periodical Accounts* 1, no. 1, 1800, 68. "Heathen" and "pagan" are terms frequently used to describe Hindus.

18. Ibid., 68.

19. Ibid., 67.

20. Carey to the BMS, January 6, 1795, *Periodical Accounts* 1, no. 1, 1800, 121.

21. Ward, Journal, November 15, 1800, BMS Archive.

22. Carey to Andrew Fuller, journal entry for November 2, 1800, in letter dated November 23, 1800, BMS Archive.

23. Carey to the Church in Harvey Lane, Leicester, February 5, 1795, *Periodical Accounts* 1, no. 2, 1800, 133.

24. Marshman, Journal, August 11–22, 1804, BMS Archive.

25. Carey to [Andrew] F[uller], January 30, 1795, *Periodical Accounts* 1, no. 2, 1800, 131–132. "Vyakaran" were grammar texts. They were a central part of the curriculum of village schools.

26. Carey, Journal, January 19, 1794, BMS Archive.

27. Extracts from Mr. Carey's Journal, January 25, 1795, *Periodical Accounts* 1, no. 3, 1800, 191.

28. Carey to [Andrew] F[uller], January 30, 1795, *Periodical Accounts* 1, no. 2, 1800, 129–130.

29. Ward, Journal, January 26, 1800, BMS Archive.

30. Ward, Journal, February 2, 1800, BMS Archive.

31. Carey, Journal, October 13, 1794, BMS Archive.

32. Carey to R. B[——, of Leicester], March 12, 1795, *Periodical Accounts* 1, no. 2, 1800, 137. Note also the use of phrases like "imperceptibly adopted" and "imaginary cast," which eliminate indigenous subjectivity and resist the notion of religion as negotiated social activity. This particular construction of the colonial subject as passively reproducing religion / tradition will be further discussed in chapter 5.

33. Carey to Mr. S(utcliff, Olney), January 16, 1798, *Periodical Accounts* 1, no. 5, 1800, 404.

34. Carey to the BMS, January 6, 1795, *Periodical Accounts* 1, no. 2, 1800, 121.

35. "Answers to Various Questions Put to Mr. Carey by the BMS," n.d., *Periodical Accounts* 1, no. 5, 1800, 411–412.

36. Ward, Journal, November 12, 1802, BMS Archive. Kali Yug refers to the contemporary period, which according to Hinduism is the age of materialism and of destruction.

37. Ward, Journal, August 9, 1801, BMS Archive.

38. Carey to [Andrew] F[uller], January 30, 1795, *Periodical Accounts* 1, no. 2, 1800, 132.

39. Marshman to his father, August 17, 1800, BMS Archive.

40. Carey to Mr. P[ of Birmingham], November 28, 1798, *Periodical Accounts* 1, no. 6, 1800, 484.

41. Carey to Mr. M [of Clipstone], September 23, 1798, *Periodical Accounts* 1, no. 6, 1800, 469.

42. Ward, Journal, June 17, 1802, BMS Archive.

43. Ibid., April 2, 1804.

44. Ibid., February 16, 1803.

45. Ibid., January 22, 1803.

46. Carey to J. Sutcliffe, journal entry for December 23, 1800, in letter dated December 29, 1800, BMS Archive.

47. Ward, Journal, October 20, 1805, BMS Archive.

48. John Wolfe, *The Protestant Crusade in Great Britain, 1829–1860,* Oxford: Clarendon Press, 1991, 109–127.

49. Carey to J. Sutcliffe, journal entry for December 23, 1800, in letter dated December 29, 1800, BMS Archive.

50. Ward, Journal, October 24, 1800, BMS Archive.

51. Ward, Journal, December 30, 1804, BMS Archive.

52. Edward Said, *Orientalism,* New York: Vintage, 1979, 7.

53. Carey to his sister, December 22, 1796, *Periodical Accounts* 1, no. 4, 1800, 344–345.

54. Carey to Mr. P [of Birmingham], June 1, 1797, *Periodical Accounts* 1, no. 5, 1800, 371–372.

55. Ward, Journal, June 1, 1800, BMS Archive.

56. Ibid., April 27, 1800.

57. Ibid., May 25, 1800.

58. Carey to the Church in Harvey Lane, February 5, 1795, *Periodical Accounts* 1, no. 2, 1800, 133.

59. Ward, Journal, October 18, 1801, BMS Archive.

60. Memorial to Lord Minto, Governor-General of India, September 30, 1807, signed by William Carey, Joshua Marshman, William Ward, William Moore, Joshua Rowe, Felix Carey, House of Commons, Parliamentary Papers, 1812–13, vol. 8, 337.

61. Carey to J. Sutcliffe, journal entry for December 18, 1800, in letter dated December 29, 1800, BMS Archive.

62. Ward, Journal, March 22, 1801, October 4, 1801, BMS Archive. The interlocutor is in the latter incident referring to the deaths of Fountain, Grant, and Brunsdon all of whom, as noted earlier, died soon after the establishment of the Serampore Mission.

63. Ward, Journal, June 23, 1804, BMS Archive.

64. Extracts from Mr. Carey's Journal, January 25, 1795, *Periodical Accounts* 1, no. 3, 1800, 191.

65. Carey to Mr. P.[, Leicester] January 2, 1797, *Periodical Accounts* 1, no. 4, 1800, 355.

66. Carey to [Andrew] F[uller], June 22, 1797, *Periodical Accounts* 1, no. 5, 1800, 376.

67. Carey, Journal, February 22, 1795, BMS Archive.

68. Carey to Mr. P[of Leicester], January 2, 1797, *Periodical Accounts* 1, no. 4, 1800, 355–356.

69. Ward, Journal, May 30, 1800, BMS Archive.

70. Ibid., August 26, 1800.

71. Carey to Mr S[utcliff of Olney], November 22, 1796, *Periodical Account* 1, no. 4, 1800, 330.

72. Ward, Journal, March 15, 1801, BMS Archive.

73. Ibid., October 2, 1801.

74. Ibid., November 26, 1803.

75. Kalikinkar Datta, *Survey of India's Social Life and Economic Condition in the Eighteenth Century, 1707–1813* (New Delhi: Mushiram Manoharlal, 1978), 19–33.

76. Sumanta Banerjee, *The Parlour and the Streets: Elite and Popular Culture in Nineteenth-Century Calcutta* (Calcutta: Seagull, 1989), 83.

77. Kalikinkar Datta, *Studies in the History of the Bengal Subah, 1740–1770* (Calcutta: Calcutta University Press, 1936), vol. 1, 92–106.

78. Ward, Journal, October 18, 1802, BMS Archive.

79. Ibid., May 27, 1802.

80. Marshman, Journal, March 11, 1803, BMS Archive.

81. Ibid., May 13, 1803.

82. Sumit Sarkar, *Bibliographical Survey of Social Reform Movements in the Eighteenth and Nineteenth Centuries* (New Delhi: Indian Council of Historical Research, 1975), 6–7.

83. Ranajit Guha, *Elementary Aspects of Peasant Insurgency in Colonial India* (Delhi: Oxford University Press, 1983); see, for example, the introduction.

84. Dharampal, *The Beautiful Tree: Indigenous Education in the Eighteenth Century* (New Delhi: Biblia Impex, 1983), 49. For a survey of education in the eighteenth century, see Kalikinkar Datta, *Studies in the History of the Bengal*

*Subah*, vol. 1, 1–28; and his *Survey of India's Social Life and Economic Condition in the Eighteenth Century, 1707–1813*, 34–50.

85. Ranajit Guha, *Elementary Aspects of Peasant Insurgency in Colonial India*, especially ch. 7.

## Chapter 4: Traveling Texts

1. Edward Said, *Orientalism* (New York: Vintage, 1979), 20.

2. The publication history of Ward's *Hindoos* is complex and difficult to reconstruct. The *National Union Catalogue Pre-1956 Imprints*, vol. 648, 357–358, notes the publication in Britain during Ward's lifetime of three two-volume editions of his text, in 1816, 1817, and 1818, and two four-volume editions, one published between 1817 and 1820 and another in 1821. The 1822 edition used here was also published in Britain but in three volumes. The 1816 edition claims to be a third edition, which suggests a second edition between 1811 and 1816. An extract from Ward's *Hindoos* appeared as a tract in 1813 in London. A U.S. edition of Ward's work appeared in 1824 and selections from Ward's text had been published by Thomas Robbins in *All Religions and Religious Ceremonies*, Hartford, 1823. The *National Union Catalogue* also notes a posthumous edition published in India in 1863. The titles of the different editions vary slightly and it is unclear whether the *National Union Catalogue* information is complete. It is entirely likely that differences similar to those found in contrasting the 1811 and 1822 editions may also be evident in comparing the intervening editions with each other and with those examined here. However, the general argument being advanced here, of a shift in missionary discourse in the course of the second decade of the nineteenth century, is well served by comparing the first with the last edition published before Ward's death and does not require analysis of each intervening edition.

3. This includes James Mill, *The History of British India*, 3 vols. (1817; reprint of 2nd ed., New Delhi: Associated Publishing House, 1972), a work that Ronald Inden has dubbed a hegemonic text within Indology, in *Imagining India* (Oxford: Basil Blackwell, 1990), 44–45. Mill's *History* cites the 1817 London edition of *Hindoos*. The way Ward is footnoted suggests that Mill probably had access to *Hindoos* only toward the completion of his work. For the influence of Ward and the Serampore Baptists on Mill, see Javed Majeed, *Ungoverned Imaginings: James Mill's* The History of British India *and Orientalism* (Oxford: Clarendon Press, 1992), 180–181.

4. Mary Louise Pratt, "Scratches on the Face of the Country; or What Mr. Barrow Saw in the Land of the Bushmen," in *"Race," Writing and Difference*, ed. Henry Louis Gates, special issue of *Critical Inquiry* 12, 1 (Fall 1985): 125.

5. Ward to Andrew Fuller, January 12, 1809, *Periodical Accounts Relative to the Baptist Missionary Society* 4, no. 19, 559.

6. Ward, Journal, March 16, 1802, BMS Archive.

7. Ibid., December 5, 1803.

8. Ibid., February 9, 1806.

9. Ibid., March 9, 1806.

10. Ibid., March 22, 1806.

11. Ibid., March 25, 1806.

12. Ibid., September 24, 1806.

13. Ibid., June 1, 1807.

14. Ibid., December 6, 1810.

15. Ibid., January 8, 1811.

16. Ibid., March 17, 1811.

17. Hayden White, "The Context in Text: Method and Ideology in Intellectual History," in White, *The Content of the Form* (Baltimore: Johns Hopkins University Press, 1987).

18. David Kopf, *British Orientalism and the Bengal Renaissance: The Dynamics of Indian Modernization, 1773–1835* (Berkeley: University of California Press, 1969).

19. S. K. Das, *Sahibs and Munshis* (Calcutta: Orion, 1978). See also B. S. Cohn, "The Command of Language and the Language of Command," *Subaltern Studies IV*, ed. Ranajit Guha (Delhi: Oxford University Press, 1985), 276–329.

20. M. A. Qayyum, *A Critical Study of Bengali Grammars: Halhed to Haughton* (Dhaka: The Asiatic Society of Bangladesh, 1982).

21. Ward, Journal, September 16, 1805, BMS Archive.

22. Das, *Sahibs and Munshis.*

23. Qayyum, *A Critical Study of Bengali Grammars,* especially chs. 3, 4.

24. For a description of this process, see Ward's letter to a friend in Edinburgh May 10, 1820, reprinted in *Baptist Magazine,* July 1820, 290–292.

25. This presumption was, as Said has argued, a defining feature of orientalist discourses; see, for instance, Said, *Orientalism,* 5–9, 40–41.

26. See the portrait by Robert Home, "William Carey and a Pandit," 1811, frontispiece to *Serampore Letters,* ed. Leighton and Mornay Williams (New York: G. P. Putnam's Sons, 1892). The pundit has been identified as Mrityunjay Vidyalankar in C. A. Bayly, ed., *An Illustrated History of Modern India, 1600–1947* (Delhi: Oxford University Press, 1991), 218.

27. Rosaldo makes this point in his analysis of Evans-Pritchard's classic monograph on the Nuer. See "From the Door of His Tent: The Fieldworker and the Inquisitor," in *Writing Culture: The Poetics and Politics of Ethnography,* ed. James Clifford and George Marcus (Berkeley: University of California Press, 1986), 89. The effacement of the "I" of the ethnographer has been critically analyzed by many critics of the rhetorical conventions of ethnography. See, for instance, James Clifford, "On Ethnographic Authority," in Clifford, *The Predicament of Culture* (Berkeley: University of California Press, 1988), 21–54, especially 38–44.

28. Homi Bhabha has argued that the colonial subject is invariably conceived as unsuccessfully mimicking a European original, in "Of Mimicry and Man: The Ambivalence of Colonial Discourse," *October* 28 (Spring 1984): 125–133. Ward's description of contemporary India, by contrast, represents it as a mimicry of its own past.

29. Charles Grant, "Observations on the State of Society among the Asiatic Subjects of Great Britain, particularly with respect to Morals, and on the Means of Improving It. Written chiefly in the Year 1792," in Ward, *Hindoos,* 1822, vol. 1,

298–312. The full text of Grant's "Observations" may be found in *Parliamentary Papers*, 1812–13, vol. 10, paper 282, 1–112.

30. Clifford, "On Ethnographic Authority," especially 26–34. Clifford analyzes late-nineteenth-century ethnography. I draw allusively on his work since it is helpful in comprehending differences between the two editions of Ward's work.

31. Ibid., 46. The reference is to evangelist R. H. Codrington's *The Melanesians*, 1891. Clifford's description suggests that it was produced in much the same way as Ward's *Hindoos*, through long-term residence and collaboration with indigenous informants and translators. Ibid., 27.

32. Robert Thornton, "The Rhetoric of Ethnographic Holism," *Cultural Anthropology* (August 1988): 285–303, especially 286. James Clifford has also noted the prominence gained by social structure in the wake of the professionalization of anthropology, as theoretical concepts were sought in order to enable the professional fieldworker to grasp the essential features of a given society more quickly than would be possible through an exhaustive inventory of customs. See Clifford, "On Ethnographic Authority," 31.

33. For critical analysis of the subsequent career of "caste" in South Asian anthropology, see Ronald Inden, "Orientalist Constructions of India," *Modern Asian Studies* (July 1986): 401–446; Inden, *Imagining India*, 49–84; Arjun Appadurai, "Putting Hierarchy in Its Place," in *Place and Voice in Anthropological Theory*, ed. Appadurai, special issue of *Cultural Anthropology* 3, 1 (February 1988): 36–49.

34. For an overview of the Clapham Sect's activities during the debates on the renewal of the East India Company charter in 1793 and 1813, see Ainslee Embree, *Charles Grant and British Rule in India* (New York: Columbia University Press, 1962), 141–157, 270–275; Ernest Marshall Howse, *Saints in Politics: The Clapham Sect and the Growth of Freedom* (Toronto: University of Toronto Press, 1952), 65–72.

35. Quoted in Howse, *Saints in Politics*, 72.

36. For discussion of the mutiny and Charles Grant's defense of the missionaries, see Embree, *Charles Grant and British Rule in India*, 237–248.

37. For a discussion of both controversies and an overview of the relationship between the Baptists and the East India Company in this period, see Daniel Potts, "The Baptist Missionaries of Serampore and the Government of India, 1792–1813," *Journal of Ecclesiastical History* (October 1964): 229–246.

38. *Missionary Register*, June 1813, 235; Embree, *Charles Grant and British Rule in India*, 271; E. M. Howse, *Saints in Politics*, 82–94; see also C. H. Philips, *The East India Company: 1784–1834* (Manchester: Manchester University Press, 1940).

39. D. W. Bebbington, *Evangelicalism in Modern Britain: A History from the 1730s to the 1980s* (London: Unwin Hyman, 1989), chs. 1–3; Richard Brown, *Church and State in Modern Britain, 1700–1850* (London: Routledge, 1991).

40. Francis G. Hutchins, "Evangelicalism, Utilitarianism and the Origin of the Idea of a Just Rule," in Hutchins, *The Illusion of Permanence: British Imperialism in India* (Princeton: Princeton University Press, 1967), 3–19; see also Majeed, *Ungoverned Imaginings*, 178–183.

41. Hutchins, *The Illusion of Permanence*, 10.

42. Mill, *The History of British India;* Majeed, *Ungoverned Imaginings*, 179.

43. Ranajit Guha, *A Rule of Property for Bengal: An Essay on the Idea of Permanent Settlement* (Paris: Mouton, 1963).

44. Grant, "Observations." For Wilberforce's debt to Grant, see Embree, *Charles Grant and British Rule in India*, 271–272.

45. William Wilberforce, Speech to the House of Commons, June 22, 1813, *Parliamentary Debates*, vol. 26, col. 865.

46. Said, *Orientalism*, 100–101. See also Johannes Fabian's classic study of the allochronic representation by the West of the non-West, *Time and the Other: How Anthropology Makes Its Object* (New York: Columbia University Press, 1983).

47. William Wilberforce, Speech to the House of Commons, June 22, 1813, *Parliamentary Debates*, vol. 26, cols. 859–862.

48. Claudius Buchanan to Wm Wilberforce, May 17, 1813, 261–262; Wm Wilberforce to Z. Macaulay, May 1812, 231–232, in *The Correspondence of William Wilberforce*, ed. R. and S. Wilberforce, vol. 2 (London: J. Murray, 1840).

49. Claudius Buchanan, *Memoir of the Expediency of an Ecclesiastical Establishment for British India*, London, 1805; William Wilberforce, Speech to the House of Commons, June 22, 1813, *Parliamentary Debates*, vol. 26, col. 863.

50. Stephen Lushington, Speech to the House of Commons, July 1, 1813, *Parliamentary Debates*, vol. 26, cols. 1018–1051.

51. Ibid., cols. 1042, 1044, 1051.

52. Embree, *Charles Grant and British Rule in India*, 273.

53. Thornton, "Narrative Ethnography in Africa, 1850–1920: The Creation and Capture of an Appropriate Domain for Anthropology," *Man* (September 1983): 503–504, 506–508.

54. "On the Burning of Women in India," *Missionary Register*, June 1813, 215–218; Ward, "Burning of Widows Alive," *Hindoos*, 1811, vol. 2, 547–550.

55. "On the Burning of Women in India," 215.

56. "Instance of the Cruelty of Hindoo Superstition," *Missionary Register*, July 1813, 268; Ward, "Burning of Widows Alive," *Hindoos*, 1811, vol. 2, 554–555.

57. Ward, "Burning of Widows Alive," *Hindoos*, 1811, vol. 2, 544–566.

58. *Missionary Register*, April 1814, 137.

59. Ibid., 137–138.

60. Ibid., 138.

61. F. K. Prochaska, *Women and Philanthropy in Nineteenth-Century England* (Oxford: Clarendon Press, 1980), 24.

62. Priscilla Robertson, *An Experience of Women: Pattern and Change in Nineteenth-Century Europe* (Philadelphia: Temple University Press, 1982); Jane Rendall, *The Origins of Modern Feminism: Women in Britain, France and the United States 1780–1860* (Houndmills, Eng.: Macmillan, 1985); Ludmilla Jordanova, "Natural Facts: A Historical Perspective on Science and Sexuality," in *Nature, Culture and Gender*, ed. Carol P. MacCormack and Marilyn Strathern (Cambridge: Cambridge University Press, 1980), 42–69; Jordanova, "Naturalizing the Family: Literature and the Bio-Medical Sciences in the Late Eighteenth Century," in *Languages of Nature: Critical Essays on Science and Literature*, ed. Jordanova (London: Free Association Books, 1986), 86–116.

63. Catherine Hall, "Private Persons vs. Public Someones: Class, Gender and Politics in England, 1780–1850," in *British Feminist Thought: A Reader,* ed. Terry Lovell (Oxford: Basil Blackwell, 1990), 51–67.

64. Prochaska, *Women and Philanthropy in Nineteenth-Century England.*

65. Ibid., 231.

66. "Human Sacrifices to Hindoo Deities," *Missionary Register,* September 1817, 405–407.

67. "Hindoo Superstitions and Cruelties," *Missionary Register,* July 1819, 326–329.

68. "Ganesa, A Hindoo Deity," *Missionary Register,* February 1819, 94–98.

69. "An Account of Juggernaut," *Missionary Register,* July 1817, 300–310 (reproducing an engraving from Ward's *Hindoos*).

70. Ward, Journal, November 9, 1800, BMS Archive.

71. Ward notes that Buchanan requests Carey "to give him the best advice he can respecting the way of putting a stop to women burning, to the aged being exposed, & to children being offered to Ganga, or drowned, or exposed." Ibid., April 7, 1803. Carey's response was finally incorporated into Buchanan's *Memoir of the Expediency of an Ecclesiastical Establishment for British India,* printed for T. Cadell and W. Davies by W. Bulmer, 1805, which was extensively cited by Wilberforce in the 1813 parliamentary debate on the East India Company charter.

72. Ward, Journal, January 5, 1802, BMS Archive.

73. Ibid., January 6, 1804.

74. Ibid., December 19, 1802.

75. Ibid., April 18, 1803.

76. Ibid., August 15, 1803.

77. Moore, September 13, 1813, *Periodical Accounts* 5, no. 23, 1812–14, 519.

78. Ward, *Farewell Letters to a Few Friends in Britain and America on Returning to Bengal in 1821,* London, 1821. See also the report on Ward's June 22, 1819 sermon at the Sion Chapel, *Missionary Register,* August 1819, 358–359.

79. Daniel Potts, *British Baptist Missionaries in India, 1793–1837* (Cambridge: Cambridge University Press, 1967), 122–126.

80. Ward, *Farewell Letters,* 67.

81. Ibid., 73.

82. Ibid., 79.

83. Ibid., 82.

84. Ibid., 97–98.

85. Ibid., 144 and passim.

86. See Inden, *Imagining India,* ch. 2, for a critical analysis of caste in colonial representations of India.

87. The monthly *Friend of India* began publication in May 1818. In September 1820, the Baptists published the first issue of the quarterly *Friend of India.* The quarterly was to be devoted to longer essays and reviews, leaving the monthly to focus on shorter pieces and news items. The monthly *Friend of India* was published until 1828, and the quarterly remained in existence until 1827.

88. *Essays Relative to the Habits, Character, and Moral Improvement of the Hindoos* (London: Kingsbury, Parbury and Allen, 1823).

89. None of the articles have named authors although, as chief editor of the journal, Joshua Marshman was known to be closely involved in the publication. In addition to articles on widow immolation, the monthly *Friend of India* also carried eyewitness accounts of *sati*. These are analyzed in chapter 5.

90. "On the Burning of Widows in India," *Friend of India*, monthly, December 1818, 301–311; "On the Burning of Widows," *Friend of India*, monthly, July 1819, 319–333; "Review of a Pamphlet on the Subject of Burning Widows," *Friend of India*, monthly, October 1819, 453–484.

91. "On Female Immolation," *Friend of India*, quarterly, vol. 1, no. 3, March 1821, 332–352; "Sketch of Popular Ideas relative to the Burning of Widows, Shraddhas or Funeral Feast &c. Taken from Recent Occurrences," *Friend of India*, quarterly, vol. 3, no. 9, 1825, 33–65; "On the Burning of Widows," *Friend of India*, quarterly, vol. 4, no. 14, 1826, 449–477.

92. "On the Burning of Widows in India," *Friend of India*, monthly, December 1818, 305–308.

93. "Review of a Pamphlet on the Subject of burning Widows," *Friend of India*, monthly, October 1819, 456–477 and passim. Rammohun's second pamphlet specifically took up and addressed the points made by the advocate of widow burning in this pro-*sati* tract. For Mrityunjay Vidyalankar's *vyawastha*, see chapter 1.

94. "On the Burning of Widows in India," *Friend of India*, monthly, December 1818, 304–305.

95. Ibid., 301–302.

96. Ibid., 302.

97. Ibid., 304.

98. "On the Burning of Widows," *Friend of India*, monthly, July 1819, 319–333.

99. Ibid., 327.

100. Ibid., 331.

101. Malek Alloula, *The Colonial Harem* (Minneapolis: University of Minnesota Press, 1986), 129 fn 11.

102. "On the State of Female Society in India," *Friend of India*, quarterly, vol. 1, no. 2, December 1820, 197.

103. This data was published in the *Circular Letters* of the Baptist Missionary Society and reprinted in William Johns, *A Collection of Facts and Opinions Relative to the Burning of Widows with The Dead Bodies of Their Husbands and to Other Destructive Customs Prevalent in British India* (Birmingham: W. H. Pearce, 1816), 37–41.

104. See, for instance, Ward, *Farewell Letters*, 65.

105. See, in particular, "On Female Immolation," *Friend of India*, quarterly, vol. 1, no. 3, March 1821, 332–352; and "On the Burning of Widows," *Friend of India*, quarterly, vol. 4, no. 14, 1826, 449–477.

106. "On Female Immolation," *Friend of India*, quarterly, vol. 1, no. 3, March 1821, 335, 350.

107. "On the Burning of Widows," *Friend of India*, quarterly, vol. 4, no. 14, 1826, 460.

108. "Burning of Widows Alive," *Friend of India*, monthly, February 1824, 45–46.

## Chapter 5: The Female Subject, the Colonial Gaze

1. Malek Alloula, *The Colonial Harem* (Minneapolis: University of Minnesota Press 1986), 5.

2. Gayatri Chakravorty Spivak, "Can the Subaltern Speak?" in *Marxism and the Interpretation of Culture,* ed. Cary Nelson and Lawrence Grossberg (Urbana: University of Illinois Press, 1988), 297.

3. Alloula, *The Colonial Harem,* 5.

4. Gayatri Chakravorty Spivak coins this phrase. See her "The Rani of Sirmur," in *Europe and its Others,* ed. Francis Barker et al., proceedings of the Essex Conference on the Sociology of Literature (Colchester: University of Essex, 1984), vol. 1, 130.

5. My concerns here intersect with those raised by Benita Parry, "Problems in Current Theories of Colonial Discourse," *Oxford Literary Review* 9, 1–2 (1987): 27–58, especially 34–39. However, where Parry draws on discourses of nationalist resistance to pose questions with respect to Spivak's analysis, my strategy in this chapter is to explore the issue through analysis of women's agency in *sati.*

6. Letter to the editor, *Calcutta Journal,* May 2, 1819, 357.

7. "Suttee," *Bengal Hurkaru,* July 29, 1823, 247.

8. "Suttee," *India Gazette,* October 23, 1828, 4.

9. "Another Suttee Rescued," *Missionary Register,* July 1829, 323–324.

10. "Prevention of a Suttee," *Asiatic Journal,* October 1823, 343–345.

11. "Another Woman Burnt Alive," *Circular Letters of the Baptist Missionary Society,* September 1811, 177.

12. "Suttees," *Bengal Hurkaru,* July 1, 1828, 2.

13. *Asiatic Journal,* May 1824, 570–577.

14. "The Burning of Two Widows on One Pile," *Friend of India,* monthly, July 1820, 204–208.

15. Ibid., 206.

16. "Suttee at Hurdwar," *Friend of India,* monthly, May 1820, 132.

17. "Suttee Prevented," *Asiatic Journal,* May 1821, 508.

18. *Bengal Hurkaru,* September 16, 1828, 2.

19. See, for instance, "Immolation of a Widow," *Bengal Hurkaru,* August 12, 1823; "Suttee," *Bengal Hurkaru,* June 20, 1829, 2.

20. Letter to the editor, *Calcutta Journal,* May 2, 1819, 357; Letter to the editor, *Bengal Hurkaru,* February 6, 1824, 3; *Quarterly Papers of the Baptist Missionary Society,* no. 12, October 1824, 47, among others.

21. "Suttee," *Bengal Hurkaru,* September 15, 1825, 2; "Horrible Suttee," *Bengal Hurkaru,* January 4, 1826, 2; "Immolation of Widows," *Bengal Hurkaru,* April 19, 1826, 2; *Bengal Hurkaru,* July 27, 1826, 2.

22. "Unsuccessful Attempt to Prevent Suttee," *Asiatic Journal,* April 1820, 387–388.

23. *Baptist Magazine,* vol. 14, February 1822, 85.

24 *Bengal Hurkaru,* November 26, 1825, 2.

25. *Baptist Magazine,* vol. 14, February 1822, 85.

26. *Missionary Register,* March 1820, 123.

27. Ibid., 123–124.

28. *Missionary Register*, 1821, 115; see also "Concremation," *Bengal Hurkaru*, February 2, 1828, 2; "Suttee at Cuttack," *Bengal Hurkaru*, August 22, 1828, 2. In this last case, the magistrate, on finding that the widow had been intoxicated by her brothers-in-law conspiring to be rid of her, refused permission for her immolation. The relatives appealed his decision, were successful, and the widow was burnt some sixteen days later.

29. "Suttee," *Asiatic Journal*, March 1823, 292.

30. See, for example, *Bengal Hurkaru*, November 26, 1825, 2.

31. "Suttee," *Bengal Hurkaru*, September 15, 1825, 2.

32. "Horrible Suttee," *Bengal Hurkaru*, January 4, 1826, 2.

33. *Calcutta Journal*, April 23, 1822, 586.

34. *Calcutta Journal*, August 14, 1821, 549.

35. William Hodges, quoted in William Johns, *A Collection of Facts and Opinions Relative to the Burning of Widows with The Dead Bodies of Their Husbands and to Other Destructive Customs Prevalent in British India* (Birmingham: W. H. Pearce, 1816), 21–22.

36. *Asiatic Journal*, December 1816, 599.

37. Alloula, *The Colonial Harem*, 49.

38. "Suttee," *Asiatic Journal*, March 1823, 292.

39. Letter to the editor, *Bengal Hurkaru*, April 2, 1823, 232.

40. See also Rajeswari Sunder Rajan's insightful analysis of the absence of a discussion of pain in the contemporary debate on *sati* in the aftermath of Roop Kanwar's burning in Deorala, Rajasthan, on September 22, 1987, "The Subject of Sati: Pain and Death in the Contemporary Discourse on Sati," *Yale Journal of Criticism* 3, 2 (Spring 1990): 1–23.

41. "Another Woman Burnt Alive," *Circular Letters of the Baptist Missionary Society*, September 1814, 178.

42. "Immolation of Widow," *Bengal Hurkaru*, August 12, 1823.

43. *Bengal Hurkaru*, February 6, 1824, 3.

44. "Suttee," *Bengal Hurkaru*, April 24, 1824, 3.

45. William Carey, in Johns, *A Collection of Facts and Opinions Relative to the Burning of Widows*, 24.

46. "Suttee," *Bengal Hurkaru*, September 15, 1825, 2.

47. D. L. R., "The Suttee," *Bengal Hurkaru*, November 16, 1829, 3.

48. According to Toby Falk and Mildred Archer, the lines of Sanskrit at the bottom of the plate are from the *Yaginavalbyasmriti*, discussing "the arguments for and against the widow joining her husband on the funeral pyre according to the circumstances, and the alternatives open to her." See Falk and Archer, *Indian Miniatures in the India Office Library* (London: Sotheby Parke Bernet, 1981), 140.

49. Letter to the editor, *Calcutta Journal*, May 2, 1819, 357.

50. Letter to the editor, *Bengal Hurkaru*, April 19, 1826, 2.

51. *Bengal Hurkaru*, July 27, 1826, 2.

52. Sunder Rajan, "The Subject of Sati: Pain and Death in the Contemporary Discourse on Sati," 9.

53. "Burning of Widows," *Friend of India*, monthly, November 1823, 348.

54. "Horrible Suttee," *Bengal Hurkaru*, January 4, 1826, 2.

55. In the discussions that followed the burning of Roop Kanwar in Deorala Rajasthan, 1987, in lieu of details of suffering are stories of the miraculous ascent of the unscathed, untouched widow to celestial regions. The widow here is said to *literally* evaporate.

56. Letter to the editor, *Asiatic Journal*, March 1818, 222.

57. James Lovewell, "Description of a Suttee," *India Gazette*, December 28, 1829, 4.

58. "Female Immolations," *Friend of India*, monthly, March 1822, 94.

59. Letter to the editor, *Calcutta Journal*, May 2, 1819, 357.

60. Lovewell, "Description of a Suttee," 4.

61. "The Burning of Two Widows on One Pile," *Friend of India*, monthly, July 1820, 208.

62. William Ward, *A View of the History, Literature, and Mythology of the Hindoos* (London, 1822), vol. 3, 327.

63. Ibid., 327.

64. Lovewell, "Description of a Suttee," 4.

65. Leonidas, "The Hindu Wife," *Bengal Hurkaru*, August 20, 1823.

66. *Samachar Darpan*, October 22, 1825, in *Bengal Hurkaru*, October 25, 1825, 2.

67. *Samachar Chundrika*, June 12, 1826, in *Bengal Hurkaru*, August 29, 1825, 2.

68. "Female Immolations in India," *Calcutta Journal*, June 13, 1822, 602.

69. Mary Louise Pratt, "Fieldwork in Common Places," in *Writing Culture: The Poetics and Politics of Ethnography*, ed. James Clifford and George Marcus (Berkeley: University of California Press, 1986), 33. For critiques of conventional ethnography, see Johannes Fabian, *Time and the Other: How Anthropology Makes Its Object* (New York: Columbia University Press, 1983); see also the essays in *Writing Culture;* James Clifford, *The Predicament of Culture* (Berkeley: University of California Press, 1988); Arjun Appadurai, ed., *Place and Voice in Anthropological Theory*, special issue of *Cultural Anthropology* 3, 1 (February 1988). In "On Ethnographic Allegory," in *Writing Culture*, 111, James Clifford writes that the ethnographic present "which is always, in fact, a past . . . effectively textualizes the other, and gives the sense of a reality not in temporal flux, not in the same ambiguous, moving, *historical* present that includes and situates the other, the ethnographer and the reader."

70. Clifford, "On Ethnographic Allegory," 111.

71. Pratt, "Fieldwork in Common Places," 35.

72. "Suttee," *Bengal Hurkaru*, October 17, 1826, 2.

73. "Unsuccessful Attempt to Prevent a Suttee," *Asiatic Journal*, April 1820, 388.

74. Mary Louise Pratt, *Imperial Eyes: Travel Writing and Transculturation* (New York: Routledge, 1992), 201 and passim.

75. "Suttee," *Friend of India*, monthly, December 1823, 381.

76. Clifford, "Introduction: Partial Truths," in *Writing Culture*, 11, argues that the privileging of sight in Western culture accounts for the predominance of "visualism" in ethnographic writing and the relative subordination of sound, touch, taste and smell; see also, Walter Ong, *The Presence of the Word*

(New Haven: Yale University Press, 1967); and Ong, *Rhetoric, Romance, and Technology: Studies on the Interaction of Expression and Culture* (Ithaca: Cornell University Press, 1971); Fabian, *Time and the Other;* Timothy Mitchell, *Colonising Egypt* (Cambridge: Cambridge University Press, 1988), discusses visual imaging of the Orient as a crucial representational strategy of colonial discourse.

77. See, for instance, "Suttee," *Bengal Hurkaru,* September 15, 1825, 2; *Bengal Hurkaru,* November 26, 1825, 2.

78. Ann Chaffin's account of *sati* was written in a letter to J. James Smith, November 27, 1814. A revised version, which failed to acknowledge her authorship, was printed in Johns, *A Collection of Facts and Opinions Relative to the Burning of Widows,* 43–49. The original, on which I draw here, is to be found in the manuscript collection at Angus Library, Oxford University. Bampton's account is "Suttee," *Baptist Magazine,* May 1825, 229–231.

79. In other accounts by women, women either arrive after the pyre is in flames (e.g., *Missionary Register,* 1821, 115) or leave before the burning takes place (e.g., *Quarterly Papers of the Baptist Missionary Society,* January 1828, 98–99). The length of Chaffin's account and its detail—it is four closely written pages—make it difficult to reproduce in full. My reading thus draws upon extracts to highlight significant similarities and differences between its representation of the practices surrounding immolation and those to be found in more standard descriptions.

80. Alloula, *The Colonial Harem,* 4.

# Glossary

| | |
|---|---|
| *anoomarana* | the burning of a widow with an article belonging to her deceased husband |
| *banian* | an Indian manager/intermediary for a European merchant or for an East India Company employee. More generally, a trader or member of the mercantile class |
| *bhadralok* | elite, "respectable" class |
| *bhadramahila* | women of the elite, "respectable" class |
| *bhakti* | devotion to deity |
| *chottolok* | non-elite classes |
| *darogah* | local-level police official, in charge of a police station |
| *debta, devta* | Hindu god |
| Diwani Adalat | provincial civil court |
| *dola jatra* | theatrical performance of a religious nature |
| *Durga puja* | annual festival worshipping the Hindu goddess Durga |
| "Hari bol" | literally, "chant the name of God" |
| *jogi* | community of weavers, supposedly descended from wandering mendicants |
| *munshi* | native teacher |
| Nizamat Adalat | provincial criminal court |
| *pir* | Sufi saint or holy person |
| pundit | Hindu scholar/theologian |

225

| | |
|---|---|
| *qazi* | Muslim scholar/theologian |
| Sadar Nizamat Adalat | superior criminal court |
| *sahamarana* | the burning of a widow along with the corpse of her husband |
| *shastras* | sacred Hindu writings |
| sudra | laboring caste; the caste designated lowest in the fourfold hierarchy outlined in brahmanic scriptures, brahmin (priestly caste), kshatriya (warrior caste), vaisya (merchant caste), sudra |
| *talukdar* | one who has the proprietary right to collect revenue in a taluk, or district/subdivision |
| *vakil* | lawyer |
| *zamindar* | in precolonial India, collectors of revenue; under the British, landowners |
| *zillah* | district |

# Bibliography

## Unpublished Primary Sources

### BAPTIST MISSIONARY SOCIETY (BMS) ARCHIVES, LONDON

Basu, R. The Gospel Messenger, English translation of Bengali verse.
    Translator unknown, mss, c. 1810, BMS Archives.
Carey, W. Letters to the BMS, 1793–1811.
Marshman, J. Letters to the BMS, 1799–1811.
Ward, W. Letters to the BMS, 1799–1811.

### REGENT'S PARK COLLEGE, OXFORD, ANGUS LIBRARY

Fuller Papers. Ann Chaffin, An Account of Suttee, 1814, Manuscript
    Collection.

### INDIA OFFICE LIBRARY AND RECORDS

Bentinck Correspondence, European Mss.

## Published Primary Sources

### PARLIAMENTARY DEBATES

Vol. 25, March 11–May 10, 1813. East India Company's (EIC) affairs, cols.
    248–249, 255–256, 415–460, 487–494, 527–531, 697–698, 764–765, 781–
    782, 904–910.
Vol. 26, May 11–July 22, 1813. EIC's affairs, cols. 238–239, 562, 827–873, 1018–
    1100, 1169–1170, 1184–1196, 1201–1207.

*New Series, commencing with the accession of George IV*

Vol. 5, April 3–July 11, 1821. Burning of Hindoo Widows, cols. 1217–1222.
Vol. 9, May 1–July 19, 1823. Burning of Hindoo Widows, cols. 1017–1021.
Vol. 13, April 19–July 6, 1825. Hindoo Widows-Female Immolation, cols.
    1043–1047.
Vol. 24, April 8–July 4, 1830. Abolition of Suttees, cols. 1355–1356.

*Third Series, commencing with the accession of William IV*

Vol. 2, December 21, 1830–March 3, 1831. Hindoo Superstitions, cols. 60–62.
Vol. 4, June 14–July 18, 1831. Suttees, cols. 576–578.

**PARLIAMENTARY PAPERS: HOUSE OF COMMONS**

1812–13         Vol. 2, Charter Renewal Bill.
                Vol. 8, Missions. Christians in Malabar. Pilgrim Tax.
                    Moral Character of Indians.
                Vol. 10, Grant's Observations. College of Fort William.
                    Charter Renewal Bill.

**PARLIAMENTARY PAPERS ON HINDU WIDOWS**

1821            Vol. 18, Paper 749
1823            Vol. 17, Paper 466
1824            Vol. 23, Paper 443
1825            Vol. 24, Papers 508, 518
1826–27         Vol. 20, Paper 354
1828            Vol. 23, Paper 547
1830            Vol. 27, Papers 178, 550

**CONTEMPORARY NEWSPAPERS AND PERIODICALS**

*London:*

*Asiatic Annual Register*
*Asiatic Journal*
*Baptist Magazine*
*Missionary Herald*
*Missionary Register*
*Oriental Herald*

*Calcutta:*

*Bengal Herald*
*Bengal Hurkaru*
*Calcutta Journal*

*India Gazette*
*John Bull*

*Serampore:*

*Friend of India* (monthly and quarterly)
*Samachar Darpan*


CONTEMPORARY TRACTS AND BOOKS

"An Account of the Proceedings at a Public Meeting, Held at the City of
    York, on the Nineteenth January 1827, to take into Consideration the Ex-
    pediency of Petitioning Parliament on the Subject of the Immolation of
    Widows in British India." York, 1827.
Bandhopadhyay, B. *Sambadpatra Sekaler Katha.* 2 vols. Calcutta: Bangiya
    Sahitya Parishad, 1949–50.
Buchanan, Claudius. *Memoir of the Expediency of an Ecclesiastical Establish-
    ment for British India.* London: printed for T. Cadell and W. Davies by W.
    Bulmer, 1805.
———, ed. *The College of Fort William in Bengal, Containing Official Papers
    and the Literary Proceedings of the College of Fort William, During its First
    Four Years.* London, 1805.
Carey, E. *Memories of William Carey.* London, 1836.
Carey, W. *An Enquiry into the Obligation of Christians to use means for the
    Conversion of Heathens in which the Religious State of the Different Nations
    of the World, the Success of Former Undertakings, and the Practicability of
    Further Undertakings, are Considered.* Leicester, 1792.
*Circular Letters of the Baptist Missionary Society, 1807–1815.*
Dubois, Abbé J. A. *A Description of the Character, Manners and Customs of the
    People of India.* London, 1817.
———. *Letters on the State of Christianity in India.* London, 1823.
*Essays by the Students of the College of Fort William.* Vol. 1. Calcutta, 1802.
    (Vols. 2 & 3, published as *Primitiae Orientalis.*)
*Essays Relative to the Habits, Character and Moral Improvement of the Hindoos.*
    London: Kingsbury, Parbury and Allen, 1823.
Fuller, A. G. *The Complete Works of the Reverend Andrew Fuller.* 5 vols. Lon-
    don, 1831.
Halhed, N. B. *A Code of Gentoo Laws, or Ordinations of the Pundits.* London,
    1776.
Johns, William. *A Collection of Facts and Opinions Relative to the Burning of
    Widows with The Dead Bodies of Their Husbands and to Other Destructive
    Customs Prevalent in British India.* Birmingham: W. H. Pearce, 1816.
Majumdar, J. K., ed. *Raja Rammohun Roy and Progressive Movements in In-
    dia: A Selection from Records, 1775–1845.* Calcutta: Art Press, 1941.
Marshman, J. C. *The Life and Times of Carey, Marshman and Ward: Embrac-
    ing the History of the Serampore Mission.* 2 vols. London: Longman, Brown,
    Green, Longmans and Roberts, 1859.

Mill, James. *The History of British India.* 3 vols. 1817. Reprint of 2nd edition. New Delhi: Associated Publishing House, 1972.

*Periodical Accounts of the Serampore Mission,* n.s., 1820–1829; 3rd ser., 1830–1836.

*Periodical Accounts Relative to the Baptist Missionary Society,* 1792–1819.

Phillips, C. H., ed. *The Correspondence of Lord William Cavendish Bentinck.* 2 vols. Oxford: Oxford University Press, 1977.

*Primitiae Orientalis. Being the Essays and Disputations of the Students of the College of Fort William.* Vols. 2 and 3. Calcutta, 1803–1804.

*Quarterly Papers for the use of the weekly and monthly contributors to the Baptist Missionary Society,* 1822–1831.

Roy, Rammohun. *Tuhfutul Muwahiddin.* Translated by Obaidullah El Obaide. Dacca, 1883. In Kissory Chand Mitter and Rammohun Roy, *Rammohun Roy and Tuhfatul Muwahiddin.* Calcutta: K. P. Bagchi, 1975.

———. *The English Works of Rammohun Roy.* Edited by K. Nag and D. Burman. 7 parts. Calcutta: Sadharan Brahmo Samaj, 1945–1958.

———. *The English Works of Rammohun Roy.* Edited by J. C. Ghose. 4 vols. New Delhi: Cosmo Publications, 1982.

*Serampore Pamphlets,* 1813–1836.

Ward, W. *An Account of the Writings, Religion and Manners of the Hindoos.* 4 vols. Serampore, 1811 (final edition published as *A View of the History, Literature and Mythology of the Hindoos.* 3 vols. London, 1822).

———. *Farewell Letters to a Few Friends in Britain and America on Returning to Bengal in 1821.* London, 1821.

———. *Brief Memoir of Krishna-Pal.* Serampore, 1822.

Wilberforce, R. and S., eds. *The Correspondence of William Wilberforce.* Vol. 2. London: J. Murray, 1840.

Williams, Leighton and Mornay. *Serampore Letters, 1800–1816.* New York: G. P. Putnam's Sons, 1892.

## Selected Secondary Sources

Ahmad, Aijaz. *In Theory: Classes, Nations, Literatures.* London: Verso, 1992.

Ahmed, A. F. Salahuddin. *Social Ideas and Social Change in Bengal, 1818–1835.* Leiden: Brill, 1965.

———. "The Bengal Renaissance and the Muslim Community." In *Reflections on the Bengal Renaissance,* ed. David Kopf and Safiuddin Joarder. Rajshahi: Institute of Bangladesh Studies, 1977, 33–41.

Alloula, Malek. *The Colonial Harem.* Minneapolis: University of Minnesota Press, 1986.

Appadurai, Arjun. "Putting Hierarchy in Its Place." In *Place and Voice in Anthropological Theory,* ed. Appadurai, special issue of *Cultural Anthropology* 3, 1 (February 1988): 36–49.

Arnold, David. "Some Observations on the Theory and Practice of the Colonial State." Paper presented at conference on "Culture Consciousness and the Colonial State," Isle of Thorns, July 23–27, 1989.

————. *Colonizing the Body: State Medicine and Epidemic Disease in Nineteenth-Century India*. Berkeley: University of California Press, 1993.

Bagchi, A. K. "De-Industrialization in India in the Nineteenth Century: Some Theoretical Implications." *Journal of Development Studies* 12 (1975– 76): 135–64.

Bandhopadhyay, B. *Bangla Samayik Patra*. 2 vols. Calcutta: Bangiya Sahitya Parishad, BS 1384, 1948.

Banerjee, Sumanta. *The Parlour and the Streets: Elite and Popular Culture in Nineteenth-Century Calcutta*. Calcutta: Seagull Books, 1989.

Bayly, C. A. "From Ritual to Ceremony: Death Ritual and Society in Hindu North India since 1600." In *Mirrors of Mortality*, ed. J. Whaley. London: Europa, 1981, 154–186.

————. *Indian Society and the Making of the British Empire*. Vol. 2, pt. 1 of *The New Cambridge History of India*. Cambridge: Cambridge University Press, 1988.

————, ed. *An Illustrated History of Modern India, 1600–1947*. Delhi: Oxford University Press, 1991.

Bebbington, D. W. *Evangelicalism in Modern Britain: A History from the 1730s to the 1980s*. London: Unwin Hyman, 1989.

Bhabha, H. "Of Mimicry and Man: The Ambivalence of Colonial Discourse." *October* 28 (Spring 1984): 125–133.

Brown, Richard. *Church and State in Modern Britain, 1700–1850*. London: Routledge, 1991.

Carey, S. P. *William Carey*. Philadelphia, 1923.

Carroll, Lucy. "Law, Custom and Statutory Social Reform: The Hindu Widow's Remarriage Act of 1856." *Indian Economic and Social History Review* 20, 4 (1983): 363–89.

Chakrabarty, Dipesh. "Postcoloniality and the Artifice of History: Who Speaks for 'Indian' Pasts?" *Representations* 37 (Winter 1992): 1–26.

Chandra, Sudhir. "Conflicted Beliefs and Men's Consciousness about Women: Widow Remarriage in Later Nineteenth-Century Indian Literature." *Economic and Political Weekly, Review of Women's Studies*, October 31, 1987, 55–62.

————. *The Oppressive Present: Literature and Social Consciousness in Colonial India*. Delhi: Oxford University Press, 1992.

Chatterjee, Partha. *Nationalist Thought and the Colonial World: A Derivative Discourse?* London: Zed Press, 1986.

Chatterjee, Ramananda. *Rammohun Roy and Modern India*. Calcutta: Sadharan Brahmo Samaj, 1918.

Chatterjee, S. K. *William Carey and Serampore*. Calcutta, 1984.

Chowdhry, Prem. "Customs in a Peasant Economy: Women in Colonial Haryana." In *Recasting Women*, ed. Sangari and Vaid, 302–336.

Clifford, J. "Introduction: Partial Truths." In *Writing Culture: The Poetics and Politics of Ethnography*, ed. Clifford and Marcus. Berkeley: University of California Press, 1986, 1–26.

————. "On Ethnographic Authority." In Clifford, *The Predicament of Culture*. Berkeley: University of California Press, 1988, 21–54.

————. *The Predicament of Culture.* Berkeley: University of California Press, 1988.

Clifford, J., and G. Marcus, eds. *Writing Culture: The Poetics and Politics of Ethnography.* Berkeley: University of California Press, 1986.

Cohn, Bernard S. "Notes on the History of the Study of Indian Society and Culture." In *Structure and Change in Indian Society,* ed. M. B. Singer and B. S. Cohn. Chicago: Aldine Publishing Co., 1968.

————. "The Command of Language and the Language of Command." In *Subaltern Studies IV,* ed. Ranajit Guha. Delhi: Oxford University Press, 1985, 276–329.

————. "The Anthropology of a Colonial State and Its Forms of Knowledge." Background paper for conference on "Culture Consciousness and the Colonial State," Isle of Thorns, July 23–27, 1989.

————. "Law and the Colonial State in India." In *History and Power in the Study of Law,* ed. Jane Collier and June Starr. Ithaca: Cornell University Press, 1989, 131–152.

————. *An Anthropologist among the Historians and Other Essays.* Delhi: Oxford University Press, 1990.

Collet, Sophia Dobson. *The Life and Letters of Raja Rammohun Roy,* eds., D. K. Biswas and P. C. Ganguli. Calcutta: Sadharan Brahmo Samaj, 1962.

Das, S. K. *Sahibs and Munshis.* Calcutta: Orion, 1978.

Datta, Kalikinkar. *Studies in the History of the Bengal Subah,* 1740–1770. Vol. 1. Calcutta: Calcutta University Press, 1936.

————. *Survey of India's Economic Life and Social Condition in the Eighteenth Century, 1707–1813.* New Delhi: Mushiram Manoharlal, 1978.

Datta, V. N. *Sati: Widow Burning in India.* Riverdale Md.: Riverdale, 1988.

Derrett, J. D. M. *Religion, Law and the State.* New York: The Free Press, 1968.

Dhagamwar, Vasudha. "Saint, Victim or Criminal." *Seminar,* no. 342 (special issue on *sati*), February 1988, 34–39.

Dharampal. *The Beautiful Tree: Indigenous Education in the Eighteenth Century.* New Delhi: Biblia Impex, 1983.

Embree, Ainslee. *Charles Grant and British Rule in India.* New York: Columbia University Press, 1962.

Everett, Jana. *Women and Social Change in India.* New Delhi: Heritage, 1981.

Fabian, Johannes. *Time and the Other: How Anthropology Makes Its Object.* New York: Columbia University Press, 1983.

Falk, Toby, and Mildred Archer. *Indian Miniatures in the India Office Library.* London: Sotheby Parke Bernet, 1981.

Foucault, Michel. *Discipline and Punish.* New York: Vintage, 1979.

Frankenberg, Ruth, and Lata Mani. "Crosscurrents, Crosstalk: Race, 'Postcoloniality' and the Politics of Location." *Cultural Studies* 7, 2 (May 1993): 292–310.

Galanter, Marc. "The Displacement of Traditional Law in Modern India." *Journal of Social Issues* 24 (1968): 65–91.

Guha, Ranajit. *A Rule of Property for Bengal: An Essay on the Idea of Permanent Settlement.* Paris: Mouton, 1963.

———. "On Some Aspects of the Historiography of Colonial India." In *Subaltern Studies I,* ed. Guha. Delhi: Oxford University Press, 1982, 1–8.

———. *Elementary Aspects of Peasant Insurgency in Colonial India.* Delhi: Oxford University Press, 1983.

———. *An Indian Historiography of India: A Nineteenth-Century Agenda and Its Implications.* Calcutta: Centre for Studies in Social Sciences, 1987.

———. "Dominance without Hegemony and Its Historiography." In *Subaltern Studies VI,* ed. Guha. Delhi: Oxford University Press, 1989, 210–309.

———, ed. *Subaltern Studies.* 6 vols. Delhi: Oxford University Press, 1982–89.

Hall, Catherine. "Private Persons vs. Public Someones: Class, Gender and Politics in England, 1780–1850." In *British Feminist Thought: A Reader,* ed. Terry Lovell. Oxford: Basil Blackwell, 1990, 51–67.

Hjejle, B. "The Social Policy of the East India Company with Regard to Sati, Slavery, Thagi and Infanticide, 1772–1858." D. Phil. thesis, Oxford University, 1958.

Howse, Ernest. *Saints in Politics: The Clapham Sect and the Growth of Freedom.* Toronto: University of Toronto Press, 1952.

Hutchins, Francis G. "Evangelicalism, Utilitarianism and the Origin of the Idea of a Just Rule." In *The Illusion of Permanence: British Imperialism in India,* ed. Hutchins. Princeton, N.J.: Princeton University Press, 1967.

Inden, Ronald. "Orientalist Constructions of India." *Modern Asian Studies* (July 1986): 401–446.

———. *Imagining India.* Oxford: Basil Blackwell, 1990.

Ingham, Kenneth. *Reformers in India, 1793–1833.* Cambridge: Cambridge University Press, 1956.

Jordanova, Ludmilla. "Natural Facts: A Historical Perspective on Science and Sexuality." In *Nature, Culture and Gender,* ed. Carol P. MacCormack and Marilyn Strathern. Cambridge: Cambridge University Press, 1980, 42–69.

———. "Naturalizing the Family: Literature and the Bio-Medical Sciences in the Late Eighteenth Century." In *Languages of Nature: Critical Essays on Science and Literature,* ed. Jordanova. London: Free Association Books, 1986, 86–116.

Joshi, Svati. "Rethinking English: An Introduction." In *Rethinking English: Essays in Literature, Language, History,* ed. Svati Joshi. New Delhi: Trianka, 1991, 1–31.

Joshi, V. C., ed. *Rammohun Roy and the Process of Modernization in India.* New Delhi: Vikas, 1975.

Karlekar, Malavika. *Voices from Within: Early Personal Narratives of Bengali Women.* Delhi: Oxford University Press, 1991.

Kaviraj, Sudipta. "The Myth of Praxis: The Construction of the Figure of Krishna in *Krishnacaritra.*" Occasional Papers on History and Society, 1st ser., no. 50. New Delhi: Nehru Memorial Museum and Library, 1987.

———. "Humour and the Prison of Reality: Kamala Kanta as the Secret Autobiography of Bankimchandra Chattopadhyay." Occasional Papers on History and Society, 2d ser., no. 4; New Delhi: Nehru Memorial Museum and Library, July 1988.

———. "Imaginary History." Occasional Papers on History and Society, 2d ser., no. 7. New Delhi: Nehru Memorial Museum and Library, September 1988.

———. "On the Construction of Colonial Power: Structure, Discourse, Hegemony." Paper presented at conference on "Imperial Hegemony," Berlin, June 1–3, 1989.

Kishwar, Madhu. "Toiling without Rights: Ho Women of Singhbum." 3 parts. *Economic and Political Weekly,* January 17, 1987, 95–101; January 24, 1987, 149–155; January 31, 1987, 194–200.

Kopf, David. *British Orientalism and the Bengal Renaissance: The Dynamics of Indian Modernization, 1773–1835.* Berkeley: University of California Press, 1969.

Kriplani, Krishna. *Dwarkanath Tagore, A Forgotten Pioneer: A Life.* Delhi: National Book Trust, 1980.

Kumar, Dharma, ed. *The Cambridge Economic History of India.* Vol. 2. Cambridge: Cambridge University Press, 1983.

Lowe, Lisa. *Critical Terrains: French and British Orientalism.* Berkeley: University of California Press, 1991.

Majeed, Javed. *Ungoverned Imaginings: James Mill's* The History of British India *and Orientalism.* Oxford: Clarendon Press, 1992.

Mani, Lata. "The Production of an Official Discourse on *Sati* in Early-Nineteenth-Century Bengal." In *Europe and Its Others,* ed. F. Barker, Peter Hume, Margaret Iversen, and Diana Loxley. Colchester: University of Essex, 1985, vol. 1, 107–127; also in *Economic and Political Weekly; Review of Women's Studies,* April 26, 1986, 32–40.

———. "Contentious Traditions: The Debate on *Sati* in Colonial India." *Cultural Critique* 7 (Fall 1987): 119–156. Also published in *Recasting Women: Essays in Colonial History,* ed. Kumkum Sangari and Sudesh Vaid. New Delhi: Kali, 1989, 88–126.

———. "Multiple Mediations: Feminist Scholarship in the Age of Multinational Reception." *Feminist Review* 35 (Summer 1990): 24–41.

———. "Cultural Theory, Colonial Texts: Eyewitness Accounts of Widow Burning." In *Cultural Studies,* ed. Lawrence Grossberg, Cary Nelson, and Paula Treichler. New York: Routledge, 1992, 392–405. Also published as "The Female Subject, the Colonial Gaze: Reading Eyewitness Accounts of Widow Burning." In *Interrogating Modernity: Culture and Colonialism in India,* ed. Tejaswini Niranjana, P. Sudhir, and Vivek Dhareshwar. Calcutta: Seagull, 1993, 273–290.

Metcalf, Thomas R. "The Indian Empire: Its Structures and Processes under the British." *Indo-British Review* 6, 2 (1973): 31–38.

Mies, Maria. *Indian Women and Patriarchy: Conflicts and Dilemmas of Students and Working Women.* Delhi: Concept, 1980.

Mitchell, Timothy. *Colonising Egypt.* Cambridge: Cambridge University Press, 1988.

Mittra, K. "Suppression of Suttee in the Province of Cuttack." *Bengal Past and Present* 46 (1933) 125–131.

Mohanty, Chandra T. "Under Western Eyes: Feminist Scholarship and Colonial Discourses." *Feminist Review* (Autumn 1988): 60–88.

Mukherjee, Hiren. *Indian Renaissance and Raja Rammohun Roy.* Poona: University of Poona, 1975.

Mukherjee, S. N. *Sir William Jones: A Study in Eighteenth-Century British Attitudes to India.* Cambridge: Cambridge University Press, 1968.

———. "Class, Caste and Politics in Calcutta, 1815–1838." In *Elites in South Asia,* ed. Edmund Leach and S. N. Mukherjee. Cambridge University Press, 1970, 33–78.

———. "Bhadralok in Bengali Language and Literature." *Bengal Past and Present* 95 (July-December 1976): 181, 225–237.

———. "Bhadralok and Their Dals—Policies of Social Factions, 1820–1856." In *The Urban Experience: Calcutta,* ed. Pradip Sinha. Calcutta: Riddhi-India, 1987, 39–58.

Mukhopadhyay, A. "Sati as a Social Institution in Bengal." *Bengal Past and Present* 75 (1957): 99–115.

Mukhopadhyay, Mokshodayani. "Bangalir Babu." In *Women Writing in India, 600 B.C. to the Present.* Vol. 1. *600 B.C. to the Early Twentieth Century,* ed. Tharu and Lalita. New York: The Feminist Press, 1991, 219–221.

Nandy, Ashis. "Sati: A Nineteenth-Century Tale of Women, Violence and Protest." In *Rammohun Roy and the Process of Modernization in India,* ed. Joshi. New Delhi: Vikas, 1975, 168–194.

Neill, S. *A History of Christianity in India, 1707–1858.* Cambridge: Cambridge University Press, 1985.

Niranjana, Tejaswini. *Siting Translation: History, Post-Structuralism and the Colonial Context.* Berkeley: University of California Press, 1992.

O'Hanlon, R. "Issues of Widowhood: Gender and Resistance in Colonial Western India." In *Contesting Power: Resistance and Everyday Social Relations in South Asia,* ed. Douglas Haynes and Gyan Prakash. Delhi: Oxford University Press, 1981, 62–108.

——— and David Washbrook. "After Orientalism: Culture, Criticism, and Politics in the Third World." *Comparative Studies in Society and History* 34, 1 (January 1992): 141–167.

Ong, Walter. *The Presence of the Word.* New Haven: Yale University Press, 1967.

———. *Rhetoric, Romance, and Technology: Studies on the Interaction of Expression and Culture.* Ithaca: Cornell University Press, 1971.

Pandey, Gyanendra. *The Construction of Communalism in Colonial North India.* Delhi: Oxford University Press, 1992.

Parry, Benita. "Problems in Current Theories of Colonial Discourse." *Oxford Literary Review* 9, 1–2, (1987): 27–58.

Patel, Sujata. "The Construction and Reconstruction of Women in Gandhi." *Economic and Political Weekly,* February 20, 1988, 377–387.

Philips, C. H. *The East India Company: 1784–1834.* Manchester: Manchester University Press, 1940.

Potts, Daniel. "The Baptist Missionaries of Serampore and the Government of India, 1792–1813." *Journal of Ecclesiastical History* (October 1964): 229–246.

———. *British Baptist Missionaries in India, 1793–1837.* Cambridge: Cambridge University Press, 1967.

Prakash, Gyan. *Bonded Histories: Genealogies of Labor Servitude in Colonial India.* Cambridge: Cambridge University Press, 1990.

———. "Can the 'Subaltern' Ride? A Reply to O'Hanlon and Washbrook." *Comparative Studies in Society and History* 34, 1 (January 1992): 168–184.

Pratt, Mary Louise. "Scratches on the Face of the Country; or What Mr. Barrow Saw in the Land of the Bushmen." In *"Race," Writing and Difference,* ed. Henry Louis Gates. Special issue of *Critical Inquiry* 12, 1 (Autumn 1985): 119–143.

———. "Fieldwork in Common Places." In *Writing Culture: The Poetics and Politics of Ethnography,* ed. Clifford and Marcus. Berkeley: University of California Press, 1986, 27–50.

———. *Imperial Eyes: Travel Writing and Transculturation.* New York: Routledge, 1992.

Prochaska, F. K. *Women and Philanthropy in Nineteenth-Century England.* Oxford: Clarendon Press, 1980.

Qayyum, M. A. *A Critical Study of Bengali Grammars: Halhed to Haughton.* Dhaka: The Asiatic Society of Bangladesh, 1982.

Ray, A. K. *The Religious Ideas of Rammohun Roy.* New Delhi: Kanak Publications, 1976.

Ray, Rajat K. "Introduction." In *Rammohun Roy and the Process of Modernization in India,* ed. Joshi. New Delhi: Vikas, 1975, 1–20.

Ray, Ratnalekha. *Change in Bengal Agrarian Society c. 1760–1850.* New Delhi: Manohar, 1979.

Rendall, Jane. *The Origins of Modern Feminism: Women in Britain, France and the United States 1780–1860.* Houndmills, Eng.: Macmillan, 1985.

Ricoeur, Paul. "The Model of the Text: Meaningful Action Considered as a Text." *Social Research* 38, 3 (Fall 1971): 529–562.

Robertson, Priscilla. *An Experience of Women: Pattern and Change in Nineteenth-Century Europe.* Philadelphia: Temple University Press, 1982.

Rosaldo, Renato. "From the Door of His Tent: The Fieldworker and the Inquisitor." In *Writing Culture: The Poetics and Politics of Ethnography,* ed. Clifford and Marcus. Berkeley: University of California Press, 1986, 77–97.

Roy, Benoy Bhusan. *Socioeconomic Impact of Sati in Bengal and the Role of Raja Rammohun Roy.* Calcutta: Naya Prokash, 1987.

Rudolph, Lloyd I., and Suzanne H. Rudolph. *The Modernity of Tradition.* Chicago: University of Chicago Press, 1967.

Said, Edward. *Orientalism.* New York: Vintage, 1979.

Sangari, Kumkum, and Sudesh Vaid, eds. *Recasting Women: Essays in Colonial History.* New Delhi: Kali, 1989.

Sarkar, Sumit. "Rammohun Roy and the Break with the Past." In *Rammohun Roy and the Process of Modernization in India,* ed. Joshi. New Delhi: Vikas, 1975, 46–68.

———. *A Critique of Colonial India.* Calcutta: Papyrus, 1985.

Sarkar, Tanika. "Bankimchandra and the Impossibility of a Political Agenda: A Predicament for Nineteenth-Century Bengal." Occasional Papers on History and Society, 2d ser., no. 40; New Delhi: Nehru Memorial Museum and Library, July 1991.

Seed, G. "The Abolition of Suttee in Bengal." *History* (October 1955): 286–299.

Sharma, Arvind. "Suttee: A Study in Western Reactions." In Sharma, *Thresholds in Hindu-Buddhist Studies.* Calcutta: Minerva, 1979, 83–111.

———, ed. *Our Religions.* San Francisco: HarperCollins, 1993.

Sharpe, Jenny. *Allegories of Empire: The Figure of Woman in the Colonial Text.* Minneapolis: University of Minnesota Press, 1993.

Shinde, Tarabai. "Stri Purush Tulana." In *Women Writing in India, 600 B.C. to the Present.* Vol. 1. *600 B.C. to the Early Twentieth Century,* ed. Tharu and Lalita. New York: The Feminist Press, 1991, 223–235.

Singh, Iqbal. *Rammohun Roy: A Biographical Inquiry into the Making of Modern India.* 3 vols. Bombay: Asia Publishing House, vol. 1, 1958, vols. 2–3, 1987.

Sinha, Mrinalini. *Colonial Masculinity: The "Manly Englishman" and the "Effeminate Bengali."* Manchester: Manchester University Press, 1995.

Sinha, N. K. *The Economic History of Bengal.* Vols. 2 and 3. Calcutta: Firma K. L. Mukhopadhyay, 1962.

Sinha, Pradip. *Calcutta in Urban History.* Calcutta: Firma KLM, 1978.

———, ed. *The Urban Experience: Calcutta.* Calcutta: Riddhi-India, 1987.

Smith, Richard Saumerez. "Rule-by-Records and Rule-by-Reports: Complementary Aspects of British Imperial Rule of Law." *Contributions to Indian Sociology,* n.s., 19, no. 1 (1985): 153–176.

Spivak, Gayatri Chakravorty. "The Rani of Sirmur." In *Europe and Its Others,* ed. F. Barker, Peter Hume, Margaret Iversen, and Diana Loxley. Colchester: University of Essex, 1985, vol. 1, 128–151.

———. "Can the Subaltern Speak?" In *Marxism and the Interpretation of Culture,* ed. Cary Nelson and Lawrence Grossberg. Urbana: University of Illinois Press, 1988, 271–311.

Stein, Dorothy K. "Women to Burn: Suttee as a Normative Institution." *Signs* 4, 2 (1978): 253–268.

Stokes, Eric. *The English Utilitarians and India.* Oxford: Oxford University Press, 1959.

Suleri, Sara. *The Rhetoric of English India.* Chicago: University of Chicago Press, 1992.

Sunder Rajan, Rajeswari. "The Subject of Sati: Pain and Death in the Contemporary Discourse on Sati." *Yale Journal of Criticism* 3, 2 (Spring 1990): 1–23.

Thapar, Romila. *The Past and Prejudice.* Delhi: National Book Trust, 1975.

Tharu, Susie, and K. Lalita. "Literature of the Reform and Nationalist Movements." In *Women Writing in India, 600 B.C. to the Present.* Vol. 1. *600 B.C. to the Early Twentieth Century,* ed. Tharu and Lalita. New York: The Feminist Press, 1991, 145–186.

———, eds. *Women Writing in India, 600 B.C. to the Present.* Vol. 1. *600 B.C. to the Early Twentieth Century.* New York: The Feminist Press, 1991.

Thornton, Robert. "Narrative Ethnography in Africa, 1850–1920: The Creation and Capture of an Appropriate Domain for Anthropology." *Man* (September 1983): 502–520.

———. "The Rhetoric of Ethnographic Holism." *Cultural Anthropology* (August 1988): 285–303.

Tillotson, Giles H. R. "Sacrifice of an Hindoo Widow upon the Funeral Pile of her Husband." In *An Illustrated History of Modern India, 1600–1947,* ed. C. A. Bayly. Delhi: Oxford University Press 1990, 220–222.

Viswanathan, Gauri. *Masks of Conquest: Literary Study and British Rule in India.* New York: Columbia University Press, 1989.

Washbrook, David A. "Law, State and Agrarian Society in Colonial India." *Modern Asian Studies* 15, 3 (1981): 649–721.

———. "Progress and Problems: South Asian Economic and Social History, c. 1720–1860." *Modern Asian Studies* 22, 1 (1988): 57–96.

White, Hayden. *The Content of the Form.* Baltimore: Johns Hopkins University Press, 1987.

Wolfe, John. *The Protestant Crusade in Great Britain, 1829–1860.* Oxford: Clarendon Press, 1991.

Young, Robert. *White Mythologies: Writing History and the West.* London and New York: Routledge, 1990.

## Bibliographies

Sarkar, Sumit. *Bibliographical Survey of Social Reform Movements in the Eighteenth and Nineteenth Centuries.* New Delhi: Indian Council of Historical Research, 1975.

Whitley, W. T. *A Baptist Bibliography.* Vol. 2, 1777–1837. London, 1922.

# Index

| | |
|---:|:---|
| Compositor: | G & S Typesetters, Inc. |
| Text: | 10/13 Galliard |
| Display: | Galliard |
| Printer and binder: | Thomson-Shore, Inc. |